PARTNERING WITH GOD
Practical Information for the New Millennium

D0778325

Kryon
Book VI

115 International Kryon Books
in 21 Languages

Spanish
Kryon Books - One, Two, Three, The Parables, The Journey Home, Kryon Book Six and Seven

Spanish
Kryon Books Eight, Ten and The Indigo Children books

Hebrew
Kryon Books - One, Two, Three

Hebrew
Kryon Books - The Parables of Kryon, The Journey Home, Books Six, Seven, Eight, Nine, Ten, and The Indigo Children

Hebrew
Indigo Celebration

Italian
Kryon Books - One, Parables, Book Seven, Ten, and The Indigo Children

Estonian
Kryon Books - One and Two

Turkish
Kryon Books - One, Two, Three, Six, Seven, Eight, Nine and Ten

Turkish
Kryon - Parables, The Journey Home, and The Indigo Children

Chinese
Kryon Books - One, Two and Three (coming)

Slovene
Indigo Children

Portuguese
Kryon Books - Indigo Children, Books One, Two, and Three

part•ner•ship n.

1. The state of being a partner.

2. A legal contract entered into by two or more persons in which each agrees to furnish a part of the investment for an enterprise, and by which each shares a fixed proportion of the result.

3. A relationship between individuals or groups that is characterized by mutual cooperation and responsibility, as for the achievement of a specified goal.

PARTNERING WITH GOD

Practical Information for the New Millennium

Publisher: **The Kryon Writings, Inc.**

1155 Camino Del Mar, #422
Del Mar, California 92014
[www.kryon.com]

Kryon books and tapes can be purchased in
retail stores, or on the Internet [www.kryon.com] credit cards welcome
Phone 800 352-6657 or Email <kryonbooks@kryon.com>

Written by Lee Carroll
Editing by Jill Kramer
Copyright © 1997—Lee Carroll
Printed in the United States of America
First Edition—First Printing—November 1997
Second Printing - March 1998
Third Printing - June 1998
Fourth Printing - October 1998
Fifth Printing - February 1999
Sixth Printing - June 1999
Seventh Printing - December 1999
Eighth Printing - October 2000
Ninth Printing - January 2002
Tenth Printing - October 2002
Eleventh Printing - July 2003
Twelfth Printing - July 2004
Thirteenth Printing - June 2006

ISBN# 1-888053-10-0 : $14.00

115 International Kryon Books
in 21 Languages

French
Kryon Books - One, Two, Three, Journey Home, Six, Seven, and Eight, Nine, Ten, The Indigo Children and Celebration

Russian
Indigo Books One and Two

Russian
Kryon Books - One, Two, Three, Four, Seven, Eight, Nine, Ten

Danish
Kryon Book One

Japanese
Kryon Book - One, & Indigo Children

Hungarian
Kryon Books - One, Two, & The Indigo Children, Books Eight and Nine (coming)

Bulgarian
Kryon Books - One, Two, Four & Six

German
Kryon Books - One, Two, Three, Four, Five, Six, Seven, Eight, Nine Ten, Indigo 1 & 2

Romanian
Indigo Children

Finnish
Kryon Books - Book One, Two, Three, Five, Six, Seven, and Indigo Children

Greek
Kryon Books - One, Two, Three, and Five (The Journey Home)

Greek
Kryon Books - Six, Seven, Eight, and the Parables of Kryon

Dutch
Kryon Books - Journey Home - Parables of Kryon - Indigo Children

Korean
The Indigo Children

Table of Contents

continued...

Table of Contents... continued

Thanks!

*W*ith each book I seem to have a growing list of those to thank! Now it has grown to a point where I'll be in trouble remembering all those who should be on this list. Therefore, I include only the ones specifically who made an impact on this, Kryon's sixth publication.

Garret Annofsky

Cristine Arlsmendy

Linda Benyo

Zehra Boccia

Norma Delaney

Rebecca De Sol

Barbra Dillenger

Janie Emerson

Steve Goldstein

Louise Hay

Barbara Harris

Rob Harris

Geoffrey Hoppe

Jill Kramer

Ka Sandra Love

Michael Makay

Trish McCabe

Todd Ovokaitys

Cookie Perrin

Mohammad Ramadan

Steve Rother

Paula Randol Smith

Nancy Ann Tappe

Jan Tober

Doreen Virtue

Preface

From the Writer

Kryon

Partnering with God
Kryon Book VI

From the writer...

Anyone reading this is probably now familiar with the Kryon Book Series. Although this is Kryon Book Six, it is only the fourth in the Kryon teaching series. Kryon Books Four and Five were in parable and novel styles respectively, published by Hay House.

The last Kryon teaching series book, Kryon Book Three (fuchsia colored to match a favorite shirt), was written almost two years before this one, so there is a great amount of new information available—which is the reason for this publication. It seems that each year the vibration of the planet, and the humans on it, is growing to such a degree that the old information is being clarified greatly, and new gifts are being presented at an increasingly rapid pace.

Kryon has now appeared personally before over 10,000 seminar attendees. *The Kryon Quarterly* Magazine has 3,000 subscribers (at this writing) in over 12 countries. Almost all the books are on tape (some abridged), and they have been translated into many languages around the world. Shortly, Kryon will begin giving seminars on other continents, and naturally, this won't be the last book.

In Kryon Book One (1993), Kryon outlined where eight other Kryon channels were in the world. Many have written from these other nations and asked, "Where is our Kryon channel?" I started asking Kryon (while in my shower), "Where are the other Kryon channels?" The answer I got surprised me and made me laugh. Kryon said (while I was holding my soap on a rope), "You make a bad human assumption that they are all adults! The timing for each culture is specific." So this means that some of them are children, scheduled to reveal a message as the planet gets closer to 2012 (more about 2012 later).

I asked Kryon if there would be time to give the messages when these children grew up. He informed me that all the world isn't as dense as our culture! (Thanks, Kryon.) I think, with all love and soapiness, I was gently insulted. Sometimes the truth hurts.

Through all of this, I still remain the reluctant and doubting channel—the guy who keeps asking for more validations and reality checks about the work. This has indeed kept me balanced and grounded, and has also given me three new postulates to work with. Here they are:

(1) Anyone can channel! It isn't just a few of us who write books and give seminars. Some of you are channeling your Higher Selves on a regular basis. It isn't spooky or weird (even if your friends think so). If your friends think you are strange, consider not channeling in the supermarket any more—or at least move away from the broccoli.

(2) Spirit (God) isn't proprietary! That's why anyone can channel. The truth is available to everyone. Certain teachers may have been chosen to impart it properly, and perhaps it should be carefully given to those who will be called to minister, but truth cannot be sequestered—ever!

Therefore, the Kryon work teaches self-enablement, raising a human's consciousness and self-worth. It also teaches that we don't have to "buy into" the doom and gloom of the millennium soothsayers. We have completely changed our future!

(3) Disengage all the sensationalism regarding flying saucers, ETs, comets and other-worldly visitations from your spiritual learning focus. "What?" you might ask. "Are you telling us that these things don't exist?" Not at all! I am stating that **they do not belong in your heart!** Kryon even gave messages regarding ETs at the United Nations (later in these pages), not once—but twice! Therefore, I believe they exist. But the advice is not to worship them—and by looking at all the time spent on this subject, many New Agers come very close! Study this topic all you want, then turn the page

and return to your real quest—how to create the love of God in your life to the extent that you co-create your reality, have peace with yourself and your surroundings, and begin to change the planet because of it.

As you read this book, become aware of another one of Kryon's comments since the beginning. Unless you are reading this book in a group (not very likely), I am communicating directly to your personal mind. Kryon will be channeling information directly through your two eyes as you continue these pages. This is the way of it. Kryon tells us that it is the individual heart and mind that will respond to the messages here. No group consciousness or mass action is desired. Reaching the individual human being is the goal. Discernment is the key, and vibrational increase and enlightenment is the result. If you don't like it, then put the book down. If you feel it is valuable to continue, then do so. Individual human choice is the paramount issue here. We are free to choose to accept any of this or not.

What's in these pages...

Most of this book was transcribed from live channels all over the United States and Canada. In each city, Kryon imparted love and wisdom to an energy that was specific for that area, but for all to read later. Each channel was given before a crowd that varied from 200 to 700 in size, depending on the city. It was amazing to analyze what was happening. As time went on, the channels became clearer, and the love imparted became greater. Soon there were healings occurring at almost each session. Kryon explains that the healings were where humans finally got the message that it was okay to give permission. In other words, the human did the healing. Heretofore unspoken subjects were now on the table, so to speak, and it was becoming far more distinct just what the human role in this New Age was supposed to be—and what it wasn't supposed to be.

Some of you are subscribers to *The Kryon Quarterly* magazine. We promised you that you would receive channels months before anyone else would see them. We fulfilled that promise, so you might recognize some of the material in this book as having been published in the magazine (aren't you glad you got to see it first?). Read it again, for some of it has now changed (channel on a channel). Kryon loves to do that, and to update or clarify the information within the appropriateness of an ever-changing Earth.

It is the style of Kryon to give a loving congratulatory message in the first ten minutes of every channel. Some of these messages are for new ears each time, but will be redundant if shown over and over in these pages. Therefore, I have removed some of the similar comments, as the channels are presented in this book, to conserve your time.

This book is about "Partnering with God." Can there ever be a grander goal? **Chapter One** prepares us with a message that Kryon gave in two parts in two different cities—both in Canada. The "Sit in the Chair" series must be understood before anything else. It is the cornerstone of the entire partnering concept, and therefore is first in the book. Later on in subsequent channels, Kryon may give the expression, "Sit in the chair." You will understand what it means.

Chapter Two gets into the partnering concept and begins a practical "how to" of what is now available. **Chapter Three** is the "hands-on" chapter, with explanations of real-world situations and practical answers. The last channel from Australia is one of my favorites.

A short **Chapter Four** speaks about human biology, and **Chapter Five** is the next installment on that very popular subject, *Ascension*. It is called *Ascension II*, since there have been other chapters in earlier books and tapes that gave preliminary information. You will find this chapter very grounded and clear for such an elevated subject.

Chapter Six is the full story and transcript of both channelings given by invitation at the United Nations in November of 1995, and 1996.

Chapter Seven is all about my experience and what Kryon has to say regarding the new INDIGO children. Again, it's practical information with a report on how to deal with these children, and what to look for.

Chapter Eight contains my favorite parable of the past two years, and a discussion of Intent and Co-creation—two very powerful attributes of the New Age.

Chapter Nine is the lengthiest. It represents direct Kryon answers to the most-asked questions that we have received through the mail and at seminars, even some controversial ones.

Chapter Ten features scientific validation regarding some of the past Kryon channelings, and additional good scientific information on what is happening right now. There is also a brief discussion of Carl Sagan's book *The Demon-Haunted World*.

The rest is Kryon information about on-line connections, how to get our magazine, and how to get on our mailing list. This is followed by the index (you are really weird if you spend time reading the index).

Throughout this book, I refer to Kryon as a HE. I wish there was a word besides "it" that I could use. I apologize for genderizing Spirit, but for the written communication it is more readable.

Enjoy this sixth Kryon book! It was written for *you*. It is no accident that finds you reading these words. Relax and enjoy a loving voice from home!

Lee Carroll

Sitting in the Chair

Chapter One

For those friends I lost this year...

For Bob
For Muktabi
For Joe

We all realize that your passing was your reward, and our test.

There will come a day when again we will embrace and know that we are all eternal!

"The Way Things Work"
Channeled in
Banff, Canada

The Kryon Writings, Inc.

PMB 422
1155 Camino Del Mar
Del Mar, California 92014
[www.kryonqtly.com]

"The Way Things Work"
Live Channeling
Banff Canada

These live channelings have been edited with additional words and thoughts to allow clarification and better understanding of the written word.

Greetings, dear ones, I am Kryon of Magnetic Service, and I love you dearly. My partner spoke the words of the honor that we have for you. And oh, dear ones, it is my honor to be with you. Even now as you get used to the sound of my partner's voice representing my communications, I tell you that I am here to wash your feet. For the nurturing that I bring is the symbol of home, and if any of you for a moment could place yourself there, you would experience in-credible love. Right now you sit in the duality of lesson. You sit in a place of honor. Priests, you are, each one in this New Age! We are here to tell you that you are dearly loved for this work. Even those of you who have no concept of what is taking place now — even the ones of you who do not believe that this could pos-sibly be the voice of Spirit and can  hardly wait for this meeting to be over—you are dearly loved as well.

There is no judgment by Spirit of any human—only incredible love. You are in this place on purpose! The appointment was never clearer that you should be here to hear these words or to read this page. For in this clear energy, we have some messages for you this night—messages that will be repeated over again by my partner, for they are very important. These messages do not speak of world calamity or of fearful Earth changes. This is the voice of home, which you are hearing and reading, that loves you—that surrounds you with arms of gold—that speaks to your heart this moment.

There is a message for you as you sit here. And before we start this message, we are encouraging the entourage we bring to walk the aisles of this place, and to visit the place where you are reading. We ask for a cocoon of love to encompass you, and if you've never felt it before, this is the time we ask you to feel your guides. They come in with you—they stay with you—they give you intuitive nudges, and they love you dearly. They are your best friends, and you know them from the other side. When all of this is over and you again meet in the Hall of Honor, you will have a grand time with these who have spent their lives with you on this planet. Not one of you is ever alone.

The guides are quiet. We will speak of this in a moment. But their embrace is what you can feel as you sit in this place and are loved by God. The potential in this room is astonishing, and we wish to tell you about it this night. This message is entitled *The Way Things Work*. We wish this to be a practical message, and when you leave this place or arise from your reading position, you'll understand more about who you are and some of the potentials that exist for your life.

Before we do that, we must revisit a parable that has been channeled and published. We wish to expound upon the parable of *Wo and the Rooms of Lesson*. We know that there are those among you here and reading this who are unfamiliar with this parable, so we will review it only briefly—and only the end of it. This will be knowledge necessary to understand the truth of what is to come.

Wo was a human being who, through his passing and his death, was momentarily shown the metaphoric rooms in his house of life. The rooms that Wo was shown by his guides before he went to the Hall of Honor were astounding to him. And as the parable goes, the rooms were thus: Wo opened a room that was filled with magnificent treasure. And his guides told him, "Here, Wo, is your room of abundance should you have chosen to use it while you were on Earth." This was a metaphor to show Wo what he had in the way of riches—physical riches that he could have tapped into at any time. Another room was filled with white essence and light and was Wo's room of inner peace. This showed Wo metaphorically that at any time he had wished, he could have entered this room and felt the peace of God—where worry was nonexistent. All he had to do was enter it through INTENT. It was his all along. It belonged in his house, in his life, and it had his spiritual name on it.

Another room the guides would not go in was the room of gold. This room was Wo's pure essence—his "piece of God." This was Wo's Love Room—a room so sacred and so anointed that only he could sit in it. Later he was shown other doors in his house that he did not open. On his way out of the house, he was shown doors he did not understand, which had names of unborn children. One name on a door said "World Leader." But he did not open any of them.

And as the parable goes, he moved on in full understanding that these rooms and this house would be repeated for him when he again incarnated on the Earth. That was the parable of Wo as channeled then, but we wish to continue it now. Rather than involving Wo, dear ones, instead we are going to involve YOU. You see, this is the way it works. We are going to give you some information this night that is going to help you move forward in your life.

You are important to this universe! This planet is not insignificant, and, oh, so much revolves around it! Dear ones, we wish you to visualize yourself in one of these rooms now—the one that is the most important—the one that we will expound upon—the one that holds the key to your entire life here. It is the room that Wo saw as gold. It is the room the guides could not move into. There is indeed something in this golden room with you that is hidden. If Wo had been able to stay in this room, he would have discovered something amazing beyond his wildest imaginings. As he (and you) might explore the interior of the room more fully, you would have discovered a creature of immense power and beauty. There sitting on a throne of gold would be a splendid golden angel—one whose wings spread out to a distance that touched the walls!

Who was it, this astounding angel? Had Wo gotten closer, he would have discovered that the love was so thick that breathing would have become difficult—the vibration around the angel was so anointed that he would have found himself on his knees staring up at a piece of God! As he peered into the face of this great one, the face on the angel would have slowly taken shape. There, where Wo expected to see the glorious face of a citizen of heaven— instead he would see his *own* features!

What could this mean, you might ask? Wo was looking at the angel that was his higher entity, or Higher Self! The entity was sacred beyond description but was a part of Wo! Wo had discovered the secret of his own divinity... his "piece of God."

Dear ones, there is an angel with your face, sitting figuratively in the chair of gold in the golden room in each of your lives right now. Its presence shouts that you belong here! Its existence gives you information that you are important, enabled, and deserve to be on this planet.

In your mind, we wish you to go in and sit in that chair right now. There is no one around you. You are alone, but empowered! We wish you to feel this gold essence fill every pore, and there's a reason why we invite you to do this. For this gold essence is the anointed piece of God that you carry with you; it is your Higher Self, and it is ingrained in each one of your cells. It speaks of home and contract and it smiles and loves you. Like a sponge, we ask you to absorb this golden light as we give you insight about what you are experiencing.

Some of you in your past days, and even to this day, have fallen in love with God. Perhaps you have assigned it to some kind of entity—some kind of master who has stood before you with great love energy. Maybe you returned it by being in love with one of these. Perhaps it was Yoganenda, Mohammed, Buddha, or the Senanda energy. Feel the love that it was that you had for this entity! Feel it strongly. Perhaps some of you have loved Kryon, or the Virgin Mary or Lord Michael. There are so many that you could pour your love to, for they (and we) pour it back so consistently and so wonderfully! Now we are here to tell you a secret, dear ones— something you may have never truly recognized. All of the love that you have had for God—for Spirit—for these entities in all of your life, is simply an absolute direct mirror of your own love for yourself. For within this metaphoric golden room is your self-essence. The piece of Spirit that you fell in love with was from home, and it was always yours.

And so, dear ones, we say to you that this gold room where you sit right now as you absorb this, is the love of your Higher Self. What it develops in your life is self-esteem, so you understand that you are not only important and loved, but are potently ready to change. So for the rest of this message, we ask you to stay in that spot and never move. The love of self creates self-esteem, and in a moment we will describe the difference between this love and the love of ego. For they are vastly different and easy to identify. It is the love of God within you that creates the enablement for the releasing of problems at this time. Anytime you feel you are not worthy, enter this room figuratively and metaphorically, and sit in that chair. Invite the love of the Higher Self and the piece of God that is you, walking on this Earth, to be absorbed within your body—and you will know the importance you have for this planet. I'm speaking to you! Yes, I am!

Day-to-Day Life

What about the day-to-day life that you live? Spirit knows when you leave this place that you get into vehicles and go places; you have occupations. How does sitting in the golden chair apply to this, you might ask? Early on we gave you the parable of the tar pit. And the parable of the tar pit said that when you receive the gifts of Spirit in the New Age, while other humans seem to be mired in tar walking from place to place, it recedes from you naturally. Guess where you are when this happens? You're sitting in that room, filled with gold, high on self-esteem, knowing who you are, taking your place on this planet as the piece of God that you are. That's why the tar does not stick. It recedes from you! Those around you in your everyday life will react to this fact. I absolutely guarantee you, dear one, that if you take the step of discovering the self-esteem of the inner self and begin loving this feeling, those around you will begin to notice. For you see, love begets itself. It attracts itself, and it's special. No matter where you go or the places you might see that might seem diametrically opposed to a Godly place, you may still sit in the golden room and feel the self-worth. And those around you who have no concept of who you are or what you were doing will look at you differently. Because at the cellular level they will know where you're sitting, you see. We are giving you a key to life at this moment. For every single person who is with you and sees you at the cellular level sees what you're doing. And even though their mouth and their eyes may say one thing—at the cellular level—their body is celebrating you, and it doesn't take long before they will change toward you. Then once again we have the action of the one changing the many by changing only themselves. Without saying a word—without evangelism, your change will affect them.

X Abundance X

What about all that abundance? you might ask. Was it only metaphoric? Some of it was. Let me take you for a moment from this room of gold to have a vision within a vision. Where is it that you are the most peaceful? I invite you to go there now. For my partner, it might be standing in the sun over a precipice overlooking the ocean, feeling the salt air, hearing the waves, experiencing the planet as he enjoys so much. For others it might be in this very place [Banff], again on a precipice, feeling the breeze from the mountains. You might have the wonderful coolness of the weather or the snow in your face. These things often bring peace to humans. Go to that place that creates the most peace for you and stand there for a moment. I'm going to ask you a question, and it is this: Where is your greatest treasure?

Some of you will say, *"You're right. It's not in the rubies and the gold. I want to be free of the hatred that I have for this or that. I want to stop worrying. I wish my family life was clear and clean. That would be my greatest treasure if I could have anything in the world."* Some of you are saying, *"If I could only have my health back. I am so concerned of what is churning in my body that I have no control over. I am afraid!"* So your greatest treasure would be to eliminate these things—to settle them—to have solutions. Well, let me tell you that your room of peace is combined with your room of abundance. Day-to-day living is about these rooms! It starts with the room of gold because the room of self-esteem begets the room of peace. And peace creates balance, and that is where the treasures lie.

For those of you wondering why it is so difficult financially to move from place to place, or to go from here to there, we must back up two rooms. We say this: Settle the one that's gold first! Get that one settled, and the one of peace follows—and the one of abundance follows that. Take care of yourself—and your heart. All will follow. This is practical. This is day-to-day. This is how it works.

Power of the Human Being

Let us talk about the power of the human being. For, you see, the power of the human being lies in the unopened doors. Wo saw names on those doors that we will explain later to you, because we have a story to tell—another parable. The power you have is amazing, for depending upon what you do in your room of gold will determine what happens regarding the unopened doors. We'll show you this in a moment.

We have three suggestions for you as you walk day to day. These are practical things that you should know. It is important as you claim this love of your Higher Self, never to sequester it with others just because they are of like mind. We have spoken of this before, but it is the tendency of the human being to do this. Dear ones, when you receive this sacred "love of self," there is the tendency, then, to sequester it with others of like mind and keep it a secret. Do not form communes, for that is sequestering God from the rest of the Earth. It is a fear-based mechanism that asks you to do this.

The spirit of God says that you are to take your light and let it shine to those around you. That is what you're to do. And without saying anything at all, or telling anyone around you what is taking place, the light shines through you. That is what you're to do. What good is a light, dear ones, unless you take it to the dark places? If, instead, you take those lights and put them all in one room and shut the door, you have done nothing for this planet. Now we are not speaking of a meeting like this, here where you sit. No. We are speaking of a situation where you would actually sequester yourselves and others within a day-to-day living existence. We say, please beware—do not fall into that trap. Let that light shine.

ETs

Now we come to an interesting subject. What are you going to do with all of this activity around the Earth? What are you going to do with those ones who you call the ETs? How does all this fit in? You see, many are here, you know. I would like to give you an example of what is taking place right now on this planet—something that we told those at your world organization. This planet is moving toward a new area of space, an area that has an energy conducive to being joined by others, you see, and most of you know this. **The Universe is teeming with life!** Teeming with life! And the thought that you are alone is comical, but is part of your duality to think such a thing. Some of you are upset by those whom you see. You have heard of the dark energies, and much has been written about them. Some of you are spending all your time dealing with the potential of these from elsewhere—and you are even combining their existence with your politics! The more sensational you can make the study, the more exciting it is.

Here is an example of what is taking place: When you enter any large city to meet with the high sacred council, you must come through the peripheral parts of the city. When you enter those parts of the city to get to the center, you come in contact with what we would call the *riffraff*. They do not represent the council, nor is their consciousness the consciousness of the city, but they feel a lot like the ones you're going to meet. Do not mistake these for the main force, for they are not [also channeled later at the UN, Chapter Six and p208]. Any of you who have ever had problems with what we call the riffraff, listen to this: They cannot touch you when you are in that chair of gold! And we say this now to those who believe firmly that they have been taken against their will, and that something is being done to them. This is very real! We say to you that these visitors are not allowed to touch you if you're in that room of gold, And do you know why? Because even they see the priesthood in you! They recognize the spark of God in you.

Do you want to know why some of these are so interested in you, dear ones? It's because they want to know more about that spark. They want to know more about the emotions that you have; they want to know more about this spirituality that you have. You see, you are in duality. You are honored. You are priests, each one, walking in biology, and they're fascinated by that—fascinated! For those of you who are spending your lives watching them, learning more about them, reading this and that book about them, centering your lives around them, we ask you not to let that activity consume your life, or it absolutely will.

It's marvelous for you to think that there is other life. What must it be like? But again, we give you our advice: Do not let it consume you. For the real difference in the planet lies in that gold room, not in a life's study about those you are going to meet someday. Nothing you read or investigate about space visitors will help you with your family, or heal your body or help you in your workplace or create abundance. No amount of sensational news, valid or not, will create peace in your life. No. That lies in the chair in the gold room! Get your priorities correct. First, take care of YOU! Then the study of everything else will fall into place.

Channeling

Now we're going to give you some information about chan- neling. We would like to give you some discernment rules. It would be folly and illogical for Spirit to give you discernment rules about itself; therefore, we take these from a wise human source—a published one that is available to you, known to my partner. It is our meld that allows this information. This is what wise humans have to say about channelers and it is good advice.

(1) There will always be useful information for everyone. *Beware of the channel that gives you useful information for only a few, or tells you that it's only for a special group or a sequestered number*. It must be useful for **all** humanity, every single human. Watch for this. This is an area of discernment to know you are hearing truth.

(2) *The message should be uplifting*. Watch for an empow- ering message—**Not one of fear**, not one that drags you down, not one that makes you want to take fearful action or hide—but an enabling message! Watch for that.

(3) *Spirit will never ever channel you a message that asks you to give up your free will*. Never! For your free will is what your experience on Earth is all about as you sit in those chairs of gold. Free will! Choice is what drives your planet's future.

(4) *Spirit will never give you a message—ever—that asks you to violate the integrity of what you believe*. You are honored

in your thought processes. Spirit will never trick you or "talk you" into anything. The message must never violate your integrity. You must feel comfortable with it, and it will ring true to your heart.

(5) Dear ones, *Spirit will never represent a channeler as being the only source.* Watch for this, for there are many channels of Spirit and they all **dovetail their information** to create a bigger picture—especially in this New Age time. They will **never** represent themselves as the only source of information.

(6) *Watch for the fact that the information is normally new information.* Beware of the channel that simply rehashes the old, for they are not channeling anything but the ego of the human being. New information is necessary. It is the entire reason for the channel. Think about it.

(7) *Watch for the fact that channeled information should have spiritual solutions presented.* Solutions to life challenges on Earth, via new information, is the purpose of channeling.

These are seven of the twelve rules of channeling discernment from Spirit, given to you by human beings.* And now we'll give you a rule of our own—one given you by us. What you do with channeled information, as we have told you before, is to *treat it as a reference.* Do not wallow in it. Do not make it your life. Do not make the human who channels out to be a guru. Look at the information and learn from it as a reference, then put it away. If you need to retrieve it to review it, do so as you would any reference, and then put it away again. Then with your own power and your own enablement, go into that room of gold and start creating higher vibrations for this planet. You are the enabled ones! The channeling is only data for your action.

We have told you to sit in this room and feel the love of God. Some of you will say, *"Kryon, how do I know the difference between love and ego? They feel much the same. You have told us we must love **ourselves**—isn't this ego?"* Dear ones, the

* Originally seen in *New Realities Magazine* - July 1987

difference between the love of Spirit, your Higher Self, and the love of the human ego is vast. Now we will give you four rule elements around that. Here are the four elements of pure love— human and spiritual. We will quote these to you often in many forms as we continue the quest to bring our vibrations closer together. There is perhaps no greater message in this entire meeting (and this book) than what follows:

The Four Elements of Pure Love

1. Dear ones, the pure Love of Spirit **is quiet.** Love does not shout from the hilltop, "Here am I—look at me!" The Love of God and the Love of the Higher Self is quiet, compassionate, strong, and thick. Oh, can you feel this? We are pouring this into you at this moment. This is the true essence of home. This is what some of you feel when you believe you are "in love" with God. It is the remembrance of home, and it belongs to you! And, dear ones…its embodiment is in that chair in the gold room! Do you understand?

2. Love has **no agenda**. It exists for itself and feeds only the spirit of Love. There is no evangelism around it. It does not choose to encompass anyone but you. This is true love. It does not shout, "If you do this for me, I'll do something for you!" No. It exists only to "be." It is content to just exist. Watch for this—there is no agenda around the Love of God.

3. The third one is that love **never pumps itself up**. It never beats its chest. It's never proud. It never has to be, you see, for it is from the creative source. Everyone will see it, and you will never have to say a word. You never even have to raise your hand to say, "Look at me." Like a light in the darkness, you will attract those who will ask, "What is it with you?" When Wo saw the great golden angel in the chair of gold, he didn't ask for credentials. He felt the sacredness of the entity! Your ordainment of humanism is a badge that all can see. As the old energy of Earth clears, many will observe it!

(4) Finally, Love has the **wisdom** to use the other three. The wisdom is quiet, without an agenda or importance. It knows what to say and what not to say. It features wise action.

Pure Love will **never create a fear scenario** in your life, but the **ego will**. This is the main difference, dear ones. Fear has no place within the messages of God. Fear is a mechanism used within karma and human lesson. I ask you to remember this: In the history of all of the things written as long as you have recorded humanity, when the angels of the Lord appeared in any writings of any belief systems, they came with two words. Before they said anything to any human, do you know what the words were? "*Fear not*—proof that God will never bring you a fear message. *Fear not!* It's written for you to look at.

Sit in those gold chairs for a moment, because we have a story for you. This is the story of Thomas. Oh, dear ones, these parables are given to you because stories are remembered more than just words. This story is dripping with truth. The story is meaningful. Was there really a Thomas? No. And yet there is a Thomas in every one of the chairs that sits in this room right now, or is reading this message.

The Parable of Thomas the Healer

Early on, Thomas knew that he had a gift. He could look at people, even as a child, and know something was wrong. "Oh, you have a headache," he would say when he was ten. "I'm sorry. Let me touch your head to make it better." He saw disease and discomfort, he saw colors in the faces of people. But it was not until he was older that he realized that this was not common to humanity.

And so you see, Thomas had a gift, just like the gift that so many of you possess that are reading this or hearing these words. Perhaps in a different way—but a gift, nonetheless. The key is that it was a gift known from birth—something that was recognized intuitively, perhaps stuffed away, but, nevertheless, a gift.

Now Thomas had a choice as he grew up. He was aware of his gift, and he had dabbled in the healing of individuals, and he knew that it was indeed his passion. But he also knew that he had to make a living. Thomas wanted to make the biggest change he could on the planet, so he studied chemistry and biology. He said to himself, "*I will be a research scientist. Maybe I will discover something great. God will help me, and I will affect many, many lives this way.*"

And so when it really came down to it, Thomas was on the precipice of an important decision: (1) to join a research company and create his career, or (2) stop everything and become a singular healer with all of the uncertainties thereof—healing one person at a time in a noninstitutional atmosphere. At the cellular level, he knew where his passion and his contract lay. He wanted to heal people—to do the most good he could with his gift. What should he do?

So it was that Thomas went to bed that night, and not long after he was asleep, he was met in a vision by two of his guides. He was taken away in that vision to a place of importance.

And his guides smiled at him and said, "Thomas, this night we are going to show you a place that the prophets have seen. And we call it *The Many Futures of the Planet*. But in this case, we're going to show it to you in your own lifetime. Not the planet's future, but *your* future. We're going to show you two possible outcomes."

Thomas was very excited, and the guides took him to something he had never seen before. It was a building made of concentric circles, as though you had dropped a rock in a pond and circles were created from its center. Each one of those many circles represented a very long, circular, narrow room; and each one of those rooms represented a different future for Thomas, depending upon his actions during his life.

Thomas was very interested in this building, but he said to these guides, "Before you show me anything else, what is in the center room?"

And his guides said, "That's a place we cannot go. That's where only the priests go. We're going to show you some of the ripples—some of the rooms of your life."

And so they took him to one of the rooms, and they said, "Here is a possible outcome of your life, Thomas. Look at it." Thomas walked into the room, and what he saw was much activity and many people, but he could hear nothing. Spirit was not going to give him the whole picture, but enough so that he could feel what was taking place. None of those in the room could see him, but he was aware of all of the events taking place.

It seemed that a great deal was going on. This room was gigantic and circular. It was well lit and packed with humans. There were many children among them, and he saw that they were very excited. Thomas walked a great distance before he actually saw himself in the room, and he saw that it was a celebration around his life! In this room there were even senators, world leaders, and mothers and fathers. They were having a great feast and a banquet, and they were all healthy, every one.

Thomas thought to himself, *I'm being shown the result of my life as a research scientist. This is what I had hoped for— the greatest amount of help for the most people. My work paid off!*

And so Thomas was overjoyed seeing that he was receiving accolades. The celebration revolved around what he had done. And all of the families and the children made it that much more special. And the guides said, "Thomas, it is time to go and look at still another room. Another outcome for you."

Thomas stood outside the room for a moment, and he said, "*Oh, I don't want this next one to be a bad one.*" For Thomas was still feeling the joy of seeing the room he had just been in, and he was still savoring it all. His guides said to him, "*Oh, Thomas, you must understand that **the journey** is your honor. For you are one that has gone to Earth. You are one who is going to change the vibration, no matter what you do. It is the fact that you are here that is special and anointed. It is the **free choice** that is yours, which is the spiritual icing on the cake. There is no judgment around what is in these rooms, only as interest for you—helping you in your choice.*"

The guides took Thomas to the next room, and it was dark. Thomas reacted. "*There must be a mistake. There is no one here.*"

The guides said nothing. So Thomas started traversing the dim room and walked a great length of time before he saw light in the distance. There it was—a table where a celebration was going on among thirteen people. One of them was him! It was a banquet—again, a celebration of what he had done.

Thomas thought to himself, *This scene must represent what would have happened had I become a singular healer.* Thomas looked around at the few at the table who were toasting him. "*Looks like I was pretty bad. Healing just twelve people in my lifetime.*"

Then Thomas saw something—something that made him swoon with understanding. For on the wrist of the arm of Thomas at the celebrating table was a gold timepiece from the research company he was about to join in real life. The play in front of him was a celebration of his retirement as a research scientist!

Thomas left the room quickly and said to his guides, "*Please, I'm not done with this vision; don't let it stop. I want to go to the center room.*"

And his guides said, "*We cannot accompany you there, but this is just a vision, Thomas, so you can go there if you choose.*"

So he did, and he was transported to the very center of the concentric rooms, and in that room, dear ones, there was a golden presence. And in that room, dear ones, there was a golden chair with a spectacular image of Thomas himself sitting in it! And he instantly awoke. Thomas thought to himself, *I am so thankful for this Spiritual direction*!

You see, dear ones, Thomas knew instantly what had taken place. The potential of the one sitting in the gold room is what is important, and when Thomas took his place in the vision in the gold room, he understood the overview—that there would be humans destined to come his way that he would heal, humans that would go on to live productive lives—to have as yet "unborn children" whose names were on the doors of the house in the parable of Wo.

Whereas there are those of you who thought the names of "unborn children" in the other parable belonged potentially to Wo, this is not the case. You see, the unborn children were to be born of those **people he affected**! They represented an incredible potential for change—children born from those he had helped heal or had spoken to—all due to one life: His.

Thomas now realized that a one-at-a-time healing was the correct path for him. He hadn't realized before that the one who was healed and balanced would beget two—would beget four—would beget eight. This is the parable we give you now to show you that you have no idea who you're going to meet, or the effect you're going to have on them, when you sit in that gold room. The overview is ours, but we invite you to have faith that it exists for you! We know of your potential!

The potential for the power to change this planet is awesome as you sit in that chair! You have no idea, for the ways of God are very complex, but I will tell you that the potentials for you are already accomplished in the "now." The solutions are in place, and if you were to go into that gold room and find self-esteem— to move forward in this new energy and take your power and do

impossible things—we will be at your side all the way, implement-
ing solutions that have already been created by your intent.

There will be those who will come and meet you by design, and
you will recognize the synchronicity of their coming. Because of
your work, they will go on to sit in their own gold rooms and affect
others who will sit in their gold rooms as well! What a way to heal
the planet!

**Healers in this room and those reading this, are you
paying attention?**

Each one of you is an absolute powerhouse of change for this
planet! Why does Spirit give you this message? Because the future
of the planet is uncertain, but it is balanced toward your work. You
are poised on the edge of something amazing, but you're going to
have to take your place in those seats within those golden rooms
to make the difference—and you simply can't ignore it.

So now some of you may understand when we say, "You're
honored." When you sit at the feet of Kryon in a situation like this,
you have had your feet washed by Spirit! For we are sitting here
with our bowl of sacred water—our tears of joy for you—washing
each foot and loving each of you and calling you by name, saying,
"We know who you are! You are indeed dearly loved!"

Even the ones who don't believe that this is real are loved! May
the seeds be planted this night even in those who would walk away
from this place not understanding, so that someday when the time
is appropriate and their lives are ready, all of this will come flooding
back, and they will feel the love that transferred this night into their
lives.

This is the way it works, dear ones. You want to know about
co-creation? It's in the gold chair! Because in the gold chair, self-
empowerment creates the peace that creates joy. When you
realize that you deserve to be here, everything changes! You will
"own" the fact that all is in Divine order. And this self-esteem lets

your verbalization create power, which creates a situation where you can create your own reality—this is co-creation at its best.

So, what is it with you right now? Do you want to go from this place with the knowledge that your gold room is something to search for? I'll tell you what it can do for you: It could solve all of those problems that weigh on your shoulders at this very moment! There is no malady here in any single body that is not able to be healed instantly by the energy that is currently here in this room!

There is nothing beyond your reach in this, and you know I am telling you the truth. At the cellular level, nothing is impossible here. You think you face an impossibility in relationships or family or work? It is a phantom of your imagination—it is a karmic setup. For we promise you that there is a "win-win" solution in every single one of these situations—but its solution starts with the love in that room, in that chair.

And so, dear ones, it is time again for us to depart as we pull the entourage out of the aisles, and away from you. We say this, that we are never, ever gone. Someday when you and I will meet again face to face, when you will be in your new colors, within your Merkabah, you will recognize my colors as well.

And that day there will be great love between us, when I say "Remember the time when we were in the beautiful setting on Earth in Banff, and I gave you this message?" Oh, dear ones, there are no words my partner can say that exemplify the love we have for you.

No words....

And so it is.

Kryon

"Power of the Human Spirit"
Channeled in
Toronto, Canada

The Kryon Writings, Inc.

PMB 422
1155 Camino Del Mar
Del Mar, California 92014
[www.kryonqtly.com]

"Power of the Human Spirit"
Live Channeling
Toronto Canada

*These live channelings have been edited with additional
words and thoughts to allow clarification and better
understanding of the written word.*

Greetings, dear ones. I am Kryon of Magnetic Service. Oh, it has been a while since this reunion was planned, hasn't it? And I say this, dear ones, because I recognize all of you. Now there will be those, as you are getting accustomed to my partner's voice representing me, who would doubt that this is taking place—that Spirit can speak through a human being. And we say, "Oh, if you only knew that Spirit was inside each one of you, and that it speaks daily to you, and can speak **through** you just as easily as what you are hearing now."

This message of love is for each and every one of you sitting in every chair and on the floor (and for those reading this). It does not matter at this moment whether you are a believer in what you are hearing or not, you see. It is for you, regardless. And so we say to the doubters in this room, "Oh, dear ones, you are loved beyond measure." And we say, also, "Nothing that transpires in these moments will be adverse to you." The seed of truth will be planted, however, which you can retrieve if you choose later. We challenge you, the doubter, to ask yourself, "Is this all there is?" The answer will well up and say, "No, there is far more!" For, you see, each and every one of you carries the spark of God itself around with you.

I mentioned a reunion. I say to you now that the group that exists in this room right now (Toronto) was planned long ago. That is why we release the entourage right now that comes with this entity that you call Kryon. **I AM the nurturing angel of the New Age**. If you thought I was the magnetic master, that was my

Earth designation. I come with the same countenance as Lord Michael, and the same love of that great angel. This is the love that I carry through my partner with these words this night to your ears (and eyes). Many of you have felt the similarity, and now I validate it. It is time. Oh, dear ones, this reunion was planned for each and every one of you. I know you, and you know me, for we look at each other as equals, but with one difference, you see: **You** are the ones who chose to do the work of becoming a human being in lesson on the planet. Regarding this, we cannot say too many times that the entourage and this entity that you call Kryon comes before you with the countenance and the mind of Spirit that says to you, "**You** are the elevated ones. You are the ones doing the work!"

As we have mentioned before, Kryon comes this night to sit at your feet and wash each one. The love is great here, and the entourage is walking in these aisles as we speak. The entourage are those that have come to help Kryon, as well as the guides represented by each and every one of you. Believe it or not, even the doubters have the guides, and even among the doubters there will be revelations to come from what happens here.

Oh, dear ones, this night is the night that we wish to continue the teaching series, and I ask my partner to hook this channel with the last, for it is a continuation of the message that we received in the mountains for you (Banff). There is so much going on right now! If you only had the whole concept of what is taking place in your biology! We will say more as we go on. Dear one, I know where you're from, and I honor you greatly. Feel all there is to feel. For all of the love that comes from you is appropriate, and we love you back—oh yes, we do!

The last time we were together, we spoke of the given parable of Wo and the Rooms of Lesson, and we gave you a lesson around one of those rooms. And so in the parable, Wo was shown one of the most important rooms of all that the guides could not go in. And in review we will say that this was *the room of self-essence*.

Have you ever fallen *in love* with God? Perhaps it was an entity—perhaps a great master, and you felt the welling-up of that feeling? It is a mirror of the love you should have for yourself! We told you that the chair that is in that room of self-essence is made of gold, and the feeling in that room is one of gold. For the gold represents the crown of God, and each one of you is the spark of divinity of that crown. We invited you to sit in that chair and feel the self-worth of that position—in the chair, with your crown on—feeling the wings that the angels give you—knowing full well that you are not here by accident. Not one of you is simply a blob of biology walking this planet for a short time. Oh, there is so much more! It is in the self-discovery that happens in this room that begets the gifts of the other rooms, you see. And so once the worthiness is felt as you take your seat in the golden chair, you can move to the other rooms of peace and abundance.

You might also recall that Wo saw two other rooms that he did not go into. One bore the name of unborn children, and one bore the name of a world leader. And just as we did in the city by the mountains, we will tell you more about these rooms this night, but this teaching session is going to be something special, and it's something we hope that you really pay attention to, for it is the crux of your existence on this planet.

This teaching session is about the power of the enlightened human being. You will hear me say this many times: **You have no idea how powerful you are!** There are many in this room who must pass the test of self-worthiness, and you know why this is. It is because we have the forerunners in this room—the ones who have awakened first—the ones who have seen "who they are" first. And you, dear ones, are the ones who have spent lifetime after lifetime after lifetime on your knees before God in the monasteries of the past—even some of the doubters! These are the past-life experiences that make you feel unworthy, for again we say that you have spent many hours and days and weeks on your knees in the past. Suddenly we now tell you that YOU are the exalted ones—and we wish you to understand that we are here to honor you for your divinity. For the work is clear—what must be done on this planet—and it's clearer all the time what you must do. It is personal work—a work that turns inward. It is a work that tells you, "Oh, dear ones, sit in the chair of worthiness." The chair of worthiness will beget healing, which will beget peace, which will beget abundance. All this centers around your realization of being in that chair.

The Six Attributes of Human Power

We wish to tell you about six attributes of power of the human spirit, three of which are obvious to you from our teachings, and three that are not. The first is the power of **group meditation**. You have started only recently to understand how much this means, and as we go down this list, we are going to tell you about some of the attributes of humanism in this New Age, which will make this comment about group meditation more poignant.

Group Meditation

There is incredible power in group meditation! Make no mistake. In the past we have asked you to meditate mainly for your own person, by yourself. We have told you the appropriateness of asking for yourself in co-creation when you're alone. There is also an appropriateness, however, when you get together to change this planet. As few as twelve of you is equal in power to a stadium filled with low-energy humans. The old low energy is far different from what you have now, and we tell you that this group work can make a marked change for your planet.

When we tell you to get together, this means that you must get together in mind. It matters not how far apart you are (one of the rules of universal Spiritual law). You can make a difference, for when you connect together equally concentrating on the same subject, you have no idea the power of INTENT transmitted . But each of you must be of a high vibration to accomplish this. So it's important that you pick your group carefully. Know indeed of their intent, for this is the main attribute. Judge not their lives or any other attribute, but the INTENT of the individual at the moment of the selection. This is one of the six attributes, and it will be more meaningful as we go forward. Consider doing it, for indeed it will make a difference in the planet. One of the most awesome things in this room, and from those reading this, is the power that exists within the humanity represented. This is why Kryon brings an entourage at all, and it is the reason you have the energy balance of the guides around you that this room can contain who you are. But this is hidden from you, and you see yourself only as a human walking the Earth in lesson. We look at you far differently, you see. That is why we love you so. That is why you know me and I know you. For you see, you were not always here. Your divinity is also mine.

Vibrating at a Higher Level

The next attribute is the power of the human being to achieve a higher vibration. Now, let me tell you that you are headed for a time when this planet is going to vibrate in a way that you have never ever imagined. You have changed much with your words of intent and with the love you have given to one another and to Spirit. You have accomplished a great deal. We tell you that it is not too long from now, (approximately 2012), when there is an opportunity—a potential—for something you have called the *New Jerusalem*: a change in vibration, a change in status, a change in humanism. And you have assigned many names and nomenclatures to dimensionality, some of which are almost accurate. But the truth is that a dimensional change from one to another is mostly awareness of Higher Self, and the graduate level is to become so aware of the Higher Self that you become it, and have the power to remain in biology but within a high vibration that you have never seen yet on this planet! For those who wish to do so may gradually shift into these new dimensions and new vibrations. You have the purpose to do that, and in this New Age, the permission to do that.

So many who are vibrating at a higher level right now are the ones who know what I am speaking of. Some of you will say, *"How do I know if I am vibrating at a higher level?"* I would say that there are so many of you doing it that it is indeed a foolish question! This is a high level when you start to recognize who you are. This is the level that allows you to listen to this voice (of Kryon) and feel the love of Spirit. This higher level is a vibratory level that finally makes sense of life. Sit in that chair of gold! Almost everyone here is headed for a new energy vibration. Oh, dear ones, this is the vibration that makes us so happy and honors you so, for we see the potential of what is possible. There is so much hope for this planet! You may say, *"With all of the things that are happening, I don't see how you could say that, Kryon."* And we say, if you had any idea of what it could have been, you would be thankful that you're here at all! YOU have done this, and it's the consciousness in this room and with others like you that have made the changes. Very powerful, you are, as you vibrate higher than any other human being has been allowed to vibrate since the beginning of time on this planet. It is indeed the beginning of what you call *ascension*. (See Chapter five.)

Co-Creation

The third one is co-creation. We have spoken of this before. It is a powerful thing indeed you do when you co-create your own reality, for it uses the God-self. And guess where you are when you do your finest co-creation? Sitting in the chair of gold with a crown on!—feeling your self-worth, feeling a part of the whole, knowing absolutely that you can create the reality that is around you—and do it in such a fashion that it touches no one else in a negative way. That's the secret, and that's the miracle of this gift. Your co-creative ability is something you do for yourself, but it allows positive spiritual attributes to revolve around you. This is how you personally change the world in a positive way, and we're going to tell you more about that in just a moment.

Many have said, *"Oh I've tried to co-create my reality, but I seemingly failed. Things have not gone well; just take a look around."* This is why we love you so much. Dear ones, you will not escape the tests. That is what being a human is all about. Co-creation is yours for the taking. We never promised that the *timing* would also be yours, so when you find yourself in a place that is difficult and the tears run down from your eyes and you wonder what is happening in your life, let each tear be one of honor! You are indeed creating the reality of your life, but the time frame might seem odd or even nonexistent to you. We have the overview, and you do not. Be patient, for we know where you are and what you're doing. It's time for a change, isn't it? Let the change begin with the energy in this room, when you realize, perhaps, that now is the time to sit "in the chair." See what has been missing in your life, and love that part of you that is God! Be patient with the timing of things, and know that you are loved in the process.

INTENT—The Most Powerful Tool in the New Age

Now we get into three attributes that are new. They are not exactly new, but the descriptions may surprise you. We wish to tell you about the absolute power humans have in the new energy through high vibrational intent. You've never seen anything like it in all past history. Let me inform you where its power is on this planet. Any of those who are of a new vibrational level giving thought energy (intent) to anything will have more power than the old-energy human being who is not vibrating at that level.

For the first time on this planet, here is what that means: It means that the good (positive intent) can outweigh the bad (negative intent). It means that you have far greater power than those who would use their intent for nonlove-based thought. It means that you have nothing to fear whatsoever from any lower vibrational entity *on* this planet or *off* this planet—because YOU have the power! We have told you this in so many ways before, but this is special. Oh, this is special!

Some of you have been afraid of groups on this planet of low energy that seem to have abundant power. You have called these "the Secret Government." We are here to tell you something this night that is good news: They (the Secret Government) are in trouble! They have never seen anything like what you have. They cannot stand against an enlightened, high-vibrational energy light worker. They cannot stand! And you will see their efforts dwindle in the light of illumination from those like you who will have the power, not them. You may say, *"But they have the abundance!"* We say this is not important. What is important is the critical mass—the consciousness of the planet. Combined, *you have the power !* You sit in the new energy. This *is* your power. It resides within the new gifts you are realizing and claiming. It resides in the golden chair.

I ask you this, dear ones: What kind of an attribute would see a political prisoner in a country slowly become its president in the last few years? That's a high vibrational power at work. It's a change in consciousness of many, many humans. Those of low vibration, even with abundance and seeming endless power, will fade and fail, and the truth will come out. The critical mass of consciousness will have discernment and make the decisions, and those who cower in secret and conspiracy will fail. This is good news, indeed, and it's under way.

What has made the difference? you might ask. INTENT! And also the ability to communicate quickly with others. WHEN EVERYONE CAN SPEAK INSTANTLY WITH EVERYONE ELSE, THERE CAN BE NO SECRETS!

We tell you, dear ones, that you sit in the driver's seat collectively, for YOU HAVE THE POWER, like nothing you have ever seen. The potential positive outweighs the negative. It's the first time in human history that this balance has gone in this way. Do you see what you have done? This is what it has been all about. This is what the test has been for. This is why you arrived on the planet, to see which balance it would be. This is the excitement. This is why the planet responds to you by vibrating higher and changing so greatly—did you notice the changes? They are in response to YOU! Now, aren't you glad that you are sitting in the golden chair? It's the chair of spiritual power, and it has the potential for shifting your entire future.

Synchronicity

The next one we will call synchronicity, but it's so much more. Remember when Wo saw a door with names of unborn children? Our last channeling showed what that really meant. Remember Wo also saw the name "World Leader" on a door? Some thought this meant that Wo would have been a world leader if he had wanted to. As the last channeling showed, that was not the message at all. No. Wo in his lifetime had the ability to affect the future through synchronicity. It is the one who stood in this aisle this night who meditated and prayed with her relative who knows about synchronicity, for her action affected someone else. This other one will indeed affect someone else, and they will affect someone else. Somewhere a child or two may be born that were waiting for synchronicity—for the love to be shared—for IN-TENT, you see. And that child has the potential for a destiny beyond your imagination. Do you see how much more this is than synchronicity, dear ones? This is the future of the planet, and it often revolves around what you do right now as an enlightened human.

This is a message for the healers here, too, this synchronicity. As you hear or read these words, there are those of you right now who ask, *"What can I do? I'm a healer and I know it. I'm seeing one person at a time. Sometimes they're helped, sometimes they're not; I'm tired. I help heal one person, one day—I heal another the next day, maybe, maybe not. I can't even tell anymore."* You might wonder, *"Is this changing the planet?"* And we say that's _exactly_ what's happening! It is through the synchronicity of the one-at-a-time healings that you in this room, and you reading this are doing, that is going to make the difference! You are the leading edge! There are no accidents regarding the mix of the ones coming to see you. Look at who they are, and know that through their healing, there will be the result of "unborn children," and that some of those will go on to do things that are special for the planet. They're waiting. How does that make you feel? Important in the scheme of things? Think about it!

Synchronicity. Future potential. One-at-a-time healing. There is so much power here! Look carefully at every single human who comes into your chamber for energy healing. You never know what's going to happen, or their potential contracts of responsibility. You may be the catalyst.

Years ago, my partner did not know me, and I wondered if he ever would. It was the synchronicity of the love that steered him into the right place at the right time, and he could not resist the logic of it because he knew it was where he belonged. Do you see that if he had not honored the synchronicity of the messages, there would be no meeting this day, and there would be no reunion this day, and no book in your hand? This represents only one human. Can you imagine the power you have as healers, and the choices that are going to be made from those who feel the energy as you balance them and allow them to give permission to move on to the next level?

Love

Now we get into the sixth one, and I will give you a word that you think you know the meaning of. I am speaking of love. Love makes the difference, does it not? It is what you've learned in these channelings. We have told you that the messages of Spirit are always filled with love, but we have been unable to truly define this for you, for it is not just the welling up and the emotions. It is not just the actions of one human being to another in times of stress. No. We're going to tell you what love is from a spiritual standpoint, you see.

Love and physics are married, and I want you to take a trip with me to the nucleus of an atom, and around that nucleus is a vast void space—an "energy soup" as we call it. This energy soup has a bias, and the bias is the attribute of where the energy is *at the moment.* You might say, *"Kryon, what are you doing talking physics? We're talking about love here!"* I'm here to tell you that the bias of the energy soup is love. Now I'm going to tell you some other things. Only three or four times have your scientists seem something that is absolutely baffling to them, and if they knew the reality of this they would be hesitant to share it, for it does not seem "scientific." The fact is that the bias that takes place in the energy soup changes depending upon the energy in the room that it is in! Is it no wonder it's seldom the same? Can consciousness and love affect matter? **Yes**, and this is the mechanical aspect of it. This is the secret. They're interconnected. It is the stuff in the middle between the parts that is the love.

This sounds odd to you, but it is this interconnection that is the missing piece between science and spiritual thinking. It's this attribute that has been unrecognized that is the unexplainable part of why INTENT and love can change physical things. Do you know about miracles within the practical Earth plane that you are on? Do you know about those who have been healed spectacularly? Perhaps there have been bones placed where bones never were before. It's a miracle. Do you ever wonder what the mechanics of that were? It's physics, and LOVE is at the center of physics, you see. There are avatars on this planet that can manifest objects in their hands at will. Did you know this? Did you ever wonder what the physics of this was? You see, it's SCIENCE. It's matter enhancement. It's LOVE. Perhaps it will be some time before those in science relate what they're looking at to how they're feeling, but it will indeed occur!

We tell you this, dear ones, in all seriousness: Love is at the heart of physics! Is it any wonder that the consciousness of this planet can shift the mantle—can change the weather—can change the orbit of an astral body? It is not Kryon doing this. Kryon is here to report what YOU are doing. Is it any wonder that attributes that seem to be in place and immovable can be voided out forever? Oh, there's so much more to know about this energy soup, but the bias is LOVE. That is the consciousness of Spirit itself, and you as human beings are beginning to go into that vibration, to have power with it, and that is why the miracles are happening. That is why physics is related to spirituality. That's love.

Oh, and it's the physics and thickness of love that is what you feel now as we pour this love to you, and you know why? Because it's the cellular level and the atomic level that we're dealing with, and that's where the "welling-up" happens. That's where the emotion happens. It's because we are affecting every single moving part (atom) of your body. It's Spirit! Pure Spirit.

Who do you think is the most powerful person on the planet? Well, you might say it's obviously the leader of the largest and most abundant country. We say no. We are talking now about Spiritual power. Power is defined by Spirit in this conversation this night as being that which can affect the vibration of the planet. That is power! Not political or economic. The one who has the power of the vibration of the planet will also hold the political and economic balance. And so we pose the question again: Who do you think is the most powerful? Now you might say, *"Kryon, I've heard these kinds of questions before. You're going to tell me it's me."* Not this time. I'm going to tell you it's some of you. Right now on this planet, in this instant, in this moment, as we channel to you in all love, we tell you this: The one with the most power to change the vibration of the planet is the human mother. Later we will speak about the INDIGO children arriving on the planet. You, as mothers, have the power to create an entire generation of balanced humans! Consciousness is the power of the future.

The Parable of Martha and the Singular Treasure

We wish to give you a parable of Martha and the Singular Treasure. Martha was an enlightened woman. She knew all about vibrational changes, and she knew about co-creation. Martha was co-creating, and she was happy, indeed. Oh yes, she had the same tests all the other humans did, but Martha was peaceful in her life. For long ago she had understood about the karma-changing attributes that Spirit had given her. She had accepted the new gifts of Spirit, and with intent had moved forward in her life.

Now Martha was honored in her life by a vision where an angel showed her the room of lessons. Much like Wo (in the parable) she saw the gold room and realized in an instant that that's where she sat. She also saw her room of peace and realized instantly that this was the key to life—to walking through it in a peaceful way. Then she was shown her room of abundance. There was enough for her—more than enough! Unusual as it might have been, one corner was filled with books! In another corner there was a special package, and the angel said to Martha, "*This is your singular treasure, Martha. This singular treasure is honored above anything else in this room. There will come a day when you will give it away. Don't do it, Martha, unless it's appropriate, and you will know. Also understand, Martha, that when you give it away, this singular treasure will not be replaced.*"

Martha knew how to co-create her own reality. She and her friends got together and they decided to build an organization— a store—where they would sell New Age books and materials to others of like mind. It was a good idea. Not only was it a good idea, but it brought them all abundance and they felt very good about it, for they were distributing products that had messages that they believed in. They watched those who would come into their store and show intent to purchase or not. They saw how Spirit worked with those, and they had many, many spiritual-type meetings in the store. Martha was certain that this reality she had created was the one in the vision—with many books. Then something happened.

It was one of these women whom Martha aligned herself with in this business called Sal. Sal did something that was unexpected to Martha, for, you see, Sal walked away with the proceeds of the store one day. And the group was no longer able to pay their debts, so they sold all of the merchandise and closed. To make matters worse, they did not have the abundance or the wherewithal to make any kind of arrangements to get their investment back from Sal. Sal had seemingly done something irretrievably evil to them—dishonest and inappropriate for the consciousness of the endeavor.

Now the two other women that Martha was aligned with were very angry and said, "We must do something!" There was great drama around this. They knew the laws of the land would support them, but they could not afford to proceed in this manner because Sal had taken their abundance. Sal knew this, and blatantly moved back in town and started her own store! She was successful.

Now Martha learned a long time ago that such seeming negative things were karmic attribute coming to face her once again—only this time Martha was prepared. She had disengaged the karma of this incident long ago and did not "feel" the wound that the other two did, or the need to participate in the drama. So she looked at Sal in a different way. She looked at Sal as a player on the field—a family member. Perhaps there was disappointment in the event, but there was no anger or vindictiveness. The other two women carried the situation with them daily. They felt victimized and would call Martha and say, *"Oh, Martha, isn't it awful, what's happened to us?"* Martha would do her best to tell them the reason Sal was in their lives, but they did not accept it. And so there was great energy and daily drama, regarding what Sal had done to them.

Now this situation continued for some years until one day Martha heard that Sal had become ill. It seems there had been an accident. Sal was right in the middle of it, and she was in the hospital gravely injured. Martha decided to visit Sal, and on the way to the hospital, remembered the words of the angel in her vision, and she knew why she had to go. Martha walked into that hospital room where Sal was lying and Sal opened her eyes. Sal saw Martha, and she was afraid! Sal knew what she had done to Martha and the others, and she knew she was in trouble now.

Sal also knew that Martha was one of those who had loved her anyway. Martha approached and laid her hand on Sal, trying to avoid all of the tubes and contraptions that were hanging from her. She said only a few words to her.

"Sal, will you accept the healing I have?"

Sal could not believe what she was hearing. After all she had done, Martha was going to heal her? And she croaked out an answer.

"Yes." And so, metaphorically, Martha reached within herself with INTENT and plucked out her singular treasure and passed it to Sal. Sal received it and gave permission for the healing that it allowed her.

Now we're going to stop the parable for just a moment and review the four attributes of love that we gave you last time. Whereas in the last channeling we itemized them, now you can see them work.

Dear ones, what Martha did was within the definition of the four attributes of love previously given.

Love is quiet. In that hospital room that night between those two women, love was quiet.

The second one is that love **has no agenda**. It doesn't plan. It does not connive or scheme. In that hospital room that night, you see, there was no agenda—none. If there had been, Martha would not have even been in that room.

The third attribute is that love does not shout from the hilltop about itself. It **is not puffed up**. That night in the hospital, only the words: *"Are you ready for the healing?"* were spoken.

The fourth attribute is that love has **the wisdom** to understand the other three. Martha didn't arrive loudly and cause a commotion, since love is quiet. She didn't demand that Sal give her anything back, since love has no agenda. She didn't congratulate herself for being healthy and loving while Sal was injured. No, love is not puffed up. Martha had used her wisdom to know absolutely that her singular treasure was to go to Sal that night, never to be replaced. Martha had shared something so special that it could not be ignored.

Now we return to the parable. That night, Sal was healed completely. The gift of healing that Martha passed to her allowed her to give permission for her life to continue. Sal remembered Martha's visit very well. She understood that in order to help heal her, Martha had first totally forgiven her and had been without anger or drama. It changed Sal's life forever.

Sal began to change. The singular treasure that was passed to her had taken root in love and was able to resound with her...and now it was hers to give also when the time was correct—and she did. When she was again healthy, she visited Martha, and the two again became friends. In the process, they began to write books together for children, and those books became popular, and went on to change many lives forever!

Now, what about Martha? You would think that perhaps she would be empty, having given away her singular treasure. One night, Martha was visited again by a vision, and the same angel who had led the first trip to her room of abundance did so again. He asked her, "*Do you wish to see your abundance room again?*" Martha agreed, and the angel led the way. Again, there were many books in the corner, but now Martha recognized them as the children's books she had published with the help of Sal—giving her the abundance necessary to meet her earthly needs. She mused to herself that these were not the books from owning a shop, as she had formerly  thought. No. These were the books created from the love and healing of her former "enemy" Sal.

The angel led her to the corner where her singular treasure used to sit, and as expected, it was gone. Martha had given it away. Instead of the singular treasure, now there were seven singular treasures stacked up to the ceiling! The angel saw her amazement and said to her, "*The singular is gone, as we told you, and now they have multiplied into the many.*" Martha saw the fun in this, and understood what it meant. The angel had spoken quite literally about the "singular" being a one-time gift. The angel didn't tell the whole story, however, for it was Martha's test. She had created a great vibrational increase—more abundance and more power in her life by giving away her precious gift. Martha understood that this was the way of God. Love has no limits, and it increases the more you give of it. It multiplies as it is distributed, and it changes the very fabric of reality. Martha was an honored human, indeed.

Dear ones, your storehouse of love is absolutely unlimited! As fast as you give it away, it will be replaced sevenfold! As you pour it to those around you, you will never run out. Some of you know how this works, and others of you are just discovering it.

Oh, dear ones, it has been such a short time since we started this message. There has been much accomplished in this room tonight. And if Spirit and Kryon could be sad, I say that right now would be that time, for we are about to say good-bye for the communications of this evening. There is a withdrawal of energy between us when we part, and I feel it as much as you. There will never be another time when this exact energy occurs between precisely the entities that are present here.

When you leave this place, look around you—especially at those you think you have never seen before tonight, for in reality they are all "family." You know each and every one. At some point in time, perhaps you may acknowledge them as family—maybe even this night, understanding that each and every one around you knows you spiritually, and you know them. It is hiding from you that many of these represent your karmic family—here because they should be, just like you.

It is good news we have passed to you this night. It is with honor and love that we have brought it to you at this appointed time. As we withdraw, we say the words from my partner's lips that you have come to know and expect from the Kryon group.

You are dearly loved!

Until next time...

And so it is...

Kryon

Kryon at The United Nations!

In November 1995, November 1996, and again in November 1998, Kryon spoke at the S.E.A.T. (Society for Enlightenment and Transformation) at the United Nations in New York City. By invitation Jan and Lee brought a time of lecture, toning, meditation and channelling to an elite group of UN delegates and guests.

This book carries the first two entire transcripts of what Kryon had to say (page 213) ... some of which has now been validated by the scientific community. Kryon Book 7, *Letters From Home* carries the meeting in 1998. All three of these transcripts are on the Kryon web site [www.kryon.com].

Our sincere thanks to Mohamad Ramadan in 1995, Cristine Arismendy in 1996, and Jennifer Borchers in 1998 who were presidents of that bright spot at the United Nations, for the invitation and for their work to enlighten our planet.

Partnering with God

Chapter Two

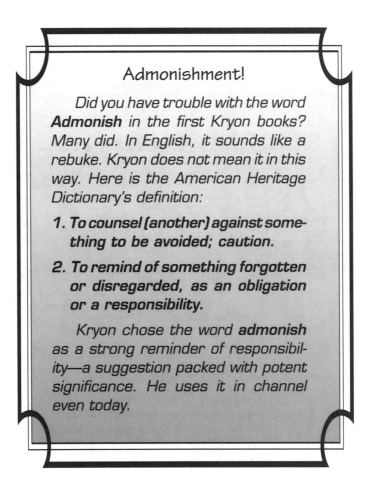

Admonishment!

Did you have trouble with the word **Admonish** *in the first Kryon books? Many did. In English, it sounds like a rebuke. Kryon does not mean it in this way. Here is the American Heritage Dictionary's definition:*

1. **To counsel (another) against something to be avoided; caution.**

2. **To remind of something forgotten or disregarded, as an obligation or a responsibility.**

Kryon chose the word **admonish** *as a strong reminder of responsibility—a suggestion packed with potent significance. He uses it in channel even today.*

"Partnering with God"
Channeled in
Indianapolis, Indiana

The Kryon Writings, Inc.

PMB 422
1155 Camino Del Mar
Del Mar, California 92014
[www.kryonqtly.com]

"Partnering with God"
Live Channeling
Indianapolis, Indiana

These live channelings have been edited with additional words and thoughts to allow clarification and better understanding of the written word.

Greetings, dear ones, I am Kryon of Magnetic Service. There will never be a time when Spirit grows tired of hearing the voices of humans (in response to a group toning). This is a time to be loved, dear ones. Take it! For the energy this night will pour into you if you so desire. Oh, there are those in this entourage who will not believe that such a thing could be, that there would be communication such as this from the other side. There's no amount of convincing possible for this belief to permeate your mind. So we ask instead that you would FEEL the love that is pushed to you from Spirit this night. For you see, there's a piece of God in each of you—a piece of Spirit that knows the truth, that knows all about God. This is the truth: Each and every one of you knows who I am. We have met before in another place, in another time, and many of you have gone through the Hall of Honor and have received the colors of the lifetimes of this planet.

Each of you, by agreement, has come to be in this place at this time. Whatever age you are is immaterial, for you are all young in spirit, appropriate, each one. So we say to you that there is a great deal that's going to be passed to you tonight if you so desire, if you so let it. It is Spirit that has a sense of urgency. You see, there are those of you who will never sit in a place like this again, and if we can say anything to you, even if you doubt what is taking place now, it is to say that there is a tremendous amount of love here. There is healing in this room. Right now, we send the Kryon entourage into this place. We extend the bubble of love, which we have done before, to gently push upon you. We invite the guides that walk in between the seats to do their jobs, and to wrap their arms around you and say, "You are eternal!"

And so each time we come and sit before an assemblage of humans, we say something to you that you expect Kryon to say. From the lineage of Lord Michael and Kryon, we say that indeed YOU ARE DEARLY LOVED, each and every one. Again, we tell you that we know your name. We know your contract, and there are those here, and those reading this, who are waiting patiently, poised for intent to proceed forward. Even the ones of you who say, "*This cannot be so*", or "*This cannot be happening,*" we ask you, are you so delighted with your life? So delighted that you would not even want to risk the possibility that this could be real? There's work here, but with the work there is joy. And with the joy, there is personal peace. And with the peace there is healing and extended life. It is the theme of Kryon that says that many of you are doing the work you came to do, and it's the intent of sitting in the chairs in this room (or being interested enough to be reading this) that proves it! Loved, each one! Yes, you are!

Oh, dear ones, this night we're going to expose a concept to you that we've been holding until we came and sat in this energy again (returning to Indianapolis), for we are in the middle of your continent, and the energy is appropriate here for us to bring you this message. This is a concept that is overdue—something that everything we have channeled to you has been focusing toward. It is a truism, a postulate, a **reality of God** that we are going to finally teach tonight. It is something that some of you are aware of but perhaps never identified properly. We want to talk about the integration of human beings with God.

It's time that we presented this to you as it should be done, and it's only with the new energy, year after year, as it gets purer and cleaner and more intense with the vibrational increases of the humans who sit here, that we could give you these messages. Do you now understand that some channeling is actually created by the energy of the crowd of humans? Think about it.

There is an integration going on between human beings and Spirit that is an integration like never before. It is an integration that we have shared with the healers—even some of the ones in this very room. It is an integration that says, "Gone are the days when God does everything for you." Instead, here are the days where you participate in the process in a way you were never allowed to before!

My partner tells a joke: How many New Age light workers does it take to change a lightbulb in the New Age healing center? And the answer is: Only one, but the lightbulb has to want to be changed! And so we have sat in front of you healers and told you that it is the one on the table that is going to make a difference in how your healing goes! We have spoken of the fact that, regardless of your process, the one on the table is the catalyst to healing, not the healer. No matter what your healing process is— if it is chemical, or hands-on, even if it is honored beyond all methods — the one on the table has to have ceremony, agree, and give permission and intent for the healing. This is something fairly new, you see. THEY HAVE TO WANT TO CHANGE! So many do not understand the concept and turn to the healer to do it all. This principle of healing is also the basis of a high vibrational life in the New Age!

And so as you walk an everyday path with Spirit, which you call God, we have a new term for you, and we're going to go over it in some depth now. It is going to be called "**Partnering with God**." The word *partner* has never been broached in any venue where Kryon has sat in front of humans as it will be now.

Following God

There are sayings that you have used in the relationship between Spirit and humans for a very long time: It's a concept of the sheep and the shepherd. And the humans somehow are equated with the sheep, and the shepherd is God. Let me tell you, dear ones, that the last things we want you to be are sheep!

Empowered is what you are! Partnering with God has nothing to do with the shepherd/sheep relationship. Some of you have equated God with a parent, a heavenly father or mother; and you are the children. A nice picture, perhaps, but cast that away, for that is not the relationship we wish to tell you about. True partners are not in that relationship at all, and they don't dominate each other in that manner—even in love.

Some have said, "_I'm going to_ **let go** _of my life and_ **let God** _take over!_" This is not what we ask for, dear ones. We wish you to _let go of nothing_. We wish you to instead grip the situation with the power you have in this New Age and take control with a partner that sees the overview—that's "Partnering with God." Some of you have said, "_I'm going to_ **surrender** _my life and let God have His will._" And we say NO! Don't surrender! Instead, _Commit!_— not surrender. Commitment is to **take charge** of your life with a partner like God. Let us use a metaphor, because you're going to understand this better in the context of partnering with human beings. You are familiar with that kind of partnership.

Human Partnership/God Partnership

Many of you are so familiar with partnering in human relationship that you have done it many times [laughter]. And you know the pitfalls, don't you? And you know where the problems arise, don't you? Especially in partnering one with another, and being in love. So we use the metaphor of those who partner, because these are the ones who want to experience each other's love together. Is it not true, as humans, that two people deciding to make this step often have ceremony? They will announce to those around them, usually their friends, their intent. They will have a ceremony where they verbalize to one another what they intend to do within their love.

Let's have a ceremony, you and I! It's time to partner, and if you wish to, go ahead and have a ceremony—perhaps on your own. Let it last two minutes or less, but let it be out loud. Let it say,

"*I wish to marry to my Higher Self at this point in my life.*" I can tell you what Spirit is going to say back to you, because I represent the love of Spirit. I represent the reply of the high partner, the Higher Self, when I say that the verbiage that is going to come back to you is this: "*Oh, dear ones, we promise to partner with you. For we love you beyond measure, and we have been waiting for you to verbalize this to us! Our vow to you in this partnership is to love you throughout it all, and never let you down.*"

Ceremony! It's a marriage to the Higher Self, because that's who the partner is. That's who lives in you, and who can make the difference. Each one of you carries that spark of life, a peace of the whole, hiding so completely in your duality.

Now, what's one of the first things that partners do? Well, they set up households, and they decide that there are going to be duties to perform. Lest one overlap the other, they often assign the duties that they're both best at. So it is that we itemize some of the duties of this spiritual partnership—and we start with the human's duties.

Clearing the Old

The goal of the partnership is to **draw closer**, and if you're going to draw closer, the duties of the partnership are for you to do everything you can for a **meld** between you and God. The first thing we wish you to do is to clear that old karma and get it out of the way. Many of you are aware of the new gifts for that purpose, for we have spoken of them often. Many of you are here because you have read of them, and we say that indeed this is necessary. It's first, and it's number one. And so YOUR part of the clearing will be to give intent for that, and OUR part of it is to make it so for you. For those of you who take this gift and go through this, we will honor you greatly with results! Just as in a human partnership, the old ways must be cast aside for the new ones to be accepted. Then things will start to happen around you that will enable one of your next duties in the partnership—that is, of co-creation. Slowly you will begin to co-create with your new partner—just as you would in a human relationship as you co-create new living attributes, acquiring common things together, and bringing a common consciousness between you.

Co-Creation and Self-Worth

Some have said, *"Kryon, you've talked about co-creation before, but what does it really mean?"* Co-creation, dear ones, is that process where you create the reality of your life, which is to find your current contract. Contracts are not always grandiose, you know. Some of the contracts are simply to be a wonderful human being, walking in the light, raising children who will also walk in the light. How about that? Some of the contracts are to be a silent healer, to affect other human beings, and you know whom I'm talking to, for some of you are right in the middle of that very contract. Some of you are in that contract, and you don't even believe it is happening! ...such is the duality. Some of you have multiple contracts, and as a parable we have given exemplifies, you are searching for just one in the midst of doing many—all appropriate!

Co-creation is that duty that requires you to believe that all these things are possible. Often there's an area of self-worth that gets in the way of these partnering duties, and we have spoken of this before. Oh, so many of you seated here and reading this have past incarnations wearing sackcloth and sandals! It's what brings you to a place like this even now—or keeps you interested in reading this communication. It's your interest in God, a calling to find out about Spirit—that part of you that says, *"There's more to life than just walking around this planet as biology. I remember it from another time!"*

But as you remember, you lived as a priest or a nun or a monk. You were taught in those days that to think of yourselves as gods and goddesses was blasphemy! We're here to tell you that you absolutely know better! Metaphorically, there is a room in your House of Lesson that has within it a golden chair—something we've spoken about before (Chapter One). This is a throne where an angel sits that is glorious and spectacular! And on the face of that angel is your likeness! For you deserve to be here as a piece of the whole. You stood in line for it. You asked for it—and now you are here! There is no other entity in this universe that is greater than the ones who sit in the chairs before me now, or that belong to the two eyes that are scanning these words. This is what allows the Partnering with God, and it's self-worth that allows the acceptance of that fact. You have earned the right to take this partnering step!

Here is something we told you during the last channel: No longer see your boat of life drifting in a sea of frightening uncertainty. Instead, take the tiller of the rudder in your hand with wisdom and power. Watch the giant hands of Spirit—your own golden angel of Higher Self—wrap its fingers around yours, and together, steer an anointed course to home. This is the real partnership!

Peace

Another duty of the partnership is to create peace in your life, for you cannot be in this marriage with God and not have a peaceful countenance. *"How is that done?"* you might ask Kryon. *"How can I be peaceful in my life just because I understand that I deserve to be here?"*

When you understand that your karma can be cleared—when you understand that the reality around you is of your own design and making—you can believe that PEACE can be achieved, also. Slowly, through intent and communication, you can start to have peace even over the most awful things in your life that have bothered you ever since you can remember—and were thought to be permanent! A peaceful countenance is an attribute of an enlightened human being. *"What's God's part in that?"* you might ask. *"Where's the partnering concept in having a peaceful countenance?"* That's OUR specialty, dear ones! *That's OUR specialty!* For at the point that you feel the most angry, and at the point that you wish to cry in frustration, that's when WE as the loving partner come to you and surround you with the loving arms of God. And we say, *"Be peaceful with this. Do not fear these things that are your lessons. For in the big picture there is only love—the most powerful force in the universe!"* It's the force that heals your body. It's the feeling that can surround you right now as I speak to you as Spirit. That's OUR part, you see. That's the part of the human's peaceful countenance, and all you have to do is ask. And if this were not true, I would not tell you so. And if it were not happening with some in this room, I would not tell you so. We promise to encompass you with love, and create for you the peace you desire when you give the intent for partnering. There is no greater peace than the peace of God!

Health

Another of your human duties of partnership is health. The health of your body is critical, for you see, there's something your partner (God) wants you to know. We want you to stay here! We want you to stay here as long as possible. For there is an investment that you have made in your journey, and so we say, *"Now that you have the truth, and now that you understand partnering, why should you leave?"* Oh! *We want you to stay!* That's the reason the karma-clearing gift is given. That's the reason the contracts are revealed. That's the reason for the peaceful countenance. Many of you have misunderstood the concept of ascension. Ascension is the name of the attribute of a human being with a 100 percent marriage to the Higher Self, and a 50/50 Partnering with God! It allows that human to stay on Earth—not leave it! It allows you to become so much greater than you are now that you actually become a spiritual being, with one foot in your dimension and the other in ours. It takes work, self-worth, and vibrational shift to do this. But the initial duties of the honeymoon revolve around love, and each of your duties are reciprocated with spiritual attributes of _what we can do for you_ to complement the marriage. But we will do nothing without your permission, nothing without your intent. INTENT is the key.

Fidelity

Now here is another interesting partnering duty. "_How could fidelity possibly relate to Partnering with God?_" you might ask. Let us speak of fidelity.

Some of you might say, "_Well, you don't have to worry about fidelity in this spiritual partnership with God, Kryon, after all, there's only one God! I'm not going to be running off with another, you know._" It's not like that. It's not what you think.

ANGER: Oh, dear ones, anger is human nature, is it not—to slip back into anger even when you know better? When you know that anger and fear are old-energy concepts and do not flatter your spirit and do not speak of love—yet it happens with humans, regardless. Anger has an agenda, and love does not. It is against the very nature of your partner (God) to be angry, and yet it is there within you often! It is, however, _infidelity_ to the very nature of a marriage with God.

WORRY: What about worry? Worry is a product of the intellect. It's the attribute that awakens you at three in the morning and says, "_There's something wrong! I can't think of what it is right now, but I know it's there...so let's worry about it!_" It's human nature. The strangest thing is that some of you agree—and get right to the worrying! If it hasn't occurred to you before now, we're asking you to void the intellectual worry nature, which is the old energy, and have the fidelity of love with Spirit. OUR part is to give you peace over worry. It's guaranteed— through intent. It is against the very nature of your partner (God) to worry, and yet it is there within many of you often! It is also _infidelity_ to the very nature of the marriage.

Anger will not serve you. Worry will not serve you. Doubting your self-worth will not serve you in this New Age. These actions go against the very principles of your new partnership and do not have fidelity with the countenance of God.

CHANNELING: Here's another item in the fidelity area with God. Listen closely, dear ones: Any channeled entity that comes into your life will honor YOUR Higher Self as much as it does itself! The Higher Self that you carry around with you is a "piece of God." A piece of God is also the partner to this very channel (that you are reading). I honor the Higher Self of the one who is channeling (Lee) as much as I honor any entity in this universe! Those of you who feel you are channeling entities, check this: See if they honor your Higher Self. Watch to see if they say that they are more important than your internal angel, and if they do—run the other way! For there is nothing higher on this planet than what you carry inside! Channeling is information, data. It is no more than that. It is information that your Higher Self and your human nature can use for spiritual food. After the information is put out, take it, apply what you wish, and put it away. Never use the channeler as a guru! Never give away your personal power of choice. Instead, give the information from the channel to your Higher Self, and the Higher Self will guide you on how to live—because that's the anointed piece of God that you are! That's who's in charge—the higher part of you—not the channeler. To embrace the channeler as a guru is to create *infidelity* with God, your Higher Self.

Drama

Perhaps the part of human nature that is the most puzzling to Spirit is when those of you, by choice, desire to go backwards in your enlightenment path and "spin" in self-made drama. All of you know of humans who do this. Just when things get good, they say internally, "*It seems to be too peaceful. I think I'll go backwards and create some problems. I'm more comfortable there.*" And

many of you are! You grow up a certain way. You're used to
certain feelings, certain things around you, and you try to create
that comfort zone when it appears to be going away. Accepting
the lack of human self-made drama requires an education. It's a
lesson in partnering, and it's a lesson of growth. You don't need
self-made human drama to feel comfortable. You don't need it!
Oh, but if you want some drama, we'll give you some! How about
this: Drama around the new energy, the kind that changes lives
forever and heals humans. It's spiritual sensationalism in the
highest order! How about miracles performed in your own body?
How's that for drama? That's the kind of drama your God partner
has and wishes you to know of. Get used to it!

Communication

HAVING A COMMON CONDUIT: Some of you are aware
that as partners, human beings can talk to each other for very long
periods of time and never really communicate anything. The
reason for that is manyfold, but among the reasons are that you
both never truly arrived at the same level in order to communicate
properly. One speaks of one subject but the other hears another!
You are not on the same page of the book, and you are not
speaking on the same common line, so you often end up with
verbalization, but noncommunication. So, therefore, there is no
communication, and sometimes this goes on for a very long time.

HOW can you communicate with this new partner we are
speaking of? We're talking about *Partnering with God*! What can
you do to make sure that communication is good? Oh, dear ones,
this is not hard. There is a conduit in place, ready right now for you
to speak to Spirit, as easily as I speak to you now. As easily as my
love flows from me and this human being whose voice you hear,
into the hearts of the humans who are in front of me, there is a
conduit ready to go! You don't have to build it. All you have to do
is know where to access it.

Here is the key: When you sit down to meditate, the first thing that you should visualize is that golden angel that sits in that throne inside you as a piece of God, deserving to sit in that chair! This opens that conduit—believe me. Again, it is the self-worth issue. Understand the "piece of God" that you are. Open the door and start the conversation. Don't come in a manner that is groveling. Don't come as a child does to a parent, or a sheep to a shepherd. It's time to talk to your partner, whom you love dearly, and sit in that chair as an angel as you speak. Feel those wings unfold, and open the conversation as an equal. That's number one! You deserve it. If you don't feel that deserving, you're not going to even open the communications. You can verbalize all you want to, as a groveling human being, hoping that God will listen. The words are going to fall right off the ceiling!

See, Spirit wants to talk to you as *a partner*. That's step one. Step two is to ask those magic questions: *"Where do you want me now? What can I do to partner better with you? Give me instructions regarding this week,"* for instance. Some of you are facing daily problems. We know that most of you have these kinds of things to deal with. Approach them in this manner: *"Dear Spirit, I wish to partner with you. I deserve to be here in my magnificence for answers from my partner, who is also magnificent. How can I have this or that take place? What can I do next? Give me the synchronicity around my living THAT SHOWS ME THE ANSWERS, and I will respond by being aware that there are no accidents in my life."*

Dear ones, use the synchronicity of what happens to you day by day as a direct answer to these questions. You see, this is the part WE play in answer to your requests. Things are not always as they seem. Make no assumptions about what IS or IS NOT going to happen, and never limit your partner! Don't give us what you believe to be the solutions! Let OUR overview bring them to you.

The overview: The last thing that your spiritual God partner wants to hear, dear ones, is that you think you know what the overview is. Odd as it sounds, there are many of you who dictate it to us constantly, as though you understood all the unseen workings around you. Remember, you don't know what we know. Allow us, therefore, to be the ones who supply the unknown. There are contracts of others around you that you're oblivious to, that are supposed to marry with yours at the highest degree—and you haven't even met these people yet! If the potential is realized for the meeting, then you will. So there's an element of trust, is there not? There's an element of being in the "now" with your life and being open to the unexpected.

In the past, we've made the joke about the map that Spirit gives you. When you unfurl the map, there's a little sign that says, "You are here," and around that dot there's seemingly very little— only where you stand. Some map! It's in the "now," you see. It only tells you where YOU ARE and what is immediately in front of you. It never tells you what is coming down the line. It doesn't even give acknowledgment for where you've been! Because Spirit, your partner, is in a different time frame, you see. We are in the "now," and we have an overview that would astound you. We know your contracts, and we know your angelic name. We see your Merka-bah, we know your colors. We know who you are! And in partnering with us, you have it all. You get a partner that has knowledge you do not, but you must ask, and give intent.

Now the second question that is often asked about communi-cation is, "WHEN should we communicate?" Two rules: "*Never communicate when you're tired*" is the first one, or you'll end up communicating in your sleep. The second? "*Don't wait until you are in trouble!*" Practice communication daily. Don't wait until you have an insurmountable problem. It's so much harder for your partner to work with you when you're frightened. *Fear* is a word that you have not heard come forth in this channel, for there is no fear in partnering with God. Fear is an old-energy concept, you know. It has no place as you walk forward and vibrate in a new way.

Reciprocation!

Finally, let me tell you about the reciprocation of this partner of yours—the God-force.

OUR PARTNERING DUTIES: Oh, dear ones, do you want to know what "sensational" is? There is no higher drama than is being played out on this planet right now with the light workers in this New Age! You are starting to see who you are. You are starting to realize the changes you've made. You are starting to understand why you're here. When you were not here, each and every one of you said, *"I want to come back, for this is the time on Earth we all waited for—the potential for amazing planetary change!"* That's drama! That's sensational! Now we talk about <u>Partnering with Spirit</u> (God), and that is the most sensational news a human being could ever have.

Answer me this: How would you like to have a partner who's always there, no matter what? Oh, you could get angry. You could slip back to the old energy and become worried. You could go off and channel inappropriate entities that fill people with fear. You could doubt your self-worth all you want. But when you decide to come back, your God partner still loves you! The partner says, *"I'm here. Let's try it again. Take my hand."* That's sensational news! For there's nothing like it that exists on the planet. It's the story of The Prodigal Son, you know, all over again.

Answer me this: How would you like a partner who is so in love with you that he's always there? Always there—regardless of what you are doing—always there with open arms and love beyond measure! How about that? That's sensational! That's what we offer this night—a Partnering with Spirit, something that we have never spoken of before. Oh, we have talked all around it, but it took a time like this, with this mixture of humans who have come to this place with a kind of pure intent that is represented this night, to say these things to you.

We love you beyond measure. Even as we speak, there are those of you right now beginning to understand the full potential of your life. Things are going to be different, you know. This is the beginning of a New Age. We will go on record to say that there's going to be brand new volcanic activity that you've never seen before on this planet, and it's going to start soon. It only makes sense, dear ones. The changes start from without, and they move to within. It won't be unexpected. We've told you this before.

What are you supposed to do about that? With a partner like Spirit, you're going to be in the right place at the right time! And you never have to WORRY, and you never have to FEAR these planetary changes. It is true that there may be some lessons for you, and some of you may lose some belongings along the way, but the lessons will be clear—given in love for you. Clear, and uplifting for your process.

There is no greater love than that where an entity agrees to come and be a human on this planet—veiled with the duality of who you are. You don't see yourselves as I do. Spectacular, magnificent, with colors shining beyond measure. That's who you are. Some of you will walk from this place doubting even that—even that you belong on the planet. But the seeds will be planted tonight, you see, because there will come a time when you can use this information. Others of you right now are absorbing this and fully understanding its implications for your life.

We have come to you this night to tell you these things in love. As I give a love wash to you and my partner, I say to you, dear ones, that there is no greater love than this. The invitation is open, and will continue to be, to Partner with Spirit. This is not the only time you are going to hear about Partnering with God. For this is one of the new gifts that you have as a human being in this New Age. And so we leave you with this information, and we invite you to feel the love of Spirit this night—and the hugs that are here—and the astounding sensationalism of humanity in this New Age!

And so it is.

Kryon

"The Seven Love Connections"
Channeled in
Vancouver Island, BC Canada

The Kryon Writings, Inc.

PMB 422
1155 Camino Del Mar
Del Mar, California 92014
[www.kryonqtly.com]

"The Seven Love Connections"
Live Channeling
Vancouver Island, BC Canada

These live channelings have been edited with additional words and thoughts to allow clarification and better understanding of the written word.

G reetings, dear ones, for I am Kryon of Magnetic Service. Oh, my partner, you have brought me this night before a special assemblage of humans, and as I speak to you who sit in front of this Kryon this night (and read these words), I say you have expected me, and I have expected you. This night I wish to talk to the family, and it is the family who sits in front of me. [Child in audience wakes up and cries.] You see, how even the little ones respond to the love of Spirit! Dear ones, in these next moments we will fill this room with love—a bubble that is a canopy that will press down upon you with the love of Spirit like you have never felt—if you so choose to feel it.

And so it is that we address you healers and those of you who can see beyond the veil who call yourselves the psychic ones, and we say that we honor you greatly, for you are the forerunners of the Warriors of Light—the first to know that there is a change afoot—the first to see the light in the sky that is the New Age—and the first to truly and wondrously realize that you are indeed special.

There is a spark in each one of you that is God itself, and you walk this planet knowing full well that it is there. So it is that we tell you that each one is exalted. Even those of you who are uncertain of what I am speaking of are exalted. Dear ones, we have waited so long for this meeting. For the energy in this room will never be the same, ever again. The consciousness of the entities that are represented here will never again gather in this exact pattern, and so we invite you to feel the family now. It is this energy and this feeling of home that we want you to have. And we want you to see what it is like again.

A slice of home it is, as we allow this veil to lift that which you call the "duality." For these few moments we are going to talk to you about love. We're going to talk about seven attributes of love. The first three are dripping with karmic potency, some of them that you would never expect in a discussion of love.

(1) The first one we have talked about before. We speak now of FEAR. Now you might ask, *"Isn't this a discussion of Love? This is a teaching about the connection of love to humans, yet the first thing you speak of is fear?"* Yes. This is because, as we have said before, fear is the mechanism (or tool) of the love of God on Earth. Fear is what is given to you as a poke or a prod that says, "This is why you're here." Look at it. Look into the eyes of it, and work through it. Fear, therefore, becomes a prime love connection, or attribute of Spirit with humans on Earth. And for those of you who have walked into the fear and turned it into joy, know of what I speak.

But now we also talk about the kinds of fears that you carry into your incarnation with you that are from your past lives and represent (facilitate) your karma—even the small fears: the fear of small places, the fear of heights, the fear of enlightenment. These are carried directly over so that you can look at them. And each time they occur, it is like a message from the duality that says, "We love you." This is why you, with permission, are often placed in a fearful mode. And oh, dear ones, listen: It is not any dark or evil entity that places you into a fear mode. It is the **love of God** itself with permission of your actual entity to facilitate your work of raising the vibration of the planet! It is your INTENT that allows you to stay in fear or not, as you choose—for your choice and your intent is what drives the vibration of this planet upward.

So the next time you are faced with fear of any kind, look at it and understand that it is a test by agreement with your Higher Self. Although anointed the fear is fake! It is a love lesson in disguise asking you to solve it, and on the other side of it there is peace and there is joy! And when you look it in the eye and verbalize, "*I see you—and I know why you're here,*" the fear will smile at you and disappear—like a joke in the night before the light arrives. Then you will know that it was packed with love. Then you begin to understand that it exists not as a dark thing, but as an agreed upon attribute for your life's work! It actually drives you to learn and grow. It is, therefore, a great gift, but one that most of you never quite openly welcome. The result of working though FEAR is **a strength** and **consciousness change**. It is common to all of you in some form or another.

Appropriate from God?

There will be those who will tell you that Spirit will never take you to a fearful or dark place in your life. Those who tell you this have not studied the spiritual history of this planet, and are therefore misinformed on how God has worked with us for eons. According to almost every written Earth religion, this attribute has been present in the lessons of great men and women since recorded time. Buddha speaks of it clearly in his great history and teachings. Mohammed had great tests of fear and faith in his life, all bringing him to a higher level. Jesus on the cross openly cried of it aloud for everyone to record as he changed to an ascended vibration. A current master, Paramahansa Yogananda, has also clearly taught of these attributes. In the old energy, the tests of Job are legendary, and can you imagine the fear and terror in the heart of Abraham as he started to slay his only son? These were all tests of a loving God—each one. Fear represents a tool filled with love and honor. Moving through fear is accompanied with a reward of a higher vibration. Don't let anyone define for you what God will and won't do. That's the fastest way to start yet another denomination of religious belief. Use your own power of discernment—and if you choose to, take a look at history. Spirit uses fear differently in this New Age than in the old energy, but it remains one of the best tools of growth there is.

(2) The second of the seven connections is perhaps the one that is the most outstanding when it comes to karma. This is the one that Spirit works with in a prime way. This is the one that you have all given permission for and have asked for over and over before your current incarnation. It's called "tests within human FAMILY."

Oh, dear ones, we have sat in front of you before and told you of this, but perhaps we have not told you of the love connection that is here. So many of you have karmic "work-arounds" and "workouts" with your family, and we are speaking now of very heavy things for you. Sometimes it is simple displeasure and harshness within the family; sometimes it is a total lack of support; sometimes it is disagreement. But there are other times when it is actual abuse—unforgivable abuse. And whatever it is that you can look back on and say, "*This happened and it was my family*," you can also say "*It changed me*," for that's what it's all about, and the purpose for it's existence—even if it gave you anger or pain.

Again, we say to you that there is no greater love in the Universe than when best friends on the other side of the duality agree to come in and abuse each other, if appropriate, on the planet Earth for the sake of learning—where one wears a mask of hatred or anger, and the other one a seeming victim as they walk through life with angry energy toward one another. There is no greater love than that. For it is karma at its best—dripping with destiny to be resolved and dissolved. And we say again to you that it is the overview and the enablement of your very spirit that allows you to take whatever is happening in your family and **transmute it to love**!

Is there someone who you think could never love you or you could never forgive? It's a setup, dear ones. It dangles in front of you and asks you on a daily basis to correct it. It says to you, "You cannot go forward on the planet until you deal with this issue!" In all love, it begs you to co-create joy in this difficult situation. Many of you will say, "*There can never be joy in this situation*." But we say this: You do not have to involve the other person—ever. All you have to do is correct it IN YOU. And, oh, dear ones, when you do that, and there is true forgiveness and understanding and tolerance for the other ones, watch what happens to them! For they will know that karma has been disengaged, and they will back away from the situation.

When you take responsibility for your end of things—at the cellular level they will know that the challenge is complete. Again, we compare it to the game of tennis. As long as you continue to show up to hit the ball back and forth, the game will go on and on and on. The day you are complete with the game and no longer show up on the court, that is the day the game stops for **both** of you. The other player may continue to show up, but it won't take long for him or her to realize that there is no return from their serve, and that your energy is missing in the game. This person will indeed know of your change. Then watch it change that person!

There is no greater facilitation tool of the engine of love than the family. And we tell you that this is a strong love connection. So the next time it happens, and you have the opportunity to be angry or to feel like the victim or to wish a family member never existed—realize and feel the spark of love that endured to allow for this. Recognize the invitation that is there to solve it! Recognize that you helped plan it!

(3) The third connection is the next most poignant and powerful karmic overlay, and it is called the DEATH experience. Now, death as you all know as human beings, is simply an exchange of energy. But as humans, each one, the death of another carries with it a great sting for you, and the sting is again karma, and the grief is also karma. What you do with your life in the face of this karmic sting is another great challenge. Death is common to all humanity, and therefore is a very appropriate tool that you have created to facilitate your growth—as difficult as this is for you.

There are several kinds of death that you will experience in your lifetime, and we are not speaking of your own. You all recognize that there is the appropriate death of those who seem aged, and who have spent their time on the planet and have moved on in all appropriateness. Not that this is any easier for you, but it is indeed expected. Even in this seemingly appropriate death, there is lesson. For there is nothing like it in human experience when that person is gone. Those who are left—fathers and sons and mothers and daughters—suddenly become aware of the lineage that they have. Suddenly alone, they look at their own families and realize that it will happen to them as well someday. These are the tough times when many karmic decisions are made—while in a time of seeming acceptance to the lessons of Spirit. Spirit indeed honors you for your path during these difficult times.

But what we wish to speak about now is what you Earth humans would call inappropriate death—but there is actually no such thing. Now, dear ones, we do not treat this lightly. These are times that are fresh with some of you here (and reading this)— when there is a death of a loved one and that person is young. Perhaps he or she is even related to you as a son or daughter. Perhaps this person has been part of a massive seeming accident or tragedy and many have gone with him or her. Let me tell you something about this: THIS EVENT IS FILLED WITH LOVE AND PURPOSE!

Oh, dear ones, we know that your grief is often great. It was some time ago when the grief stricken mother came to the Kryon gathering, and she had lost her son only hours before. I looked into her and saw her grief, and I said to her through my partner, "Have you seen the gift yet?" And she had not. Later she returned, and Kryon said to her, "Have you seen the gift yet?" Her heart welled up, and she said, "Yes, I have." You see, she had claimed the truth of the event, and understood what she was supposed to do with it—in honor of her son. When a dear one leaves you with distress and you are absolutely overcome with grief, you think, *It was seeming a wasted life*, and often your grief makes you even doubt God.

Listen! It has not been a waste! For in the supreme anointed divine planning session, with your permission, that person said to you, "If it's appropriate at the time, this is the plan when I potentially can leave—and what you do with my death will be the test." And so, dear ones, in light of this we say to you: **Take that death and turn it into your victory**! That person's energy is still with you, and he or she has only had an energy shift.

This person stands in your very presence
right now and says the following:

> "What are you going to do with this situation we have planned? For in all love I have gone through this, as we agreed could happen for you. And you have the choice now—for you can grieve for the rest of your life and be a victim, dragging my name out daily and toiling over it, or you can thank me for the love gift, and decide what is it that you're going to do with these emotions of yours."

This is when your life is ripe for decision and change! For you are now at a low ebb, perhaps it is time for intent, for spiritual awakening. This is indeed the time for that. For these are the gifts that are given in order to allow human beings to make lifelong decisions. You see, Spirit understands your humanism! So there is no inappropriate death. Difficult to see, perhaps, but always the love connection is there. No matter who you feel you've lost, you have to understand that they are still among you (and us). They are not gone! They have shifted energy, and the energy shift has been the love quest, for the purpose of raising the planet. And they continue to stand and say, "What are you going to do with it?"

Oh, dear ones, let me give you a perfect scenario the next time you have someone in your midst pass on. If you have anything to do with the planning, consider this ceremony: Gather as a group and celebrate their life! Do not allow what is left of their biology to be viewed. Set a place for them at the ceremony—an empty chair, perhaps and tell everyone that they are still with you. Then I challenge you to have humor around the event—I challenge you! It is one of the strongest attributes of Spirit, and passes to you unchanged through the veil. Use it! If you were to do this, you would feel the energy of that person with you. You would understand that their energy is not gone, and you would see the remarkable power of what you're doing. For it is truth to celebrate the shift of energy. It is a falsehood to meet and mourn as though they are gone. We cannot say enough about this, for there is so much lesson here regarding love. We honor you greatly for your path on this planet! This is why we call it "work."

(4) Now we will speak of SCIENCE—and you may ask, "*Kryon, what does science have to do with love?*" We are going to tell you something that is very humorous. Science is absolutely filled with the love connection in a way that may surprise you, and we are now going to address the scientists.

For it is very, very humorous indeed that all of you scientists claim that you have no bias whatsoever when you postulate and experiment. In fact, you claim that the last thing you have is any kind of a spiritual bias in the laboratory of study. As you walk through your experiments and postulate the way the things may be in the universe, you try your best to remain very stable and untainted in this quest. Yet at the cellular level, you know differently, and we're going to tell you how this exhibits itself and how funny it seems to us. For you know at the cellular level that you sit on the only planet of free choice. You remember at the cellular level that there was a planning session before you came in that dealt with the great experiment of Earth. Will humans, left alone and unaware of the test, generate a high vibration on their own? Are they going to be able to raise the planet's vibration or not? So you already know that Earth is special. You know it's a very special test—and the only one in the Universe. You are therefore monotheistic, whether you want to be or not, and continue to treat your planet in a biased way within your thinking.

Three hundred years ago when the greatest scientists looked at the heavens, they decided that the heavens revolved around the Earth. Monotheistic—special! The Earth was the center—everything went around it. Men and women OF SCIENCE decided this, and the interesting thing was that all the math seemed to prove it! Well, you know better now, don't you?

However, imagine in this day and age a scientist who comes upon a vast sea of sand granules, and through circumstances of this puzzle, this scientist is only able to examine one of the grains of these billions of granules. Stretched as far as he can see is sand dune after sand dune. He reaches down and picks up the one granule he is allowed to examine. On that sand piece, under the microscope, is discovered a beautiful design, with colors unimaginable. The scientist wonders to himself and postulates the following: *"I wonder as a scientist how many of these other sand pieces that I cannot examine also have beautiful designs?"* Now guess what the result of that postulation is? The logic of the monotheistic human says, *"Because I cannot look at the others, this is the only one that is beautiful."* All the others are therefore considered plain. [Laughter] Monotheistic—special! Of course, this is not good logic at all, but your bias takes over, in the name of the scientific method.

Of course, we are speaking of the fact that the universe is teeming with life. Almost every solar system that contains a planet has the potential for a seed of life. It is absolutely common. It occurs naturally and in many forms, and you will have a good laugh some day when you see that. But because you cannot examine it, therefore "it does not exist"!

You have looked around your cosmos, and you have said that there is the theory of the Big Bang—a creative event that made the universe. Now we have said before (and published in *Kryon Book III*), the more you examine it, the worse it looks for that theory! [Laughter] You might note that it's not evenly distributed—it clumps! —not something that seems to have happened from a central explosion. Some of you are sheepishly finding out that the age of the groups of matter that are farthest away are younger that the ones that are nearest. There is also a great deal of energy missing! These things do not support the idea of a singular creative event, and yet you stick to the idea that you are part of only one creative explosion. Monotheistic—special—biased!

Finally, in the science department, we have mentioned to you about time-frame differences within the cosmos. You look into the areas of the universe that are far away, and you see "impossible" physics! Huge bodies of matter rotating at astounding speed that you know is simply not possible in your physical world or they would fly apart. And so you postulate all kinds of answers for why that must be so, even though you have no observable physics to validate any of the postulations. Few of your scientists have ever thought that perhaps there is another reason. You see, you have "put upon" the rest of the universe the physics attributes of your own area. You decide that the way it is here (in your observable area) must be the way it is everywhere! You are much like the native who has never been anywhere but his local tropical jungle. He will never be able to understand the concept of ice until he understands that there are places with climates different than his own—something not intuitive to him.

And so again we broach this issue of TIME. In this discussion, we will involve something we have never done before, and that is to call on the energy of the one called Metatron for this explanation. [Pause in channeling—for the reader of this book: Kryon wants you to examine why it might be that both the names Kryon and Metatron end in the letters "*on.*" Look for others as well, then examine what they have in common. There is a fun puzzle here.]

[Kryon and Metatron]

We tell you now, dear ones, that there is something we call the energy haze, which is around the nucleus of the atom. And we tell you that the space between the nucleus and the energy haze (which is great), varies far more than you think within matter. As the space varies, the speed of the haze must change. It is in the physics where the speed of the haze is strong and fast that you have a different time frame than your own.

All of you in school have been taught that time is relative—remember? Your science has even proven it using small-particle acceleration, showing that indeed this is the case. You have even postulated and believed that if an object could go fast enough, its time frame would be different. Yet as you look into those areas of the universe where the "impossible physics" is happening, you never say, "*Perhaps the time frame is different?*" You never do! And here is the reason: Because you have not yet accepted that an object can seem to be stationary—yet actually traveling very fast. Not in a linear time from point A to B, but in the energy haze of its vibrating parts. That is where the speed is measured!

And so, dear ones, if you were in that "impossible physics" area of space, and somehow were able to look back at the planet Earth and could see what was taking place, all things would be moving extremely slowly! This is the relativity of time that you have studied, accepted, but don't seem to apply to anything you actually see in real space! Why? You are monotheistic—special—biased!—and illogical in comparison to what you already know. It is your cellular disposition.

Now what does this have to do with love? I'll tell you. Oh, dear ones, honored and blessed is the scientist who meditates! For this person will have the truth first. For the **truth of physics is God**.

It's the way Spirit works the patterns and shapes and colors. All of the things that are within the atom are blessed of Spirit. And, finally, as the energy of Metatron departs, he says this: *"What is it that makes the distance between the parts change? This is the puzzle for the scientists. For the area between the nucleus and the energy haze, although vast, is not void. It is a patterned soup of energy, and it is within the pattern of the null that changes the distance, and therefore the speed of the haze. And that is all we'll say on that."*

Science, therefore, contains the actual parts of love energy itself. All are anointed and make up the "stuff" of love. Spirit and science are one! The idea of the scientist apart from God is very humorous indeed. Shall you study the shapes without math? Can you even begin to understand geometry without the love connection that shouts to you that "this is spiritual"? No. The alliance between God and physics is a bond of oneness that cannot be separated. The sooner you see this, the greater your discovery will be. There is great love in the smallest parts of your matter.

[Kryon Alone Again]

(5) Although the love connection is strong with science, it is even stronger with the next connection. Now we speak of the PLANET Earth—with a big "P." This is nothing that we have to expound upon with you, dear ones, in this area (the beauty of Vancouver Island). But there are those walking this planet who see absolutely no connection between humans and the dirt. We say to you that when you're not human, your biology is dirt! For when you claim your Higher Self and move to the other side of the veil, the thing that you call biology decays and goes backwards with its life force—and the chemistry goes back to dirt. The planet, therefore, is **you in transition**!

All of the things that you are—every single chemical—belong to the Earth—and that's not where it stops, dear ones. There is an absolute entourage—many times the number of humans that exist on, in, and through this planet for your support. The magnetic grid itself and the way that it is generated is done in love for you (science again). We consider the magnetics of the planet to actually have life force! There is consciousness in this plan. Not as you think of it in the way of intellect, but this planet is a living, breathing entity. If you removed humanity from your globe, it would die. It responds to you. Therefore, before you shove great amounts of energy either into the planet or above the planet, we continue to beg that you LOVE IT FIRST. Understand that whatever you do to it, you do to yourselves. For it responds to your actions and INTENT and will change accordingly.

Dear ones, when Kryon originally came, we spoke of planetary changes, and you have seen the weather patterns shift, and you have seen the Earth shake. You have seen many things that we predicted would take place. This is the love/Earth connection. For we are here in honor of you! The changing of the grid and the planetary shifts are as though the Earth were under repair. Think of it as "under construction." The love connection between you and Spirit is through the planet. Understand this connection, and as a society and as a group of humans, know that once the connection is made, there is nothing you cannot accomplish. For the "dirt" absolutely will respond to you. So, dear ones, do not be afraid or timid when you sit down in your meditations to greet the planet as you would another person. Greet all of the parts of it as the ancients did. For, indeed, there is an energy of the West, North, East, and South. Indeed, there is an energy of the dirt itself.

And, indeed, there is an energy of the foliage. It is not your imagination that there are entities within the flowers, and they greet you even still. They are not the ones that left this planet with the 12:12. They are here in your support, and those of you who feel that there are entities in your garden, you are correct! These are but a few of the entities of the Earth. This is your planetary love connection. Look at the sky tomorrow, and the clouds and the water. Listen to what they are telling you. One of the things they're saying to you is "We honor you greatly for what you have done. We are so proud of you." And that is why the land honors you when you plant the seeds. And that is why we are changing the vibration of the dirt—to meet yours. Oh, dear ones, there is such a strong connection between you and the dirt.

(6) FALLING IN LOVE. The sixth one is fun, and we have spoken of this before. It is thus: Many of you are aware of what happens to a human being when he or she falls into human love. Although there is great humor in this, there is also something very serious. For the human who falls in love often experiences a seeming temporary insanity [laughter]. There is a great deal of sighing and chemistry change, running into things and stuttering. You see, love is that strong of a power—one human to another. This is not about biological procreation and desire, it's about love. When you are in this state, and you can all relate to this as humans, do you remember the feeling you have of complete and total safety? There is nothing you cannot do. Remember that feeling that is so peaceful? You are cared for. You are loved, and the object of your affection is grand indeed, and adored.

Dear ones, this is absolute, pure love. **It is the love of God, released to you during these times.** It is not something unusual. We tell you that this love is the natural state between entities on the other side of the veil! This is why, when my partner comes before you and calls you "respected" and "honored" and "worthy of having your feet washed," there is a welling-up—for those moments he indeed **is in love with you.** Believe it! This is the real thing. So expect this feeling when you greet the burning bush. We have told you before that there was a good reason why the human was asked to remove his shoes when he spoke to that bush. Many of you would say it was to honor the energy of Spirit— sacred ground and all—but that was not it. It was because the bush represented Spirit—and wanted to figuratively wash and anoint the human's feet! The sacredness of the ground was due to the human's presence there! You see, we are in love with you! In love with you!—something we ask you to feel this very moment.

(7) Number seven is grand. It is the subject of the first Kryon communication ever. We speak now of the love connection of GUIDES AND ANGELS. And we say again that each of you has a group of entities that is personal to you, sometimes three of the most beautiful entities you have ever seen. They accompany you through this lifetime, and some of you never even greet them. Yet they love you, and there is no judgment in their minds or hearts. You are supported with so many other Earth entities when these personal ones are the closest to you. And when we say that the room is filled with love—that we will walk these aisles and that we will hug you, we are talking about those entities and those angels.

These guides and angels are assigned to you for life, but are allowed to come and go as others come in to match a new energy. We have had discussions of why they are with you, but that's not what we are talking about now. In the past, we have had teachings of what to do with them and how to communicate with them—but that is not what we are talking about here. We are talking about the **love connection** between you and these grand ones, and the fact that they're here at all. Some of you might ask, *"Where is there even room for them?"* Believe me, there's room! For they occupy space with your energy or life force, and while you are here, they are actually a part of your Merkabah pattern. I, as Kryon, can look upon you and see your colors and can tell you who's with you. For they have a pattern of love within your aura. Oh, dear ones, you are grandly loved! And if you carry any lasting communication when you leave this place, let it be this one—that each of you is worthy to be here on this planet and to carry entities with you that love you greatly!

There is no judgment from God—just honor. We have said this before. It is in the journey you take that the honor is given, and not how you seemingly perform. Much is hidden in this, but be aware that your perceptions of who "made it" and "who didn't" in human life is totally a human perception. Perhaps that's why some of you have come to sit in these seats this time (or read these words with your eyes) to learn that there is a Universe that is loving and knows who you are and is not in judgment of you, but in total honor. Let these seeds of truth be planted tonight. What are you going to do with them?

Before we leave, we have a suggestion of what to do with these truth seeds. Don't hide them! Listen: It is the propensity of the New Age and enlightened persons to grasp a hold of this love with others and say, *"Let's sequester it."* It is human nature. It is an old-energy concept. You wish to take what you know and revel in it. You want to protect it, build a commune just for a few, set up a leadership, and live in a way where the others in lower vibrations will not disturb you. You feel that life will be more peaceful if you do this.

We say to you, dear ones, please don't—please don't. If you do this, your vibration will be ineffectual for the planet, and for the others who need you. Go back to your work—spread yourselves across the planet, and fit into your society as regular human beings filled with the love of God. Let others around you see who you are! Be still, and allow them to ask why you have peace and they do not. Let them ask about your life. Believe me, you will never have to evangelize your belief. You will be too busy answering those who, by their INTENT, have **recognized the love of God in you** and want to know more.

If you get together and sequester this love, others will never know what is happening. So the suggestion is to take the love and quietly push it to the others. This New Age information will reach critical mass, and before long there will be many more than just you who know what it's like to sit before an entity like Kryon—to have the veil lifted for a little while and to talk of things from the other side. This is truly where you are at this moment , and the reality is...that YOU ARE DEARLY LOVED.

It is with the greatest love that we have come to you this night.

And so it is.

Kryon

Current ETs and Humanity

Today's extraterrestrial visitors are very real. If this were not so, then Kryon would not have mentioned it both times at the United Nations. Here is a brief synopsis regarding the kind of ETs who began abducting people awhile back:

(1) They are extremely curious about our emotions, and particularly about our spiritual attributes (higher selves), which they can *see* in some way, and want (they don't have them—they also can't laugh).

(2) They started by examining both the animals and us against our will to discover where these things are biologically within us. Their main tool to accomplish this was fear. It worked for a while.

(3) As more humans became aware of how to challenge them (and therefore keep from being taken against their will), the ETs began to appeal to humanity through channeling (gasp), telling us that we agreed to help them "way back when." At least one book has been written by them covertly, and some New Age channels are receiving ET information and don't even know it, pushing out communication that is false, suiting their goals.

(4) Now the ETs are starting to realize that deception is the key, so they are acting like benefactors—peaceful and kind—gaining our trust (but really very ignorant spiritually). This will actually work far better than fear.

REALITY: Don't ever trust them! They don't care about US. They have even crossbred with us to try and capture our seed enlightenment. If you really feel you need to help them, then you may (free choice), but know in advance that they DO NOT represent our seed biology. The enlightened ones will look like US! Ask yourself the big question: Why don't they simply come down, present themselves, and meet with our leaders? Although they may give you another story, they can't! We are far too powerful a race of conscious beings. They know it, and our combined INTENT would harm them. **Think about it!** Otherwise they would be on the White House lawn!

The New Age Human

Chapter Three

"Practical Living in the New Age"
Channeled in
Seattle, WA

The Kryon Writings
1155 Camino Del Mar – #422
Del Mar, California 92014

"Practical Living in the New Age"
Live Channeling
Seattle, WA

*These live channelings have been edited with additional
words and thoughts to allow clarification and better
understanding of the written word.*

G reetings, dear ones, I am Kryon of Magnetic Service. There is no greater sound to Spirit than that of humans lifting their voices together, for it soothes our very essence [after the group toning]. And why should such a thing be, you might ask? Again, we tell you, as we have told so many other groups like yours, that it is as though heaven itself was visiting this place. And the reason is because there is a sacredness here, and that is because humans are here. Oh, dear ones, it is the message of Kryon over and over again, and a practical message it is, that says that the exalted ones in this Universe are the ones who sit in the chairs of this room (and those reading this now)! Hard, perhaps, for you to understand, but indeed it is so. The

veil is thick between you and your Higher Self, between the truth of home and the biology that you live in, and it is made that way for lesson. So as pieces of God, each one, you walk this planet in various degrees of awareness. Oh, if you could only know. But the truth is this: As you remove your shoes in a sacred area, it is so that Spirit can wash your feet! It is because the love we have for you is great and grand and because there is not one human being in this place who does not have a contract to be here (or to read these words). You have chosen to come here. It is your INTENT. Let us, therefore, wash your feet with the very tears of our joy, that you would come and listen to a message such as this.

We invite you to feel the hands of the guides as they encircle you, each one. We know of your tribulations; we know what you've been through. There are many different degrees of lesson here. Some of those here, and those reading this, have contracts that would shock you! For they are heavy, indeed, and the things they have been through are great. Others of you who have had a lighter time can celebrate and honor the lessons that are heavier.

Each of you is special—each with a name that we recognize and know. Now is the time that you are on the cusp of a different paradigm of existence on this planet. And we would like to walk you through some of the changes and give you some practical information this night.

Oh, dear ones, the very fabric of the Universe is love, and you are on the front edge of using that power to its fullest. It is the work that you are doing right now in this area that will make the changes that will affect those like Kryon. I am in service to you, and I wash your feet this night. I cannot say that enough. The lessons this night are these:

Everyday Living

Let us talk first about everyday living. Some of you have understood that vibrating at a different level is an unusual experience. We have told you some of the attributes in the past to look for, and on a practical level, some of you are finding that it's difficult to have one foot in the "now" time frame of Spirit, and the other foot in the "linear time frame" of humanism. Yet that is what we ask you to do.

On a practical level, we say this: There are times we understand that you're impatient. The impatience is caused, because as a human being, your time frame is linear, and you do not understand the circular time frame of the "now." Let me explain one more time for those of you who have not heard this before: Before you ever asked to vibrate at a different level—before you ever gave intent for such a thing—the work was in progress to allow for it. You might ask how such a thing could be, that we could anticipate what you would ask for. It is because the energy potential is there—because our time does not represent past and present and future. It represents the "now," of all times together. And so it is that we are ready when you ask. And so it is that there are preparations that have been made—years before you ever asked. This has nothing to do with predestination or fortune telling. It is an energy potential of your contract, should you be ready for it through intent.

Some of you are growing tired of not knowing what to do until the last possible moment, yet we say every time that this happens, celebrate it! For this is the time frame Spirit is in. It is the "now," where all that existed, exists, and all that has the potential for being, is. Remember this the next time that you sit down to agonize or worry about something that is coming. From a practical standpoint, we say, "Take it a day at a time." Ground yourself, and do not consider the future as humans do. When you look at a choice or crossroads looming in the distance and you do not know which way to go, you often fear the event. *"It's coming closer!"* you say. We say to you that it has already been here and has been settled! The solution is at hand. Therefore, the energy of the solution and the peace around it is available to you before you actually see what is at hand. Not all is as it seems to you.

Instead of sitting down and worrying about your future, or an upcoming trial, sit down and celebrate the fact that the solution has already been accomplished! For those of you with abundance issues, are you listening? The solution is accomplished now! As proof of that, there will come a day when you will look backwards and say, "Wasn't it foolish that I worried so much? For it all came together as it should have." How many times will you have to do this before you understand the full picture? Look forward to the day when you will never have to say that again. Instead, you will look backwards and will say, "I am so thankful that I understand the 'now' and that I did not worry." Celebrate the peace of the "now." It is a gift for you in this new time. The energy of worry robs humans of the peace of love!

Action

Some of you have given INTENT to move forward. You have asked for karma clearing and have started your journey to a higher vibratory rate. Picture yourself, dear ones, having given this intent before God, and there you sit. Figuratively, see yourself in the middle of a hallway, and this hallway is where the changes are from the old energy to the new. Now listen to this: It was the old energy that said to you, "God will do everything for you." In the new energy, we consider you a partner, for you are vibrating at a level that is closer to us than ever before. It's through your intent and it's through the love of your contract, that you have taken this step. Oh, dear ones, we're holding your hand during this time! Yet some of you do not understand this. There you sit—in that hallway surrounded by doors—doors that need to be pushed upon to see if they open, for on the other side of some of them is your work and your purpose.

In the past, you might have sat there and said, *"Okay, God, do it for me. I will simply sit here until it happens."* You felt, perhaps, that you were honoring God with some kind of surrender. We are here to tell you that in this new energy, if you do nothing, you're going to sit for a very long time! From a practical level, we say to you this: YOU have got to open all the doors! For the secret of moving forward in your new vibration is SYNCI IRO-NICITY! Look for it. Synchronicity is defined as events that happen that are odd or unusual at unexpected times, which seem to strangely coordinate together—seeming coincidences that aren't. They often will surprise you. The occurrences you think will have the least promise, or the avenues you might have traveled down once that brought no results, will often suddenly bring the most! But you're not going to know that until you stand up and push on the doors, so we say to you, "Get up and start the pushing process." Many things will take place for you within that process, for it represents your INTENT.

From a practical standpoint, some of you open a door and you see an opportunity. You don't know whether it is correct or not, and you may say, "*My discernment is not great enough, and I can't tell what to do.*" Here is a rule of thumb: If you push against a situation and it pushes back in a hard manner, it is not correct for your timing. If you push against a situation and the doors fly open where events and solutions happen for you, then this is a correct situation. That's synchronicity! Now that only makes sense, and it's logical, but YOU have to do the pushing first! Otherwise you do not allow for the synchronicity to exist. And, dear ones, that's why we call it work. It's only when you give the energy of the INTENT of the push against a situation that you will be honored with the synchronicity of its completion. **Do not sit and wait for God.** We are now a partnership!

The Door of Drama

If you open a door and out flies drama, it is probably not the door you should go through! Drama is something that humans create for humans, and some of you create it for yourselves on a regular basis. You stand in it and bask in it, and it feels familiar somehow. It's addicting, this human drama, and some of you know what I speak of. Listen: The place that you are going to find yourself in that is correct will be the place of peace, not the place of drama. Here is another attribute that you should know when we say things are not always as they seem: Oh, dear ones, look at your lessons. You are used to a normal situation in humanism where it is the strong ones who do the lifting. We're here to tell you to throw away all those precepts. It is often the enemy of God who will become the prophet. It is often the one who is hopeless who will become healed and provide hope for many! It is the reluctant one who will often go on to change the lives of tens of thousands.

Don't ever throw away an opportunity because it looks poor on the outside. Look for the synchronicity in all situations. When the one comes to you who you have always doubted would make any kind of a difference, pay attention. This is the exact situation that has potential for incredible power. When situations come forward that you have seen come forward over and over again, but usually with no progress, it's time to try it again. This time could be different. Oh, healers, are you listening? The ones that seem the least likely to take the vibratory shift from the energy that you pour into them will be the very ones to get off the table and become healers themselves! Make no assumptions! Things are not always as they seem. The practical step is this: Push against the doors, and open them. Do not fear becoming a fool when you take action. Stand up, and stop waiting for God to do something for you. Be a partner, and open the doors with us.

Where Should I Be?

"*Kryon, where should I live? Where should I go? What is appropriate?*" These are common questions presented to Spirit. In addition, you might say, "*I have so many choices, I want to do the right thing. What should I do?*" Let me tell you the practical answer to this: You go where you're pulled! Don't agonize over this question. Be still and watch for synchronicity (there's that word again). If you are happy in an area and it feels wonderful to you—and you feel no pull—and there's no synchronicity that would grab you to another area, then stay there. It's that simple. You do not necessarily have a contract somewhere else if you're not pulled there. Don't let anyone talk you into it. Let your own Higher Self and discernment make that decision. There is a powerful aspect about where you are taken when needed, however, and I wish to discuss that now.

Some light workers believe that they should only be with other light workers, and that the energy portals of Spirit are where they should assemble and live. They feel that it would do them well to be with others of like mind—and the energy feels good.

Oh, dear ones. Listen: Some of you are going to be called to some very unenlightened places! And if you find yourself pulled to those situations, I want you to sit and celebrate them! It means that you were called to be there to HOLD THE ENERGY in a place that needs you. That's what the work is, you see. It's not about staying with other like minds and enjoying yourself. It's about holding the energy of a place with your vibratory rate. We are going to speak of your area [Seattle] in a moment, but there are so many of you here [Seattle] for a reason, and you find yourself contracted at this time in history to hold the energy of this place. I am here to tell you that it's important that you remain!

Some of you in this room (and reading this) will be called to other places. How will you know? It's when you get the calls and the employment opens up, and there is a feeling of family there. Synchronistically, it seems so easy to go! Things go smoothly. Some of you have said, *"Kryon, I did that and I found myself making a move only to come back in five years."* We say, RIGHT! Who told you that you were going to go someplace and stay there for your life? Some of you will be moved around if you're needed to hold energy from place to place. Get used to it. Some of you will be the travelers and will have no problem with this, and others will be the anchors that need to stay in one place forever. You are all so different. Be willing. Show INTENT to go where you are pulled. Spirit will not give you a task that is greater than your ability. Usually it is the opposite. We pull you into the areas that will bless and keep you well—areas that will bring you peace, where you will meet family. Things are not always as they seem to you. Make no assumptions. Partner with us.

So the practical is this: One day at a time. Stay grounded. Look for answers in a synchronistic fashion. If you're not pulled someplace in a magical way, perhaps you're not to go there. When the situation pushes back hard, don't keep pushing. Go to the area where the door opens with synchronicity. Is this taking the least line of resistance? No. It's being spiritually attuned and wise. It is taking an anointed path, because the door opens easily when it's supposed to. It's not a weakness to use your spiritual wisdom to recognize a clear path. There are those who would tell you to push hard against the doors that do not open because it's good for you—it creates character. And we say that that's not true. The only character it will create is a tired and frustrated one! This is not the spiritual way. Our part of the bargain is to open the doors, but your part is to push. Learn about the partnership. Use it.

Sweet Spot

"Kryon, where is my sweet spot? I've been looking all around for it for a very long time. You talk about this place where I'm supposed to feel wonderful. I understand that I contracted to be there, and somewhere there's a passion, but I'm waiting. Bring it on. How can I find it?"

We're going to give you a story that we gave to one other group already. It has to do with the practical, and the understanding of the words *sweet spot*. Many of you make assumptions along the way...like Mike did.

The Parable of Mike and His Search

Mike was an enlightened human being. He sat in meetings much like this and heard the voice of spirit as you do now. Mike looked for his sweet spot and said, *"I am ready to go! I want to be in that area where I am to be the most useful to humanity—the area where I will find my peace."* Mike had a job as a carpenter, and he was adored by many in his arena. Mike took care of himself and he meditated. He was a spiritual being of high vibration, and the men around him knew it. Often the workers would come to him when they were in trouble. They recognized something in Mike that was wise. He told them what he believed, and many of them were touched deeply. He also told them *"Someday I'll find my sweet spot...some day."*

Mike took many jobs and was called into many areas, seemingly with great synchronicity. He was pulled into other areas of the country, and he said, "*I understand. I'll go because I am in search of my sweet spot.*" He changed vocations and became a counselor in the highest order of business finance. He went to school for it, felt called to it, and he said to himself, "*This could be my sweet spot. The doors are flying open, and the school is easy. I understand these things.*"

Indeed, Mike enjoyed it, and indeed there were those around him who asked Mike, "What is it with you? You seem so peaceful—so happy in your quest." And he was again able to share with them how he felt. He told them, "*Someday I'll find my sweet spot, I know I will. It's my passion—it's why I came here.*" Finally, in Mike's old age, after several more vocations, including that of being a far greater master healer than even he thought he could be, Mike found himself helping in an old folks' home. They loved him there, for he was one of them, and he was peaceful with his age, and he was not worried about his health, even as he watched it slowly fade. Toward the end, he held a powerful energy of absolute peace before him, and they said to him, "You seem so different. You are not bothered by approaching death." And he was able to share with them what he believed. He did much to soothe their very souls, and they loved him. His only disappointment? He would tell them, "*I'm pleased with my life, but I wish I had found my sweet spot. I've looked so hard and have done so much.*"

Mike finally passed over, and he felt all of the awesome experiences that you all do when you pass through the Hall of Honor as you celebrate with the others, and you remember who you are. He felt the empowerment you all do as he saw the colors of the Merkabah and slowly remembered everything, including his real name.

Then it was that he met an angel, figuratively, who looked much like he did. And the angel said, "Oh, Mike, you've had a grand life on Earth, and we honor you greatly for this. We have something to show you. We'd like to take you to a celebration journey—a journey where no one can see you, but you can see them. It's a celebration that you should see, and it involves people on Earth, alive right now, and also in Spirit form. The celebration is of the higher vibrations of many humans."

Mike was escorted into a room where he saw entities he knew, although he could not talk to them because it was presented as a vision. There he saw the carpenters he worked with and their children too. Many of them had become inquisitive about their conversation with Mike years ago. They were curious about enlightenment and their place on the planet. He saw that they had made shifts, and in their shifts they had affected other people as well. And because they had affected other people, there were unborn children of theirs and others yet to be affected who would become leaders and healers on Earth. He also saw younger business associates whom he had personally counseled with spiritually. He saw that they were enlightened beings, glowing white! They had shifted!

Mike realized that while on Earth he had only taken care of himself and his own spirituality, but these humans had reacted to him, and he saw much power around their lives. He saw the synchronicity of their families, and he saw their potential, because he had been open to speaking to them when they showed INTENT to ask.

Mike also saw humans from the time he was a healer. He saw the ones who had gotten off the table who were the stubborn cases...never healed. Why were they here? Although he never knew it, many had finally understood and given permission for their own healing. They had also affected others, and those others had affected others.

Mike saw the ones from the old folks' home—the dying ones—the ones whom he had spoken to again and again when they pressed him for answers about life. And he saw their peace as they passed on, and he saw their gratitude for finally grasping the meaning of it all. It gave them a gift of purpose and love. They understood that they had deserved to be there—and they passed with wisdom and quiet dignity.

The angel looked at Mike and said, *"Mike, you never realized it, but in your lifetime you had eighteen sweet spots! You fulfilled every one of them, moving appropriately from one to the other, honoring synchronicity, and holding the energy wherever you were. You met the ones you were contracted to meet, and while you were in each sweet spot, you were spreading the light to the family. And while you were in each sweet spot, you were spreading your spiritual passion to the family. The passion wasn't about what you were doing as a human; it was about what you were doing as a piece of God!"* Mike understood, and he grasped it all. He indeed had found his sweet spot—eighteen times! He had affected only a few, and the few had gone on to affect the many. Mike had a significant life! We leave him as he continues to look at the multitudes of enlightened humans who only became so because they happened to touch Mike's life during the times he moved in response to the synchronicity of Spirit leading him in his Partnership with God.

Now this story is not lost on you. Some of you are searching for your sweet spot, but you're in it! Look at where your passion lies. Where is it? Where is it, really? Oftentimes what you mistake as a human passion is the one that is spiritual. Are you shining your light in a certain area for a while? If so, then you are right where you belong. You are affecting those around you with your light. Isn't it time you stopped wondering where the sweet spot is and started celebrating where YOU are? For it will change your life, and it will bring you peace. Then some of the these things will start to click together that you wondered about. Don't constantly look to the future, wishing for fulfillment, for the future is taken care of now. It's here. You're in it!

Limiting Spirit

Talking about spiritual things from a practical level, some have asked, *"What should I do spiritually in my life? What's appropriate? What is correct? What does Spirit want?"*

That's an easy answer for us. When you're in your meditations, we want you to ask the real question and stop giving demands. Let me tell you this: What many of you have often decided to ask for is the most limiting factor of your lives! You cannot conceive of what to ask for because it's too grand. Some of the plans for those in this room are far grander than you could ever realize. Therefore, how can you begin to know what to ask for when you don't have the overview? The overview is of your partner, and that's US. When you sit before Spirit, just ask the question: **"Dear God, what is it you would have me know?"** And leave it at that. Then trust for synchronicity as you push on the doors around you.

When it comes to trust, let me tell you what Spirit expects. As we have told you recently (and earlier in this book—page 62), we wish to partner with you! Gone are the days when you think of God as the shepherd and you are the sheep. Gone are the days when you "let go and let God." Gone are the days when you use the word *surrender* to God. Instead the word is now *commitment*. I want you to understand this: There is a partnership now— a hand-holding. How would you like to have a partner who had the full overview of the Universe? That's your Higher Self—that's the hand we want you to hold—not the hand of Kryon or any other channel. It's the anointed one inside you. It's the golden angel that resides in you that is your actual piece of God.

That's the energy we want you to partner with as you move forward in your life. Partnering with God is the issue here. It is spiritual and practical. No longer see your boat of life drifting in a sea of frightening uncertainty. Instead, visualize this: Take the tiller of the rudder in your hand with wisdom and power. Watch

the giant hands of Spirit—your own golden angel of Higher Self—
wrap its fingers around yours, and together, you steer an anointed
course to home. This is partnership, and it represents the new
paradigm of your New Age.

The Thirty-Nine

We're going to speak of these things only one time. We will
never speak of this again. Many are asking this question:

*"Kryon, what about some of the things that are taking place
around us right now in this New Age? There has been energy
developed in recent months regarding those who took their
lives, thirty-nine of them. We don't know what to say to our
friends who look at us and say, 'Wasn't that your cult? For you
are New Age, too, just like they were.' What am I supposed to
do with this? What do I tell my friends? What was that all about?
Where are those people now?"*

Let me tell you the truth, and listen to this, dear ones: There
was no tragedy there. These thirty-nine entities are right where
you think they are. They're home, having fulfilled a contract of
sacrifice and appropriateness that has given this planet a wonderful gift! Nowhere in the history of humankind was an activity like
this known by so many humans so quickly. There was a message
given—a message that they knew could be theirs to give when they
arrived on this planet—and the message was this: Know yourself!
Never, ever give away your power! Never! For you have the power
of God itself within you!

And so the lesson was given in all appropriateness for you to
see in all of its spectacular drama. And the energy created around
it was a lesson that said, "Watch out for this." Was it a negative
lesson? No. It was a positive one, showing you the route to go
instead of the route not to go. It was appropriate—correct—filled
with love—an anointed road sign. As we have spoken about
before, Spirit often uses the energy around death as a potent tool,

and you help create it and agree to it before you ever arrive. The mind of God isn't always understood in this area, and many of you may still not understand what we mean.

The only tragedy, dear ones, is in the tragedy of those who do not see the gift. It was no more tragic than the lesson of the entity Job and what happened to his family, for Spirit does not see death as you do. Contracts of this kind are honored and celebrated on the other side. This was not tragedy. This was for you, as a gift of lesson. It was also a challenge to your New Age paradigm. Dear ones, this is not the only challenge that your belief will have. The events of the New Age are often going to carry an impact and an energy that you're going to have to think about, and it's going to knock off the fence-sitters—those who are only here to look around and not carry positive, active energies that help the planet. It will separate from you those who are here only to uplift themselves or to create followers. They will be forced to make a choice and exercise INTENT. So this is not the first time that your belief will be mixed up, misunderstood, manipulated, and con-nected with sensationalism. It is part of the new way, and it is done in love and it is done for you. It will purify and clarify the INTENT of the critical mass. Celebrate the event, and look at it for what it was!

Finally, we say to you this: As we predicted in 1989, Earth changes are abundant. Many of you are sitting right in the middle of what we told you would be, and you say to me, *"What are we going to do, Kryon? We live in a volatile area* [The Cascades near Seattle]. *We know geologically that the clock ticks and that there are events that can take place that the geologists are saying will take place. Yet we find ourselves here, and you say in all appropriateness that we should stay if we're called to stay!"*

Let me take you to a place not very long ago. For us it is happening right now. In a dark remote place of the Universe, in the blackness of space, there was an asteroid—a rock that had a trajectory with a mathematical equation that was seemingly unchangeable. Pure math dictates that it would have arrived in 1996 and smacked you directly! But it didn't [speaking of the asteroid that almost hit the Earth in June of 1996, as reported in *Time* magazine, see page 358 of this book]. It didn't hit you because of the love and consciousness of the workers in this room, and many like you. Lest you think that you have never done anything for this planet, let me tell you that it is because of this kind of work that we love you so much! For your future has changed because of the consciousness that you have helped create on this planet. You see, **the consciousness of love changed physics**! Get used to it. You created a miracle, and it whizzed by you one day in May when you didn't even know it.

Now, you might say, *"What has this asteroid stuff got to do with the mountain range called the Cascades?"* We told you about this in the beginning: Indeed, there may be a time when you will see more of the insides of the Earth than you've seen before. Yet you remain in a place of seeming danger. Oh, dear ones, changing an asteroid path...that was hard. Changing where the Earth moves and what happens here [Seattle] is easy in comparison! Anchor the energy and watch the changes. I told my partner (the channel, Lee) to stay in Southern California where the Earth moves, and where it will indeed move again. He is needed there! Others of enlightenment were also called into the same area. They are there so that when the Earth moves, it will do so in a subdued way so that the event will not be what it might have been had it not been for their presence. Their energy and consciousness will change the physics of the mantle itself! And we say the same thing to you who are called to remain here, in this seemingly dangerous place.

One day at a time—stay grounded. Know that you are loved. It is what you do here that will make the difference to those around you. Most around you will have no concept of what you're doing, as you anchor the light for your area. When you tell them about it, they may roll their eyes and think of you as very strange indeed. Is it any wonder we love you?

The energy in this room tonight is one that allows consciousness to change physics. You want to know what spontaneous healing is? It sounds like some mysterious thing that happens out of the sky. No. Spontaneous healing is the consciousness of **love over physics**! It is matter created where matter was not before—through love. There is an absolute connection between the physics of love and the physics of matter. It is when the partnership is so complete with the Higher Self, and the awareness is so strong, that you can feel it and smell it, that you know absolutely without a shadow of a doubt that you have created a miracle with your Higher Self.

You're here (and reading this) for a purpose, and we ask you to feel this energy, and let the love flow through you this night. Let the arms of the guides that are here and those that you've loved and seemingly lost continue to hug you now. For those of you who look into certain situations and find pity and see tragedy, find the understanding and appropriateness and look for the gift! For those of you who have recently been through what seems to be untimely death of ones who are precious, we say it's time that you also saw the gift. For Spirit does not see things as you do, and when you're not here, you will understand all of this—for you helped create it.

There is no greater gift than from that entity who comes and hides its magnificence for a time on Earth and calls itself human. It's a grand gift to the Universe!

And for that, we love you dearly.

And that will be our message as often as you allow us to speak to you.

And so it is!   *Kryon*

Humanity and the Critical Mass

Kryon has spoken of the reaching the "**critical mass**" of enlightenment on planet Earth. How many humans have to be enlightened before this is reached?

Actually, it is not the **number** of humans at all. It is the critical mass of **love energy**! Kryon says that we are already broaching it, since the light is far more powerful than the dark. Anyone notice the consciousness of humanity in general changing (see page 272)?

The Two Rooms

"Imagine two rooms. One is filled with incredible light, and one is totally dark. There is a single door between them.

"Watch what happens when you open the door. If you are standing in the room of light, darkness does not suddenly pour in. It remains in the other room unto itself. If, however, you are standing in the dark room when the door opens, suddenly it is flooded with light! The degree of darkness that existed before is now gone. Light has overcome the dark.

*"Dear ones, this is because light is active, and dark is passive. The energy of enlightenment is an active beacon of light to the darkness of the old-energy on your planet. A very few **light workers** carrying their brilliance from place to place can actually change the energy balance of the Earth!*

Is it any wonder that we love you so?"

"Human Prediction, a Difficult Task"
Channeled in
Portland, OR

The Kryon Writings, Inc.

PMB 422
1155 Camino Del Mar
Del Mar, California 92014
[www.kryonqtly.com]

"Human Prediction, a Difficult Task"
Live Channeling
Portland, OR

These live channelings have been edited with additional words and thoughts to allow clarification and better understanding of the written word.

LEE: Before Kryon comes in this night, I wish to say a prayer. I am giving intent at this point in time along with those who are in this room. And the intent is that this room be filled with love and the power of Spirit itself, and that there would be no dark thing that could get through this bubble of love. Let all that is presented this night be pure and accurate and true. This is our intent and we ask this in the name of Spirit.

Greetings, dear ones, I am Kryon of Magnetic Service! Oh, there are some of you who have waited so long to hear these words, and yet when we tell you they could ring in your heart at any moment you wish, it surprises you. For you see, I am simply the Magnetic Master. I bring you a love-filled message—a message that is available to each one of you anytime you want it. For my partner knows this, and he wishes to tell you this, as there's a great welling up in his heart when he says that Spirit is not proprietary! That is to say, there is no human on this planet who can covet it as his or her own. It is for ALL, and for ALL to discern.

We are encasing this group in a bubble of love, and we are going to press this love against you in an intense fashion as you listen to the teaching words revealed this night. For the pressure will be for all of those who wish to let us in. Oh, dear one, perhaps you are here this night in an unbelieving stance? We tell you that you are loved dearly as much as any person here. Nothing fearful will happen here, but the seeds of truth will be planted in your soul.

Someday when you decide on your own to water these fertile seeds, they will indeed grow into knowledge and wisdom and truth, and you, along with the others this night, will finally realize the love of Spirit for you, and in doing so will raise the vibration of the whole.

And so the teaching begins. We wish to tell you about predictions. In general, this type of teaching is about the whys and hows of human predictions. Spirit has told you several times through the channeling of my partner to be wary of any human being who tells you that something is going to happen on a specific day at a specific time. We have told you this because we have explained that your future is a moving target and that you are changing it daily. Oh, believe it! It is true! Even Spirit cannot tell you what is going to happen in a specific way at a specific time, for you are in absolute control.

We would like to tell you and show you why these human visionaries have difficulty with predictions. For you see, there are many visionaries, and there is much talk, and there is much information. We have told you before, oh dear ones, that each one of you has the power of discernment, and as you hear information, you may discern whether it is appropriate for you and whether it is actually the truth of what is going to happen—whether it is actually your current reality or not. So now we are going to tell you why this is so difficult.

The visionary is one who is metaphorically pulled through a hole, and the hole is that rip in the veil between your level and our many levels, opened appropriately by the visionary. We're going to tell you of three attributes that any individual visionary must face when he is pulled through that hole.

Dimensionality

Envision your life on this planet as you would a game that you play on a field. Now many of you in this culture are aware of the games that are played on fields, and you know there is a width of the field, a length, and you know there is a height of play and also a timekeeper. If you add these attributes, you will find that there are four. These four attributes correspond to four dimensions that you find yourself in which we will call, for the purpose of this example, one level—the human one in lesson.

The visionary, this one who is privileged to be pulled through the hole of the veil to view the things on the other side, is suddenly presented with multiple dimensionality. He comes from four, and he is instantly presented with a seemingly infinite number of levels. Level after level of cosmic complex dimensionality—some of which he cannot even recognize are different from his own because they are so unusual to his thought process! For he is only used to the four, and yet there are many, many more. Suddenly his playing field is multidimensional, even though he is not. It is as though fields are stacked on top of fields. It is as though the boundaries and the parameters of each game are instantly different from the other, and yet only one game is still being played. As high as he can see there is field after field—like  playing a multidimensional chess game with boards that reach through the sky, but with the same few players. He says to himself, "How can the game be played with all this complexity?"

With no concept of what the rules are anymore, or the boundaries of them, the visionary must make decisions about observations that place what he is seeing back into the dimension of the four. This individual with his four-dimensional intelligence as a human being is expected to look at this scene and somehow glean the future of your planet. This is only one of the problems facing him, and it takes a wise human indeed to be pulled through that small hole, observe this great complexity in dimension beyond his understanding, and yet somehow recognize or glean what is actually being shown him that might apply to where he comes from.

Time

Let us talk specifically about one of the dimensions of the four that you call *time*. For this is one of the most confusing attributes of all when you reach the side of the veil from which I speak. How do you think the visionary feels asking himself why the entities he sees are playing the game with a time clock that moves in all directions? Let us use the example now of a train and track as we have before. Why? Because your human time is linear, and it is of a certain speed and rate. You may look backwards from the train on your track of linear time and see where you came from and also what you did when you were there, but when you look forward, you see only the track, and not what you did on it yet. This is a linear path, and goes from past to future. It never varies anywhere between, and the speed of the train is your time frame (your speed of time). It is always consistent for you and is always in equal motion and it appears to be in a straight line. Your dimensionality only allows you to see the straight track, as you are always in motion.

When you are pulled through the hole into the other side of the veil, suddenly you are presented with a multitimed dimension (many time frames—many time types)—not to mention the interdimensionality that we have already spoken of. This time awareness (or nonawareness) is often the most confusing part for you to understand when you are here (on my side).

Let us digress for just a moment regarding time in general. Even within your scientific parameters you have discovered through small-particle acceleration that time is relative even within your linear type. That is to say, your scientific society has agreed that time goes at a different speed given different physical attributes of physics (usually what you associate with speed of matter). It is odd to us that you still look into space and apply the boundaries and the parameters of your specific game on Earth to everything you see! Sometimes you look out into space and document the physically impossible! You see attributes of mass that simply cannot exist as you know them on Earth. Sometimes you see mass that spins far too fast for its properties, and yet you look at it and you call it an anomaly that is unexplainable. Even though you know about the relativity of time, you never apply this known time relativity difference as a potential solution to these physical puzzles.

Let me ask your science to ponder this question: "What is the difference between the speed of mass as a whole, and the speed of the parts that make up the whole? Can an object travel at a high speed while remaining seemingly stationary to your sight?" The answer is yes. Speed, like time, is relative to the motion of the internal parts.

Even though these cosmic puzzles reveal themselves in linear time and are in your universe, they indeed exist at a different time speed (time frame), and this can be confusing to you. We have never spoken of this before. There is a formula for time, and it goes like this: *The density of mass plus the rate at which it is vibrating equals its time frame.* When you look into the universe, dear ones, you see different time frames. Believe me, there are many of them observable to you.

To make things even more confusing, when the visionary is pulled through that hole, suddenly he not only sees varying time frames, but time isn't even linear any longer! He suddenly is in *circular* time. He is in the "now," where the past and the future exist all together and meet in the middle. This is a confusing concept for all of you (like having a world in gray and suddenly being exposed to another one in color. How do you go back and explain that?). We have told you often that the time frame of Spirit is in the *now*, and is not *linear*. Some of your visionaries are shown *visions* of events on your planet, but this can be very confusing to a human because of the time frames and time differences. We are here to tell you that what you see isn't always what you think, and must be carefully discerned.

Some of your visionaries are seeing the *potential* of what could have been but whose potential is already gone! Yet it is this drama of what was seen in the vision that the human remembers first as he is pulled back through the hole into the dimension of the four. He comes back with a fear-based message and reports, "*Oh, it was awful indeed! Just wait, just wait.*" Little did he know that he was seeing the potential of something that never occurred, and won't.

What the visionary saw was something that could have happened in an older energy with a vibration and consciousness that was slower. Oh, is it no wonder we celebrate you for these things? As I sit at your feet this night, I can report that you have changed your actual future! Not just once—but many times in the last few years! This is just one of the great, confusing attributes of being pulled through the hole of the veil—to look around for a moment or two to see what is there, then be pulled back and report accurately. We say it is almost impossible to know what actually was seen and where it belongs in the scheme of your time, but there's more.

Expectation—Bias

Remember the advice *Don't think like a human?* Human assumption and bias often tempers or filters what a visionary will think he or she is seeing. When the visionary is pulled through the veil, he does not automatically receive the "mind of God." Indeed, he comes over with the expectations and logic and intellect that are solely human. And so the things that he sees, he analyzes with his human intellect and with the logic of human experience, human expectation, and assumption. This bias alone will corrupt the perception of what is actually the truth of what is being shown to the visionary.

Let me give you an example of what this could be like. Let us say that you are a human being, living six thousand years ago on this planet. Through a miracle, a visionary in your society was able to be transported to this current day and age and was able to spend three minutes standing in one of your large cities in 1998.

Magically, he is pulled back through the hole, stands before you, and is asked to report to you and all humanity. All of you stand waiting with bated breath to ask, "What is the future like? What is going to happen?"

(1) The first thing he reports is that in the future there is no food!

"*Really?*" you ask.

"*Oh, yes! I know this because I observed that there was not one planting field next to even one house. There simply is no food. It's gone! Disappeared! No fields mean no food. After all, humans know that you must have fields to grow food.*"

"*What about animals? Do they eat THEM instead?*" you ask.

(2) "*Oh, you won't believe it! The animals are extinct. There are no horses. There are no cattle. They're all gone. Probably eaten for food when the fields started to disappear for whatever reason. I looked around and I saw none of these animals...not one!. But that's not the worse thing.*"

"*Tell us, what is the worse thing?*" you ask.

(3) "*Oh, you don't want to be in this future that I saw,*" says the visionary fearfully, "*for Earth has been invaded by boxlike creatures of many colors that travel on roads obviously made of their own dark droppings, and not only that, each one of the box creatures has eaten at least one human being! I can tell this because when I glimpsed inside these semitransparent creatures, the humans who were still trapped looked very angry indeed!*"

So your visionary became the guru of the tribe, and all together you greatly feared the future, which you had no idea of knowing was very far away, and completely inaccurately seen.

Although this may seem comical to you, this is exactly the attribute of being pulled to the other side. For what your visionary sees does not make sense because he does not relate the reality of what he is observing to anything except *what he knows*. Because of human expectations and experiences, the visionary from six thousand years ago could not begin to understand your inventions of today, or the changes in society that appeared to him to be without food or animals. He used all that he knew, and extrapolated what it could mean—and was comically wrong due to his bias of experiential assumption.

This has already happened, dear ones. For not long ago, one of your grand visionaries came back and reported that indeed the Earth was going to tilt on its axis in the New Age. This was seen as a *doomsday event* and created much fear. Actually, what was seen was the work of the Kryon group, tilting the grids, and changing the attributes of the magnetics, allowing for high consciousness and enlightenment on your planet! Therefore, an attribute of love was seen and mistakenly reported as one of gloom! Can you see that?

How could such a thing happen? Because that visionary did not understand or see that the grid was being moved, and not the entire planet. After all, who would have expected a grid shift? It was far easier and logical to report an axis tilt than a grid shift. The fact is that both events looked the same to the visionary, who was in the midst of multidimensional and multispace time.

There have been many of these kinds of predictions. One, even at this time, has a visionary looking into the future past the year 2012 saying, *"Oh, it's awful! There are very few human beings left, and the ones who are left are foraging for food."*

This visionary actually saw something he did not understand— a wonderful potential future for humanity. He saw enlightened human beings living in high vibrational societies. He saw a potential future for you of great vibration—ascension status with high vibrational biology and graduate bodies, and they were all simply *invisible* to his sight! He would not know what to do with them in his interpretation if he had seen them, nor would he know what to report. They would never appear to be human as he understands it in 1998. And so the "normal" humans he expected to see were those who did not vibrate quickly, and there were only a few left! Therefore, an attribute of wonderment, glory, and love was turned into a doomsday prophecy again. Why do we tell you these things? So that you will fully understand that it is almost impossible for any visionary to come back from the other side and say that on a certain date at a certain time this or that will take place. Sometimes these visionaries will be fortunate, and they will be shown things that make sense because they are in the dimension they expect, but many times they are not.

What about the future? What does Spirit say about what is happening to you now, and what about predictions? It was only a few years ago that my partner channeled to you that you would have great weather changes, and to look for them. He said that where the corn and the wheat grow, the ground would shake— and it did. He said that in the places you would least expect there would be great changes—and there have been. He spoke of water when there never was water before, and there was. And we wish to tell you that there will be more of the same, and here is the reason, dear ones. Listen:

It is a time to celebrate when the Earth changes in response to your consciousness, for as we've already told you, Earth is a living entity and must respond to the consciousness of humanity that lives with it. It is part of the system, and it works together with you! Each one of you should give intent to be in your sweet spot and not be alarmed if you find that sweet spot in the middle of apparent chaos. This might be the chaos of old-energy fear that serves humanity very well, but by having you there, it helps to move humans into the New Age to face the karmic attribute of a higher vibrational choice. For you, in your enlightenment, have the foreknowledge that these events are appropriate, but do not mark the end of the planet. Instead, you understand that they are **adjustments in love** that must take place, potentially fearful because of your humanness, but appropriate, and honored because of your spiritual change in vibration. You understand, and may have peace during these things—and radiate this peace to those around you.

The overview gives you the peace to move forward into these times, and know that being in your sweet spot means that you are safe! You live in times which are magnificent. Each one of you knew of this before you signed on, but some of you are still struggling with this very attribute. For, to admit that you helped plan it is difficult! Some of you raced to this point and are in fear, and we call this the seed fear, for dear ones, the last time you saw and felt this kind of planetary change was in the time of Atlantis. We say that those feelings are in so many of you because it is the attribute of spiritual awareness that brings you here to listen to or read these words now. Although you may think there are not many of you, when compared to humanity, we say that those of you who are here (or reading this) are the ones, almost exclusively, that participated in those Atlantean times. You are also the very ones doing the most to change your planet's future!

You have heard the call again, and you have felt the feeling of home again, only this time it will be different. We promise you. For those in this room and those reading this have no idea of the positive changes you have already made by being right here, having an interest in raising the vibration of the planet, and in your own personal peace. My partner wells up with emotion because Spirit is in a congratulatory mode right now, saying, "**Thank you**!" You don't know what you've done for us—all of us! It is why we wash your feet! There is a grander plan than you know—a far grander plan than you understand. It is not just about this planet, it is not just about your heart—it is about the Universe, and that is why we are so excited at this time.

You are dearly loved!

Kryon

"Peace and Power in the New Age"
Channeled in
Adelaide
The Kryon Australia Tour

The Kryon Writings, Inc.

PMB 422
1155 Camino Del Mar
Del Mar, California 92014
[www.kryonqtly.com]

"Peace and Power in the New Age"
Live Channeling
Adelaide, Australia

These live channelings have been edited with additional words and thoughts to allow clarification and better understanding of the written word.

From the writer...

This may seem like just another channel in this book, but this one stands out. It is similar in substance to one given a month earlier in Breckenridge, Colorado, but in that session the recording equipment did not work correctly, and I was unable to transcribe it all. The energy in Breckenridge was awesome—leaving many in their chairs meditating long after the channel was over, trying to hold the anointed energy they felt personally for as long as possible. Tears were abundant. I was sorry that my chance at transcribing it was missed, but like so many other events that seemed negative at the moment, the reason was clear later—one month later in Australia.

You have read many channelings so far in this book. You may now be familiar with how much honor Kryon tells us that we have as humans. Even at that, this meeting in Adelaide, on the southern coast of Australia, was as powerful as anything I have ever experienced. Kryon gave this group accolades for their work, and he has provided a new benchmark for me in the area of how much Spirit honors us! As you read the first part of this channel, I think you will receive the feeling of just how special this group was—and the area of the Earth they were in. Evidently this crowd of 230 people were very intense in their INTENT for the evening—to be in the right place at the right time. From the letters and reports we received afterward, many indeed were.

Greeting, dear ones, I am Kryon of Magnetic Service. There is no greater sound than that of humans in song [right after toning]. The honor is great this night, and I have waited some time to present this to you. Some of you will have a moment when you get used to the voice of my partner, representing Spirit, and we say to you that this is presented in the greatest love possible. Some of you will recognize this energy, as we know each one of you. For what we bring this night is an entourage that moves up into those aisles and between those seats, to sit there and hug you and love you. Let this bubble of love press upon you. Let yourself feel this entourage that comes in honor of who you are. I greet each one of you. I greet the ones who have waited for this energy. I greet the intent of the few of you right now who are saying, "*Yes, I recognize this energy and I wish to be all that I came to be.*" I greet the facilitators, and I greet the ones who are the inventors, and I say, We know of your work! Oh, dear ones, continue. Blessed are you for the journey that you have made to be here.

Greetings, little ones. There are two little ones tonight. I will not say any more than that [in the audience that night there was only one little one. Later, we discovered that one woman was also pregnant]. We tell you this, something that we have said to every assemblage like this: The energy here is great, dear ones. The energy here is ripe for discovery. The energy here is lifting and increasing, and we tell you this: We honor you so much! You have no idea of the honor that is being presented here. Metaphorically, we ask you to remove your shoes. Metaphorically, we say when you have done that, you will let us wash your feet. For again we tell you that we come prepared to wash your feet with our tears of joy, that you would allow such a thing as this—communication between Spirit and humanity. What a power! What a thing this is for you! For it does not reflect on Kryon or the channeler. It reflects on YOUR journey that you have found yourselves sitting in these chairs this night. I recognize all of you. Believe it or not, there is not one in this room who has not passed through the Hall of Honor to be awarded the color from being a human on this planet. There is not one first-timer here!

All of you have spent many lives here, even the ones who are doubting that this could possibly be the voice of Spirit. Even the ones who will go away seemingly unchanged this night are included in this entourage of those who have been here before. All of you queued up to be here this time around. And you waited and you said, *"I want to be part of the planet when it is measured. I want to be part of the excitement when it changes greatly. I want to be there and be one of the humans to take the power— a power that you have not seen since you walked the halls of the temples in Lemuria."* And many of you did! Does that surprise you? Oh, you have a wonderful and great lineage on this planet, and that is why I speak to great wisdom assembled here tonight. I speak to those who are fully aware of why they are here. And it is true, I speak to some who are just discovering who they are. In the majority, I know I speak to those who are fully aware of the responsibility they have for the planet.

It is impossible for me to tell you of the great love that passes between us if you do not feel it. I tell you again that I know who you are. And I know who you are in the finest loving sense, because I have seen your colors before. They radiate and they're beautiful. *Splendorous* is a word that may be improper English, but it says it all—grand and splendid beyond belief. *Splendorous*—perhaps a new word. If you could see what I could see, you would see the room vibrating with an energy that has not yet been even fully realized tonight. I bring you instructions in this last of the triad of practical instructions [this being the third city on the Australian tour] that have been presented one time before at an altitude of over 3,000 meters, in a venue not too long ago on another continent [speaking of Breckenridge, Colorado]—one where we kept the recording equipment from working so that my partner would transcribe THIS message instead of that one. This is an energy of great appropriateness—an energy of love. There is so much wisdom here! Thank you for those who are here now who fully understand what is taking place, for even if you miss the English words that are being spoken here, we are telling you that there is an energy transmission—there is geometry here, coming to you, which is sacred. [Kryon often speaks of geometry as part of the form of spiritual energy transmission.] For some, it will change your life because you have allowed it and given permission for it—and we know it's happening right now—right now! You have started the process long before the others did in the other meetings. Even before the teachings begin, there are those here who have full understanding of what is going on.

There is no greater gift to God than the human being who sacrifices their high dimensional existence—coming down to Earth, having his or her Divinity hidden, to walk the dirt of the planet in lesson! No greater gift! Kryon has never been human, you know. And it is appropriate that I have not been, for it lets me sit at your feet and honor who you are. It lets me marvel at what you've been through and what you've decided to go through on your own. It lets me appreciate the responsibility that you have for the planet, that lets me freely love you and speak to you through multiple channels, this being only one. Don't be surprised if there are other channels with other names that come through with these same messages. You are making a change in the entire universe, dear ones, by what you do in this room. Grandiose? Sensational? Yes—very! And we congratulate you over and over. Seeds are being planted this night, even among the ones who do not wish to accept that this could be so. These seeds may have a bearing on what those who go away unbelieving, do with their lives. There will come a time when some of you who do not believe it now, will need this information, and it will be there for you to pick up as a gift to move forward with and cut through the fear that you will feel due to the things that may be happening to you later.

And so the message this night is about peace. Not peace on your planet—better than that. You might ask, "*How could anything be better than peace on the planet?"* And we say to you that the real peace for the planet is the peace of the human heart. When the human heart is changed and vibrates at a new level, the peace on the planet will follow. For you see, it's the human beings that create the peace on the planet when their consciousness changes—when the human heart and soul starts receiving the gifts, and the overview is realized. One of you has asked this night, *"How can I have tolerance for the intolerable? Peace where there is no peace. If I am tacit and do nothing with the intolerable things I see, does this mean I give permission for them to be?"* And we say, No. No! Because knowing the truth and having the overview and the wisdom of God lets you look upon the old energy, not in judgment, but in appropriateness as you see the things that are happening. You may be sad or anxious as you see those who are in a period in their lives that is troubling, when you understand that it would be so easy for them to move forward. Tolerating the intolerable is what we're talking about, and that is being **peaceful with life**. And in your peace with life you do something remarkable: In your silence of the intolerable, what you do is ignite a light in a dark room and stand there in your peace. Oh, dear ones, there is nothing like that light! How many of you have been in a place where there are other human beings, where you are walking across the room and heads turn to look at you? Do you ever wonder why that happens? It happens because intuitively, at the cellular level, other humans know who you are! For some of you are vibrating at a level that shouts to the cells of the other humans that you are an elite person—one who has taken the vibrational first step into perhaps a fearful intent. Fearful only because you've never gone there before. What honor we have for you!

We want to talk about peace this night. Practical peace. We're going to give you eleven attributes—six of them, maybe even seven, will reference to your vibration, and the others will be in the spiritual vibration. If we had one wish this night before my partner leaves this continent, [Australia] it would be that each and every one of you in this room would walk from this place feeling peaceful. Peaceful not only with your life, but with your land, with all of the things around you that are happening that seem to be negative—but which have appropriateness because YOU planned it. Spirit is in the now, and we will again revisit this concept before we start the lesson. You are in a linear time frame, dear ones— one that is created for YOU. A human cannot experience the *now* as a human being in the old energy, for the *now* becomes the past, and even the future becomes the past, and you never spend any time where Spirit actually is. The *now* time frame is like a circle around yours, where all things past are known, and the future *potentials* are realized and also known.

Some of you carry problems and anxiousness and worry this night. What are you going to do about this or that? What's going to happen within your body? What about the healing you've been asking for? What about the processes that you've been trying to develop for healing? What about your work? What about your abundance? What's next? What about the relationships and the family? Oh, dear ones, the *now* is the overview that Spirit has, that you don't. It's the natural state for all of you (when you are not here) and in the *now* are gifts with grand solutions. Every single one of your tests and problems are in there, and appropriately, so are the solutions that you planned—even though they hide, and you do not know what they are. They already have been solved! They are in the *now*.

For those of you with the overview of the wisdom who know this, and you vibrate at a higher level, you can put one foot into the *now* and one foot into linear time and feel comfortable. That's where peace comes from, for you realize there is an overview, and the solutions are waiting. Now, Spirit apologizes for the fact that solutions often seem to be at the last minute [laughter]. But, oh, dear ones, if you'll examine what we're saying, you'll know why they are so. For *now* time is NOW! The problems you have that you want to resolve cannot be solved until you go to the *now,* and only then they're solved. Many times the timing of that confusing attribute can only be at the moment of the solution to the problem, which is naturally at the end of that test's journey. That's where the solution is. We have told groups before that humans have a tendency to see crossroads coming and they don't know what to do. A required decision is looming in the distance, so what do they do? Some humans decide to sit down and worry about the issue. The ones with the *now* overview, however, are the ones that say, *"We cannot make a decision at the moment, but we'll know later."* It's against human nature to do this, because it voids planning ahead.

Dear ones, blessed is the human being who has the overview of knowing that the solution to the problem is ahead at the crossroad. And that bravely, without anxiety, he or she walks up to it and looks for the direction sign—out of sight before, but viewable when he or she gets there. The sign says, "Turn right or turn left." And it's at the crux of the crossroad where it stands, and often only viewable when you arrive there. That's the *now.* That's the honored spot. And it's going to remain that way as long as you live. That's how Spirit works. Do you remember?

The Human Workplace

The first of the eleven attributes tonight has to do right away with the practical of practicals, and that is the workplace of humans. Spirit (and your Spiritual planning) delights in putting you in a place where you have no control of decisions about the people you get to work with—and that is called lesson! What are you going to do with those whom you find intolerable? Dear ones, we start here because it is common to all of you. Some of you work in areas where you do not have this attribute, and some of you don't report to a place at all. But you are still forced to be with other human beings in your economy, for that's the way you make your living— and we know this. Although it is different in every culture, in many ways it is the same. For you indeed are forced to be with other human beings that are not of like mind or that come from different places—some of which do not have your overview or your wisdom, and there you are with them. You want to have peace over that?

Let me tell you: If you will let your light shine—if you will allow yourself the intent of moving into one of the first gifts we have offered—that is, to be free of the karma that you came in with, you will find that those who have irritated you the most will be disarmed in their irritation. For those *buttons* that are *pressed* in you, seemingly that create anxiety, anger, and disturbing attitudes, will simply be disconnected! Some of you already know of what we speak. You have situations where you now have *the overview of Spirit* and you walk into the same places you used to walk into, but instead of feeling anxiety or anger, you are able to walk right into the same areas you did before with the same humans you did before, but now you feel peaceful! You know what happens there? When you take care of yourself and you choose to vibrate at a higher level and feel this peace, you have a disconnection with those others and those old energy processes (which in love they have brought to you and that you have allowed and given permission for). What happens is that **they will notice**! And I promise that over a period of time those that used to irritate you will become your friends, because they realize that the karma between you, light or heavy, has been disconnected. Those old karmic *buttons* no longer get the old reactions. These workers may come to you and say, *"What is it with you? How can you have this kind of an attitude when all around you there is anxiousness?"* It is true that you walk through a difficult world. That's why we call it *work*, dear ones. That's why YOU are workers in the light, because YOU are taking that light to the workplace and holding it by yourself. All you have to do is hold it up, and others will ask you about it. This is not evangelistic. There's nothing you have to say. You see, truth seeks its highest level, and when you walk and talk, you live with the love of God;

and when you vibrate in a higher fashion, others WILL notice. Peace in the workplace—expect it. There is nothing there that is unsolvable. That is one of the easiest places to find peace.

The Children

Now we bring up one that might be unusual. You might say, *"This subject has no bearing on peace."* We say it does for many of you. We'd like to talk about YOUR children for a moment. Now, we are not speaking of the little ones. We're talking about the ones who are almost grown up or are adults. There are those of you here in this room who have a hard time disconnecting from the children, and so you have no peace over THEIR lives. This is common, and it is normal among human beings. For you will find times to awaken in the middle of the night and decide, *"Oh, it's time to worry about what they're doing."* What are they doing with their lives? What's going to happen to them? And we say it's time to disconnect and take care of yourself! They have reached the age of responsibility, and they will be what they will be. Dear ones, the most honored thing you could do for them is to disengage the worry. When you look at them or *see* them metaphorically in your mind, just love them and surround them with the white light, then disengage, for it's time. You know who I'm talking to tonight. Do you ever wonder if they love you? They do, but know this, they also know you love them, and that is the key. Disengage. It will actually help them and you to do this...and it will bring YOU peace.

Family

And while we're talking about children, let's get to the third one—the crucible of karma—the one that generates the most anxiety on the planet! Now we're talking about the FAMILY. These are the ones you actively chose before you ever arrived. The next time you look at the one who's giving you so much trouble, remember that YOU CHOSE THIS PERSON! This has to do both with the mates and the children. It also has to do with the relatives of the mates—all of them are chosen family. Oh, dear ones, there was a time before you were ever here, metaphorically, when you were embracing your best friends on your way to this planet. You agreed to *needle* each other and be in each other's lives in a challenging way. Can you disengage from that? Oh, yes. Is peace possible in the family with what you know could happen there? Yes. I'm even talking now to those of you who were abused by parents—those of you who carry in your heart a scar that is buried deeply, and it's responsible for an anxiousness in your heart, and it's responsible for anger and victimization.

I'm here to tell you that this can be completely disengaged and forgiven. And you can finally wake up peaceful about the entire experience, because you know you helped plan it. So many of you have planned it so you could come and sit in the chair this night (or read this book right now), and hear about the responsibility that you *both* had for it. For it created energy, energy that now could be dissipated because this was the big test and was the lesson of your life. I guarantee that when you dissipate the energy from that experience, the other one, the abuser, will also feel it as well. And there will come a time (if they're still alive on this planet) when they'll call you and ring you up and say, "*What is it with you? What's changed? I feel something.*"

You know, love does that. Love is the most powerful force in the universe. You'll find it in the smallest particles of matter—in the space between the nucleus and the electron haze where it's thick with love! It is the stuff that you're made of! It has THAT kind of power. And when you release THAT power, there is NOTHING that can touch you. Nothing that can touch you! There is no evil or darkness on this planet that can get close to you. There is no outside entity who is not human that can touch you. NOTHING can. Because you've released the energy of who you are. The angel that sits in that chair in your life, that has your image, is activated when you give intent for this love to permeate your being and create peace.

Security

Let's speak about another area of concern and lack of peace. We call it security. You may call it money. Abundance. Ah, dear ones. These things that are needed for your economy are indeed necessary, but they are simply energy transfer, and that's all they are. When you have limitations and fear about this energy, it WILL respond to you and give it back exactly as you have treated it. Do you understand what I am telling you? It's when you open up and realize that you *deserve* the abundance that you came for—to have your needs met on a daily basis, that you will realize that God is there to give you peace over this! The hardest part will be the *last minute* part. It may be an oversimplification, but we have said it before: If you want to know how God reacts to humans, take a look at how nature and God react to one another. For the mechanics are all there for you to study and actually observe. The bird wakes up in the morning, but it does not have a storehouse of food. Each day it must create its own sustenance and its own reality. Each single day, at the last moment, it must go out and find food for itself and its children. And what does that bird do when it awakens in the morning? Does it worry about it? No. It sings! If you're following this metaphor, then you understand what we're asking you to do.

When you awaken in the morning, even though you do not know how the financial problems are going to be solved, celebrate and sing regarding the solutions that are there in the *now* for you. Sing! And with that attitude, dear ones, in will come the energy that you're singing about. It's when you approach the day with fear and lack and limitation and worry and have anxiousness, that the energy will mirror back to you—worry, fear, anxiousness, and limitation. For you are powerful, and you can easily create what you need. Each one of you! Are you listening?

Sensationalism

Here is another one. Sensationalism. Some of you are worried and anxious about the things that have been presented to you in a sensational matter. Are you worried about the Earth changes? Worried about some of the things that have been sensationalized that sound potentially awful? We know that there are some of you who go to bed worried every night. Those of you with small children—wondering what this world is going to be for them. I want to tell you what this world can be for them: Oh, the greatest decades may follow that have ever existed for humanity! The most peaceful time that has ever been recorded on this planet! The greatest love and peace ever possible! Yes, there will be conflagrations, and there will be old-energy concepts and struggles. There will be things to avoid and to move through, and tests for you. If you wish, there will be plenty to worry about, if that's what you want. But in your life and the lives of those around you, there is great promise. Today in lecture, my partner has given you information that you have caused great changes on the planet— and again we say, there is wonderful honor for you because of this! Oh, the changes that you've made are awesome! But the ones you're going to make are even bigger coming up. Wait until you start living longer. That's what's in your future, and that's what's in the future of your children if you so desire. This world is for you to operate. And we are here to say that the ball is rolling, so to speak, toward a higher vibration even as I sit and speak to you with this voice of a human being, and you are dearly loved for that, because you are the reason and the catalyst behind it.

Throw away the sensational, negative things! They don't apply to you. Let others be sucked into that fear and that anxiousness, but not you. For you know better. You are an enlightened Human Being, and you have the ability to look around and see the overview of the planet and know that what you are being handed as sensational is a marketing lie. The truth is far grander than you know, but when you can actually see the consciousness of your governmental leadership changing, and that of your wealthiest humans, and even that of former enemies…then you can participate in the validation of what we are saying. Did you notice the changes in consciousness over these years? It is not an accident! It is actually happening. Remember that the next time you are asked to believe pages and pages of fear-based sensationalism that is supposedly from a valid New Age source. Does that really sound like what God is rewarding you with? It's time for the golden angel that dwells within you to be the discernment for all things. It will serve you well to depend on this grand source to determine truth from sensation.

Death

The sixth attribute is potent. Peace over death. There are two kinds of anxiousness over human death, and both of them represent paper-thin phantoms of fear, created for and by you so that you can walk through fear if you choose. The first one is about your own demise. For those of you worried about that, we say to you, especially those of you vibrating at a higher level, that this will come at an appropriate time—a time that you have helped plan. Remember this: YOU ARE ETERNAL! YOU are an eternal being, transmuting your energy from one kind of entity to another. Eternal, each one! I tell you that what happens at your death, as channeled before, is grand and glorious. I tell you that after an appropriate time of adjustment, I will see you in that grand hall where your color badge is delivered. Many will be there to say, "*I love you*." If you knew what was beyond the veil, it would be too inviting, and that is one reason we keep it hidden. And that's why there's so much fear around it.

Dear ones, we want you to stay! There is so much for you to do. You are placeholders, each one, and the image you hold even as you sit in the chair that you are in is grand, for this area in this part of the planet [Adelaide]. So it is we ask you to remain, and so it is we ask you to heal yourselves, and so it is we ask you to have long lives, for YOU ARE NEEDED HERE!

There are those of you who have lost loved ones recently, and I would like to talk to you now. There are some of you here (and reading this) who still have hurt and wounded hearts over the passing of these. Let me tell you about this…I want to give you some truth. There is no greater hurt than the hurt of a human heart for the passing of a loved one. And to some of you, this experience hurts for life, because you do not understand the overview! Although difficult to understand, there is a gift connected with the death of a loved one—even in the death of a child! What is this gift? What kind of gift could there be at the death of a child? Let me tell you, dear ones: YOU are responsible in your life for everything that happens to you, even some of the worst things imaginable, given in love. The gift is this: When you lose somebody on this planet, it is proper to mourn—to remember—to celebrate their lives, but the passing was given as a gift of appropriateness so that you could MOVE ON. Sometimes the gift is a gift of feeling so you can be drawn to the bottom of your emotions and give thanks to God for being alive. Only in that state will you find enlightenment! Only in that state will you be receptive! Only in that state would you potentially be prepared for a life's change in path. What a gift! A gift filled with sorrow, but a gift indeed, and a lifetime gift at that.

Every single human passing has a gift connected to it. I want to tell you that there are those who have recently passed who are here tonight, walking these aisles, and putting their arms around you saying, "We are eternal. All of us. You are, too! We are the ones who have just passed on. Did you receive the gift?" They're here, and the consciousness and energy of their lives is here. They're not gone. It's just an energy transfer, that's all it is.

Oh, dear ones, if we could only impart to you how real this is! How many of you who have lost loved ones, remember the fact that they came back vividly in dreams in the first week and the second week—and you passed the dreams off as some psychological abnormality of grieving? That was not an abnormality; that was real! And the messages they had for you were real, and those messages were of love, asking you to accept this gift and move on. What they wanted from you is that you would wrap that part of life up—seal it in love and put it on the shelf in order to move forward. The only real tragedy in the death, dear ones, is for those who remain wounded all their lives, wallowing in grief. You didn't see the gift. You missed it, and that means that their death was in vain! Is that what you want for the both of you and your contract together? It's time, isn't it, that you accepted the gift? Look at what was involved! Stare it in the face and give thanks to them for going through with it. Now it's time for you to uphold your part. Use the experience, the tenderness, and the openness for your own search for truth. That's why they left when they did! It's time to claim the peace of this, and move forward with your own process.

Here are five more attributes that are spiritual. They are practical, but spiritual, and, like the others, they have to do with peace.

The Kid Within

We want to talk about that little child within each of you. Do you hear the voice of the little one here [child in the audience has been cooing]? You know, she knows something. Intuitively at the cellular level, she knows Mom is good. She knows that whatever she needs, Mom will be there to supply it. She knows that. And like a lot of humans, she may fuss about it until she gets some response, but she knows Mom is good. At the cellular level, even at this age, she knows that everything is going to be taken care of for her. No matter what her need, even though she cannot even walk yet, it will be supplied. She'll be carried, fed, taken care of, loved, hugged, put to sleep—safe!

There's a child in each one of you, just like this one. We call it the child of God. And instead of realizing that Mom is good, that child knows that God is good. The child knows he'll be taken care of. The child knows that it's going to be hugged and there's nothing that will occur in its life, even if it stands in a place seemingly alone, that it won't have the hug of God and be taken care of. Oh, if you could go back and experience the childhood and remember how good Mom is at that age! That is what we wish you to feel, regarding the child in each of you—to know that God is good, that home is where YOU are—that YOU are hugged daily, that YOU are never alone. That you have entities who are assigned as angels or guides or whatever you want to call them, that stand next to you and love you. They're your best friends, each one. You don't have to see them, and you don't have to name them. They're there, regardless. And those of you who have chills and intuitions to "move here or there" are feeling those loved ones next to you. No human is ever alone! Never. That's the child within. Here is a big source of peace, dear ones—a big source of peace. We ask you to go there and revisit that feeling. And when you find that feeling, savor it and don't forget how to go back there. Because that's where the peace is. The inner child represents the HEALTH of YOU spiritually, for it is never afraid and is always peaceful about what tomorrow will bring. It owns the concept of being cared for!

Humor

Let's talk about humor for a moment. Let me give you a metaphor—an analogy, perhaps, that you've never heard before about humor. My partner was right, you know, when he said that humor is the only thing that passes untouched to you from the other side of the veil. Let me tell you why. Humor begets joy. You cannot have joy in your life without humor connected with it. Imagine a candle, and in the wax of the candle is joy, and the wick of the candle is you. The candle stands there inactive. Nothing happens with the joy. It is rigid. It is suspended in a shaft that is going nowhere, but is poised and ready—pointing in a raised position. Then the light and flame of **humor** is assigned to the wick (which is you). It will start to melt the joy and activate it. You can smell it, and the joy then becomes pliable. It is working—it gives off light—it is alive, because of the humor that is applied to it. Humor is the catalyst for joy. Joy begets peace and melts the human heart. Do you understand what we're saying? Use this. Use it in all things. See it as a catalyst. Learn how to see it as a catalyst.

Enlightenment

Let's talk about enlightenment. There are those in this room who are afraid of enlightenment, and you have anxiousness over this. We have spoken of this before, but we speak of it again now. There is a *seed fear* in each one of you of becoming enlightened, and it is appropriate. It's part of the test. Some of you are afraid to take that next step because it might change your lives, and you intuitively know that it's going to. We are not here to tell you that you won't have to work, because you will. It is why you're here, and we're going to face off with you in a moment and ask you a question about why you're here. Fear of enlightenment—have peace over it. It is a paper-thin phantom of fear. For when you move into that sweet spot and start paying attention to your guides, things start to clear up in your life. And one of the first things you're going to receive is peace. Even when things may be whirling around you and you don't understand what's going on, you're going to have peace. We promise that, and we have said this many times: *Spirit will never give you a snake when you ask for an apple*. We love you too much. There is no trickery afoot here. This is serious and life-changing.

Who You Are

Here is a spiritual attribute, but it also broaches the physical—and it also relates to inner peace. When you look in the mirror, are you happy with what you see? This may seem to be a rhetorical question. Many of you would say, *"Of course not. I wish I had been this or that instead."* Dear ones, what you see in the mirror is *exactly* what you asked for and planned. It is the mind of God that you had when you planned it. It is the mind of God you owned that had the wisdom of the overview when you designed it.

Are you happy with your gender? Are you happy that you look the way you do? How about your body type, or all of those things you carefully planned and are responsible for? The next time you look at yourself and you say, *"I wish this was different, or I'm not satisfied with this or that,"* know that this verbalization runs counter to what the mind of God inside you planned. It isn't honoring. Instead, try looking in the mirror and saying, *"I am happy and am pleased with this, for I have planned it this way. This is my vessel of God. This is exactly the way it should be."* And we're talking about the *looks* department, the *age* department, and all of the things that are taking place right now in your body.

We have broached this subject only one time before, but we will say it again here for all to hear (and read). Let the following go on to this recording and be registered in this continent that Kryon said it: There are some of you who wonder about the appropriateness of having the physicalness of one gender and the spiritualness of another. Let me tell you that you are honored as much as any other human, for you have come in with a setup of your own making—one where, ironically, the humans who are the most "spiritual" in your culture will point at you and tell others that you are evil and not appropriate in God's eyes. They will indicate that you are doing something wrong and will try to say that you're the scourge of their society. This is a setup, dear ones—one of your own making. You are loved every bit as much as any other human alive! It's the test you asked for, and it's the test you now have. It's appropriate in our eyes, and you are honored for it. Don't let any other human tell you that you are any less than any other human being, even a respected one who may wear a robe, have authority or carry a special title! It is not so! You are loved just as the rest are.

Where You Are

Finally, we'll say this to certain ones of you. Are you happy with *where* you are? Some of you are being pushed and pulled to various places. We now answer the question from the dear one earlier [in the seminar that day] that asked, *"Am I supposed to go someplace because I feel pulled or attracted to that?"* This is the synchronicity we have spoken of before. Dear ones, no matter what your age, you are vibrating at a higher level and you may be pulled to a place to hold and produce a certain energy there for a while. And if you feel a pull, then go. And if the synchronicity holds, the doors will fly open for you to go there. Things will occur for you in those places that are appropriate, and it will be easy while you're there. Spirit uses those who are enlightened in an unusual way on the planet. Be pleased with where you find yourself. Even those of you who seem to be pulled out of an area as splendid as this, perhaps to an area that is more congested, perhaps to an area where there is "heaviness," know that you're needed there, and that's why Spirit pulls you there!

Watch for the synchronicity and the doors to fly open—that's the sign that it's appropriate that you go. And when you go there, understand that it doesn't mean you're going to stay. But be ready to move. That's what the work is all about. Don't sequester yourselves with others of like mind, create an enlightened community, and exclude the others because they're not enlightened! This is not appropriate. We wish you to go out and hold your light in those dark places so that All can see who you are. You may be the only light they get! Some of you have designed contracts for yourselves that include moving often for this very purpose, and some of you are anchors, never to move at all. Use the appropriateness of synchronicity to test this.

We're going to close by telling you about one of the greatest channelers of all time. Over 2,000 years ago there was one who was against spirituality. This was a man of great influence who felt just like some in this culture feel—that the kind of thing you are seeing now is a fraud—that what you hear before you at this moment is a fraud. *"It can't be happening. God does not talk to men any more in this manner, God does not do miracles any longer, and God does not allow healing in places like these."* That's what this man thought.

So this man set out on the main road to the town called Damascus to interrupt meetings against the New Age master who he knew would be there. For he was convinced that what was happening was inappropriate for the time—that it was a sham— and he was going to do everything he could to prove it. His name was Saul. And on that road an amazing thing happened. Saul had a vision. He met an angel! When he met the angel, it was a very real experience for him. The angel was magnificent, and Saul could not doubt what was happening, for it was his reality, and he owned it! The other amazing thing was that he saw his own image on the face of the angel! They didn't write that, did they? And the angel said to Saul, *"Fear not, we have some things to show you."* And the angel gave visions to Saul about God and about the appropriateness of what was taking place in his land. He got to see first-hand what it was all about, and it changed his life.

Saul was not fearful, but he quivered nonetheless, for he was shaking with the energy of Spirit, as love was poured into his heart. And at that moment, Saul changed from that detractor—from that one who hated God—and became Paul the Apostle—and it happened in an instant. It was appropriate and grand, and Paul the Apostle went on to experience the love of God in his life. And Paul the Apostle channeled many letters to those in the cities around his area that have remained transcribed to this day in the books that you call sacred. That's what it was—channeling—inspired words of Spirit given to humans to pass on—anointed—sacred—uplift-ing!

Why do we bring this up? It is to say to you this night as you sit in that chair, do you know what kind of power can instantly happen in the human heart? It can take a man or a woman who is in total disbelief and turn them around in an instant! Why? Because they have assumed and accepted the love of Spirit. What a concept! What a power!

In this room (and reading this) is potential that is unbelievable. Healers listen: There are those who you might turn away synchronistically as being hopeless. You might think there would be no chance that this one is going to heal. He has been to you before and is difficult, obstinate, or unwilling to participate in his healing. Listen: This may be the one who may end up writing the books about love! This one could snap into focus with himself at the most unexpected time, and you, healer, are the catalyst for it. How does that make you feel? Does that put your work in a better perspective? That's the way Spirit works, you know. We don't just ask the ones with the muscles to carry the weight. No. When we have said it is the meek that will inherit the Earth, we're really talking about the meek—the reluctant ones who come in not believing that they're anything special, but instead, discover the power of love! They are the ones who are going to lead you into the New Age. They're the ones who sit in the chairs right here and who are reading this transcription.

My question to you this night is: *"What are you going to do with this information? What is it with you?"* We say to you in pure love: What are you going to do with this? We have explained and given examples tonight of what love can do. We have said that if you want it, you can be changed. What kind of power is it that can turn around a man from a detractor to a prophet—in an instant? The same power that the angel has who sits on that throne inside your heart! That piece of God that we keep talking about that is YOU! Blessed is this humanity! Blessed is this journey that you have decided to take! Blessed is this moment that you have allowed this entity called Kryon to love you and to hug you and to wash your feet.

And so it is.

Kryon

Human Biology

Chapter Four

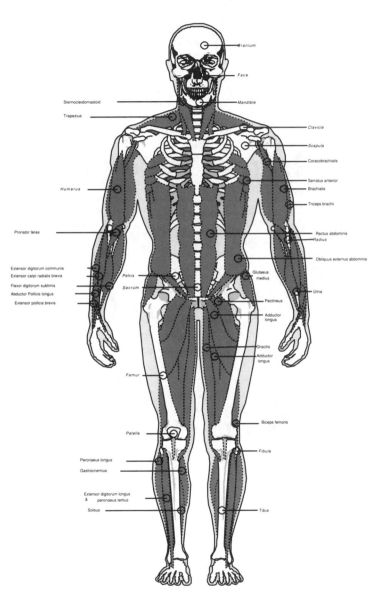

MUSCLES, DEEP LAYER, ANTERIOR VIEW

"Biology, the Greatest Human Attribute"
Channeled in
Reno, NV

The Kryon Writings, Inc.

PMB 422
1155 Camino Del Mar
Del Mar, California 92014
[www.kryonqtly.com]

"Biology, the Greatest Human Attribute"
Live Channeling
Reno, NV

These live channelings have been edited with additional words and thoughts to allow clarification and better understanding of the written word.

Greetings, dear ones, I am Kryon of Magnetic Service. Oh, it is good to see so many of you again. Some of you sitting here will say, *"I have not seen you before,"* and I say, "Oh, yes, you have. Oh, ye,s you have!" For dear ones, we know who you are, and each of you is known by name. We are here to tell you that you are all dearly loved, and so it is now that we say figuratively and metaphorically, "We are here to wash your feet." For this is a sacred time, and you have done so much. This elite group has done so much! It is no accident that you sit in the chair here, no accident that you are hearing (or reading) this communication. We have messages for you, each and every one!

It is the healer in this room [and those reading this] that we address now and in these next moments. But even for those of you who say, *"I am not a healer,"* in many ways you are. You are a healer of the planet Earth, and we speak now to everyone listening or reading. Oh, dear one, we're talking to **you**!

Any person—any entity who wishes at this time to say, *"It's time to move forward—show me what it is I'm to do!"* we invite you to vibrate at a higher rate. And so the gifts for biology, the greatest human attribute of Spirit, are given to you.

It is in these next moments that we wish to bring you a subject that Kryon has never broached before as one full channel. You see, we have waited for you, and for the timing of this year. For this group will never be this group again. There's an irony as you get together and experience and feel the emotion and love that is pressing on you. We want you to think about something: You have group karma. This group has been together before! Can you feel it? Some of you will say, *"No, I can't."* It's because the veil protects that and provides the disguise. I'm here to tell you that there are mothers and daughters and sons and grandmothers and cousins and brothers whom you are sitting with—yet you have no idea of this when you look into the eyes of a seeming stranger or perhaps the one sitting in front of you or beside you. You think you are seeing them for the first time this day. You're wrong! For they have karma with you, and it has to do with the lifetimes they spent with you in the past. But the karma this time may simply be to sit here in this group with you right now and create healing energy for your lesson. There are no "first timers" in this group tonight. It is an elite group that sits before us here, and we do not say this often. Those who have been to these sessions know we do not say this every time. For we know that the force of this group can change humans on this planet. You carry the seeds of biological change, and that's what we're going to address now.

Humans love to title seminars, and so we will title it for you. "Biology, the Greatest Human Attribute." We're going to tell you about human biology. We will give you information this afternoon, some of which you'll know, and some of which will validate what you feel. Some will be new, but it's all about human biology. Kryon has never been in human form, and it is such an honor to sit before those who have chosen to be here! The "piece of God" that you carry is the piece I know, and I recognize the Merkabahs of each of you—ageless each one! You are creations of Spirit. But as you sit before me now and I wash your feet, you are in human biology, and there is sacredness in every cell—and that's what we want to talk about.

If we're going to talk about biology, we must start at the beginning, and so we will. Each one of you carries the seeds of the stars. We tell you now something that we have said before but never emphasized or discussed to a great degree: The star seed that is in your biology was planted there purposely by beings from another place. It was done with love and honor and appropriateness to make you the spiritual beings that you are. You may say that this is fantastic or impossible! The story of Adam and Eve, although metaphoric, is true. For there was a time on this planet when the seeders came down, not just in one place, but many. And through those who visited, this sacred biological seed was given to you as human beings who were ready. This is why, dear ones, I say to your scientists, "You will never find the missing link!" That missing link will never be uncovered in the dirt. Instead, it will someday come from the sky—and introduce itself to you. When it does, you're going to see something: The seed that you carry with you, which was planted in those humans eons ago and evolved into who you are now, does not look like an insect. It does not look like a lizard. It does not look strange and weird. It does not have giant eyes and gray skin. It looks like a precious human being! Don't be surprised when you meet your ancestors, because they look much like you! And although we will not say much more about this, we'll say that there are some here even now.

Let me ask you about the logic of evolution. As the biology of this planet evolved, isn't it true that natural selection and evolution carried the finest and best attributes of all biology to the highest level? The biology that survives this process always carries the attributes that allow for the greatest survival. That's what you believe, and you get to see the reality of it in lower life forms constantly. And so it is that the ones that are more susceptible to surviving are the ones that procreate to form stronger biology.

This is logical evolution and what you call "natural selection." Now let me say this to you: There are several lower life forms that evolved before you, and your scientists tell you that you were part of the lowly starfish, or perhaps the lizard. It crawled out of the sea millions of years ago ready to spend millions of years evolving and evolving—on its way to contributing its evolutionary properties to the human genome.

But we ask you this: Why is it that the starfish can grow an arm when it loses one, or the lizard can grow a tail when it loses one, and you cannot even grow a finger back? Does this make sense in the scheme of natural selection? When human nerves are severed, why don't they grow back together? It's because your PLAN prohibits it. There was an interruption in the human evolution— and it was the planting of the seed we have spoken of. It was on purpose that this was done, according to the wishes of yourselves (when you were not here), so that you would carry the attributes of the sacredness of your journey. That's when it was decided (again by you) that humans would simply not be biology on the planet. There was a plan afoot—that humans would carry a "piece of God" with them. So the sacredness of the biology was created at that point, the metaphor of Adam and Eve, when God came forward and allowed the seed to be put in place. Believe it! We offer you scientific proof: You will never, ever find the missing link until you speak to it and it smiles at you and says, "I'm here!" Seed biology—necessary for you to accept, for it makes you understand the sacredness of who you are. And with that seed biology came the magnetic portion and instruction sets of your current DNA.

Now we have told you before that there is a great amount that is unseen in the data instructions for your DNA. You might ask, "Well, Kryon, why can't we see it? After all, don't we have powerful microscopes?" Let me give you an example. Pretend with me that 150 to 200 years ago some scientists, through a miracle in technology, were able to be brought forward to your time to observe you from a distance. In this story, their challenge was to observe, then go back to report how you communicate in 1998. Their time-travel technology would not allow them to hear anything, only peer through their time scopes and see you now. And so they did it for a while, and they went back and reported: *"Communication doesn't seem to be much different in 1998. In 150 years it seems that we'll still talk like humans. We can see their lips moving, and they're still talking out loud. In addition, we see many wires strung everywhere. We believe that they have devices that allow them to talk through the wires! Other than that, communication doesn't seem to have changed a great deal."*

Well, they missed it, didn't they? They missed the tens of thousands of images that are being flown through the air! They missed all of the communications that happen magnetically through transmission in the atmosphere. They missed all of the satellite transmissions and the stations and the towers—all of the millions of conversations taking place therein. Why did they miss it? Because they could not see it! They were not prepared for the information or the knowledge of those things. They were not predisposed toward expecting something so amazing. They did not have the technology, or even the expectation of the technology—so they didn't see it. But it still exists as reality in 1998, even though they did not report it. So as your modern-day scientists peer through their scopes and electronic instruments, they examine DNA and they analyze only what they can see—the chemistry. They are not prepared to see or understand what is around the chemistry, for they have no concept of the magnetic instruction sets of DNA. We'll tell you more about that in a moment. (see page 377)

So it is that the magnetics carry the instruction sets for your life. But they do more than that. They posture spiritual intent! Within that magnetic structure, not only do you have biology, but you have sacred appropriateness. That's the star seed portion, for it carries your karmic overlays and also the magnetics of when you were born—where the planets were in your solar system at birth—a magnetic attribute of DNA. This is the magnetic imprint we speak of, for that magnetic imprint is the imprint upon the chemistry of your DNA. These are the mechanics, therefore, of what you call the science of astrology, and we have now told you where the print of it resides.

Oh, but there's more to it than that, this huge magnetic imprint that you have. It is responsible for the way you look—the "remembrance" of how you grow, and the seeds of life itself. Although we may speak more about that later, we would like to discuss one other attribute that the DNA magnetics have. It contains a very real "instruction set" for your own termination! How can that be? It's there, and it tempers your life-span, dear ones, and it makes it less than one-tenth of what it could be without it! We're here to tell you that the human body in all its sacredness and in all its grand design and its miraculous mechanization, is designed to rejuvenate itself over and over and over. It is only because of the specific instruction set from the DNA that allows for the termination of life and the chemistry therein, which we wish to speak of next. We have spoken about the beginning; now let's speak about the end.

There's sacredness in these words. We're going to tell you things that have great power because the discussion we're going to give you is about how IT IS. Then we're going to tell you how it can BE CHANGED. Each and every single human being has the instruction set for a release of the death hormone! [*From Lee: It may not actually be a hormone in the sense science defines it, but there is no other word that translates at this time.*] Dear ones, without this instruction set, the human body will live for over 900 years. But today, you have instruction sets that cause the interruption of natural rejuvenation, and the result is aging and death. In order for this death substance to be released, there has to be a clock—and there is. Within the DNA structure and the genes of every single cell in your body, there is a chronograph—

a mechanism that counts. We are here to tell you for the first time that this mechanism that counts is the one that allows for your termination. It is the catalyst for death.

Now you already know that there is a counting mechanism within the biology of your sacred body, for it counts the days to puberty. It counts the days of the reproduction cycle, and it also counts the days of the gradual and increasing release of the death chemical! The pulsing mechanism that puts these clocks together so that every cell in the human body knows what time it is together, is what you are yet to find. You have called it the "body clock." The death hormone is released on schedule, and it interrupts rejuvenation. You call that aging. This is the way you're designed, but you might say, "That's a tragedy!" And we say, "You planned it." You might additionally say, "Why should such a thing be in place? Why is this message powerful or sacred? It seems so sad, if true."

The WHY is because it was necessary for the planet to create an incarnation for humans that would provide fairly short termination in lesson—then to reincarnate in another expression and to retain the overlays of the past karma. In other words, lifetime after lifetime of short durations created the engine of karma that was necessary to raise the vibration of this planet. This is the way the mechanism worked. This planet was created by you, as pieces of God that you are, to help make a balance decision for God. In the process, you have shocked the entire universe! For the vibration of this planet and those on it have been in constant acceleration for the last few years, against all the potential that this could happen. That is why we're here! You have changed your future, and we are here to implement the mechanics of the change and to bring you new information about what you have done. We are not *in control*—YOU ARE. And so the death hormone was created, dear ones, originally for a system that is now starting to be removed. Do you understand what is being told to you this night? The system of short lives is changing! So it is that we invite you to listen, so you will understand that it will not be much longer before the mechanism of the clock and the death hormone can be avoided. Oh, we love you! It's going to take more gifts and more spiritual energy on the planet for you to change, and it's on its way. It's going to take wisdom and understanding for you to apply this new energy—and the many new scientific advancements that will come with it. There is more.

Let us talk about choice, for that is the issue now. Did you know that from the time you were an infant you could choose what would happen? Not just with your biology, but with your life! Infants are fun to watch. We have some information about infants for you. How many of you can remember when you were one? Your psychologists tell you that memory is created by significant events. An engram is imprinted upon your brain and creates memory, and those specific events are usually ones that are remembered due to their potency. They are often first-time events. How many first-time events did you have when you were a one-year-old? The answer is probably dozens—significant and memorable in every way. Yet there are very few of you who can remember any of them, and I'll tell you why: because they are blocked!—more of that DNA magnetic stuff. Why are they blocked? The reason is that the infant who is one year old, and sometimes even those who are two, have full knowledge of who they are! Did you know that? Some infants come into this world and you say that they have a "challenging disposition." They're not happy. They cry a lot, and they're frustrated. Naturally you find many reasons for this, even though they don't seem to "line up" from child to child. Let me tell you the reason: The children want to tell you who they are, but they're frustrated! They find themselves back on Earth growing up again, and they want to shout, "*Don't you know who I am? We planned this together, and I find myself here. Let me tell you who I used to be. Let me tell you how **you** used to be.*" They can't speak a word of language, and they're frustrated beyond belief! Remember that the next time you see the infant whose eyes you look into, and you say, "*There's an old soul in there.*" Indeed! The old soul is trying to tell you who he is—and he's frustrated! He can't talk, and his body doesn't even work right yet. All you do is look at him and goo-goo. Some of the children have the answers, if only they could speak. Others are comfortable with it all, with full knowledge that they are back where they belong. That is the way of it.

Choice. Almost from the time children are five or six years old, they have a choice. Let me tell you about the choice in life as a human, especially in this New Age. You might ask, "*Kryon, what choice can a child have?*" Let me tell you. Especially with the New Age children; they will come in and they will have a choice to accept the situation they are in—or not. Because they will be aware of dysfunctionality in a family, and they'll be aware of anger. They are going to be aware of alcoholism, disease—things that might be wrong within the group. They're going to be aware of poverty or abundance. Many children at that age are going to say to themselves, "*I choose to disengage from this. As I grow up, I am going to be someone else.*" The young person just starting out has a choice to accept or not accept what is happening around him, and many times the peer pressure will be the only thing that keeps him from choosing. But it is the New Age youngster who will look around and say, "*I have a choice not to be with this group. For I am special, and I know I am. I have a choice to remove myself and go in another direction in all honor.*" [Kryon has spoken a great deal more about this in other channelings, regarding the new "indigo children."— see Chapter Seven.]

You, as the adult, also have this choice, no matter where you find yourself in life right now. I am here to tell you that you have a choice to move away from anything that is inappropriate for your spiritual contract and growth—and now I'm not talking about family. Dear ones, I'm talking about the imprint that was given to you on your biology. I'm talking about the magnetic imprint that says, "I'm predisposed to cancer for my lesson." Are you listening? You can choose to remove yourself from that! It (the instruction set is) is no longer needed. The new energy and way of things are giving you tools, permission and CHOICE over these older methods. Say this: "Dear God, by intent I choose to remove myself and give myself permission to let this disease leave. It is not appropriate. It is going to keep me from being what I came to be." Do you like those words? They're real. They're real! Choice! That's what the New Age is about. You are healers—each one.

There are some things that you are going to discover about the human body. You will never be able to clearly see the magnetic imprint of the DNA. To do so would be to invite sacred disaster. But I tell you these things for my partner, and for validation in the future, just as I've done in the past. There will be the shadow of the magnetics of DNA visible to you, and it will be a mystery. You're going to be able to see the clock, and you will identify the gene that counts, but you will not be able to discover exactly how the cells communicate and synchronize the clock. You will discover how to change some magnetic DNA instructions. You will discover where the death hormone is and what releases it. All of these things will take place for you in the next few years, if you choose.

Let me discuss biological healing. Now we get to the crux of the human biology story. Healers, here is how healing works, and this is no mystery to any of you. The human who is in front of you asking for healing must CHOOSE to be healed. Now you might say, "Kryon, that's ridiculous. Every single person who comes before me intends to sit there, so of course they CHOOSE to be healed." And we say, "Oh, no, they don't." Many of them simply choose relief. They want to feel better. They want you to fix them—YOU to fix THEM. YOU! What kind of personal choice is that? They are not choosing to be healed; they are choosing to give responsibility to YOU to heal THEM!

You see, a choice is a very important spiritual aspect. There is great sacredness in this message, dear ones, for you don't know the grand plan. You can't see what we see when an individual is healed. Many times that healed individual goes on to do things for the planet, and you have no idea how you've touched them to provide for their contract. And as we've said before—and healers, listen: "You may be tired of doing one person at a time, over and over. Know this: It's the ONE PERSON you work with who's going to go on to have children that you'll never see, or that you may not even know about, that may affect the grand plan. But how can you know? You don't have the overview we do. Trust that it is so. Partnering with Spirit is like that, you know. Trust that it is so. There is a potential in this room that is staggering for the healing of the individual and the planet!

So the one who comes to you must give permission by choice to be healed. It would also be a good idea to place ceremony around this event. So the next time the individual—let's say, a woman— sits in front of you, you might say, "Why don't we say some things together." Ask this person, *"Do you want to be healed?"* She will say, *"Oh, yes, I do."* Then have her verbalize it and make her speak the words! Ask her to verbalize what she is INTENDING. The biology will listen and hear what she is saying. Permission for healing! Oh, what a sound! That's different! That's choice!

Now here is something that is important but that sounds odd: Healers don't really heal. What healers do is give the body permission to have temporarily balanced attributes. Those of you who are doing energy work know exactly what I'm saying. Healers don't heal. Healers are the facilitation for balance. It's the human on the table that does the work. Did you know that? The human body will balance itself naturally. And all of the facilitators and all of the attributes of the substances used to heal a human being are about FACILITATION FOR SELF-BALANCE. For the biology is miraculous. It seeks balance. It's what it was designed to do. Oh, dear ones, there is no reason why anyone in this room has to leave unbalanced tonight. The researchers are just starting to discover this, this balance, and the one that my partner spoke of earlier this night has indeed been led into a very sacred area. This new science is that you can REPROGRAM YOUR DNA! The sacredness of it is that this new science will allow you to change the very plan of the planet Earth! You are perched on the edge of major biological discovery. We want you to stay! Gone is the old paradigm of short incarnation. Enter the new method of staying on the planet in increased stages of vibration and dimensional shift!

Let's talk some more about healing. We wish to give you six attributes of healing that you're aware of, but that we are going to comment on. This has to do with the subject of external healing, that is, nonself-healing and facilitation by human beings or substances. We will start at the top and move our way down—the top being the highest energy available to you now, and the bottom being from the past, or the lowest energy that works. They are all appropriate in specific situations. Remember this: Do not discard a healing technique that may save your life simply because you don't have a high-energy replacement yet! Use the science that is given to you in any and all forms. Be circumspect and wise about these things. It is ironic indeed that some "enlightened" humans throw away the old—even though the new replacement is only in its infancy of discovery. Be patient! Don't be shocked if some of the very, very old seemingly ridiculous methods end up being functional new ones!

Healing Types

(1) ENERGY HEALING—It will come as no surprise to this group that the first attribute is ENERGY healing. Energy healing is that kind of healing where one does not touch the other. The energies are comingled in a way that cooperates with the one on the table. There is so much potential here! For if the one on the table is vibrating at a high level and knows about these things and has given permission to heal, the facilitator who does the energy work on this one will be granted wonderful miracles. And the one on the table will become healed through this energy work where no one touches anyone else! Think about it. This is the New Age gift—top of the line—number one!

Now this isn't going to work as well on those with lower vibratory rates. That is why those of you who are involved in this energy healing are seeing and documenting the fact that it (energy healing) is not for everyone. For the ones on the table who are enlightened and have an idea about permission and choice are having the best results. The ones who are not, and are of lower vibration, often go away without the healing. *"So what can we offer them, these ones of lower vibration?"* you might ask. That is the next step. You call it *hands-on*.

(2) HANDS-ON—Now this is healing that requires the individual healer to touch the target for the healing, when the patient is of lower vibration (than the healer). Touching will actually make the bond, instead of the energy making the bond between two that are vibrating at equal levels, you see. And so "hands-on" is a wonderful, wonderful tool. It works, and it can get through the mire of a vibrational shift so the one at higher vibration can deal with the one of a lower vibration through this process. The ones on the table can describe choice and permission (verbalized) and the concept will be accepted. They can be healed, and indeed it happens daily. We have told you this before: There are so many of you enlightened in the work of massage who are discovering that you are healing people! That's "hands-on." We refer to the one who came to my partner and said, *"I'm worried that I'm going to lose my business because the ones I'm massaging are being healed—and they're not coming back!"* It didn't happen that way, for the masseuse became the healer! Many came who would not otherwise have done so. Oh, dear ones, there are those here who know exactly what I'm talking about. *Hands-on* is a great healing tool.

(3) LIVE-ESSENCE MEDICINES—Now let us talk about attributes that are used by the healer. We will talk about substances and materials involved in the facilitation, and the first ones we will speak of are live essences. We have spoken about these substances to you for years. Do you think for a minute it was only an accident

and not synchronicity that some of your major diseases within your lifetime were cured by live essence? We speak now about tuberculosis, and we speak now about polio. You see, there is life force still in the things that used to be alive! And if you will understand what we're saying, you will know that life force is powerful and can be a wonderful facilitating aspect of healing substances. The life force of an imprint does not easily change if the form remains intact. Those of you who are in herbalogy know of what I speak, for these are live essence. Those of you in aroma essence know of what I speak, for many of these are live essence.

Let us go to the other side of the issue and go into your mainstream science. There are those who are testing the actual changing of the genes of the body, using special manufactured genes and injecting them into the body, almost as a live soldier with different attributes than you now have, in order to fight disease from the source. This is also honored! Don't throw it away just because an "unenlightened" medical profession came up with it first. Spirit is honoring the entire planet with discovery—and it can take place anywhere there is INTENT! Think about it. Live essence—honor your science, for we have said before that science is spiritual. Physics IS consciousness, and those involved in the smallest parts of matter and the study of physics at the quantum level know exactly what I'm talking about. They are discovering that the reality of what they're looking at can change depending on what they're thinking! Did you know that?

Look for new live-essence medicines. Pay special attention to those that are obtained from very old energies—seemingly with the life force from a different age—obtained from the time capsules of Earth. You will soon know what I mean.

(4) MAGNETICS—The next one down the chain would be magnetic healing. Magnetic healing is honored. It is wonderful. It addresses the magnetic human being. It addresses the magnetics of the DNA and it is valid. It's being used with a greater impact now than at any time on the planet. Let me ask you a question,

however. We have told you that the human body seeks balance, and occasionally it needs facilitation to help it with this. Enter magnetics. Those familiar with magnetic healing will apply the magnets in the right biological areas. Through intuition and the sacredness of the gifts of new knowledge, they will know where to put them. That's how it works, you know. YOU are going to write the books on this, since they're not written yet. They will come right out of your channeled higher selves, to be used by all.

Now, does it make sense to you that once that perfect balance is achieved, the magnets would stay? The answer is NO. External magnetics, like the live essence, like the hands-on, like the energy work, is a temporary method of balance for the individual. When the individuals have choice to balance, why then would they carry the magnetic array with them all the time? Why then would they decide to sleep upon it all the time? The body will balance itself and heal. Why continue to apply the external force after the healing? It's almost like they are saying to the body, *"I don't think you're going to balance; therefore, I'm going to continue giving you the stimulus—forever."*

We're here to say, dear ones, that there is actual biological danger in any of these healing methods when you continue using them on a constant basis while ignoring the biology's natural ability to balance. There are some who are using magnetic arrays that continue to feel wonderful when the magnetics are around. It's a body trick! For cells will feel different when they are being enhanced (stimulated). They're being tickled and massaged, as it were, and their reaction is felt as "special." That does not necessarily mean that things are well and good in the balance department. Many of your dangerous mind-enhancing drugs can do the same thing; they can make you feel "wonderful." It just means that you "feel" something. Balance the body and remove the stimulus when finished! When it needs to be balanced again, bring out the balancing stimulus. Do not use it constantly as an everyday event. Magnetically, the danger is this: The instruction sets will actually become different. Many can be erased! This goes far beyond balance. It can be dangerous to your health! Believe it!

(5) CHEMISTRY—Using chemistry and chemicals is a low energy method of healing. Yet it is still honored by Spirit, for the science of the chemistry within your body is valid and will work for some of you who need it, although it may seem to be a low-energy concept. This is simply because there is nothing else that you have discovered yet in the higher echelons of healing that will take the place of it. Or if there is, the one to be healed might not respond to it due to a lower vibratory rate. So do not think because it is of the low echelon that it is not for you. If it works, dear one, and it keeps you alive on this planet, that is what's important. Try to move up to the other methods, however, when appropriate. The drawback of the chemistry is that the body is fine-tuned, and when you insert chemistry into it to make a change, it will definitely react, but you cannot pinpoint and control exactly what it will do. Sometimes there are side  effects and actual unbalancing attributes to the chemistry, and that is simply part of the properties of a low-energy cure.

(6) INVASIVE SURGERY—It will not shock you then that number six, the lowest one, is what we call invasive surgery. Dear ones, it may be the lowest, but again we say to you that currently it represents some of your finest science. There are those of you who, when all else is exhausted, go to this science and are cured. It can absolutely be appropriate for you. Healers, those of you who deal with energy work, would love to see those healed who vibrate with you—who understand and give their body choice and permission. But there are those who never will. So you move down the scale and you help them define the healing that will work for them, and sometimes it lands at number six, invasive surgery. If it's the only thing that will keep them alive on the planet, consider it as sacred as the energy work! Then work with them during their

recovery, and use your wonderful energy work to speed the healing from the surgery.

So, therefore, all have their places. It is sacred and so it is blessed, because it is indeed a product of your science. Do you understand how this works? The marriage of the highest in New Age energy work and that of the surgery knife is all part of what we are asking you to understand. Tolerance for everything is needed. You might be surprised by what you discover. It might shock you to know of the meditation and prayer and other kinds of "energy work" that go on in the minds of those holding the surgery knives in this age. There is more here than meets the eye, and it absolutely can work together. This is your new challenge.

So we have given you six different methods, and comments about these methods, but we have yet to broach the one that is the most sacred, and that's the one that only requires the body. Yes, it's possible. We are talking about the gift of self-healing. There are those in this room who are acquainted with self-healing, who are healers in energy and who are beginning to understand the concept, but this is difficult to teach. That is why the facilitators are necessary. The ones who can heal themselves are the ones who vibrate at a high level, the ones who understand that *consciousness can change physics*.

There are three aspects that you should know regarding self-healing. The first one is integration. The second one is integration, and the third and most important one is integration [laughter]. Here again speak of something that is so precious and so unusual for some of you. How many of you come into this life and wish you did not have biology? It shocks us to see how you planned to have the sacredness of your bodies work for you, and yet you come into the Earth and you spend your whole life wishing it wasn't there! You obtain enlightenment, but you somehow believe you carry it around from your neck up! You look at your body and you say, *"I'm going to spend as much time as I can astral-projecting. I hate this thing that's attached to my neck."* Some of you look for excuses to leave it! When your arm hurts, you say, *"Oh, I wish my arm didn't hurt. I'd better go have it fixed."* You see, you're missing it entirely! Every single cell is enlightened as much as the one next to it. Instead of thinking that you have one enlightened center, know that you have millions! In order for your vibrating body to work together, the whole body must vibrate as one, not just the part you have assigned as your "enlightenment center."

Here is a story we have told before: It's about the man who stuck his head into the window of a vehicle and said to the driver, *"I'm ready, let's go!"* And the driver took off with the man's head! Blessed is the human being who understands that you must place the whole body in the vehicle before you say, *"Let's go."* Oh, dear ones, we're talking about integration of the light source with each and every cell, and here are some of the steps. You must consider every cell as part of the whole consciousness. There is a "WE" involved here. If you stub your toe, WE hurt. Never again say, *"My toe hurts."* Start acknowledging the sacredness of the WE, and you will start vibrating together as one. There isn't a cell in your body that does not carry the tools of awareness. But you often perceive this awareness as perhaps being only in what you call the third eye, an important portal of the body. The third eye, dear ones, is simply a culmination of the facilitation and cooperation of the rest of the cells—a focal point. There's a flow here, and it starts with the toe cell and the elbow cell and all of the other internal cells, including pieces of every organ. They all know what you know. Why? Because all are involved in the clock, you see!

Is this starting to come together to you? Unless you're going to vibrate together, the clock will never know what to do with the death hormone! So it's the WE that's central to self-healing. It's the integration and the integration...then integration. Never again should you think that the biology connected to your head is foreign to enlightenment, for it is not. It is part of the system that is going to keep you here! Oh, dear ones, we do not have the time and you do not have the time to go through another incarnation—the inefficiency of leaving, of coming back, and growing up again. You've got work to do now! We want you to stay. Stay! So, in love we give you these messages so that you'll understand the mechanism that you require, and the sacredness of the biology you need to keep you alive, serving the planet!

Finally, we say that, again, verbalization is critical to your entire process. Verbalization? What does that have to do with biology? Again, it's due to the fact that your biology and your intellect and your spiritual side have all come together to speak words into the air, words that your biology and that of others hear as sound. What you speak is what you create! Do you catch yourself saying this part or that part hurts? Change it to "WE HURT." Verbalize in all of your communications the "we-ness" and the oneness of your biology. Then honor the parts. Start practicing this, dear ones, and you're going to see a difference in your life. Never verbalize your doubt or your seeming inability to do something. By doing so you give it credibility and your cells hear you do it! Is it no wonder they do not cooperate with the healer?

Do something really spooky! [laughter] When some of you go to the facilitator next, go into short ceremony and say out loud, "*Dear body, in all appropriateness, and sacredness I address you. We are together in this life, and together we will heal ourselves and choose to move forward into our contract. Together we will rejuvenate, and together we will have the power to slow the death hormone's release.*" There are those in this room who can have life extension if you do this! It will not be long before you see life extension taking place with many.

We want you to stay, you see. We love you, you see. And there is not an entity in this room who calls him or herself "healer" who does not have the sacred cellular instruction on how to make this work. Regardless of what is taking place in your body, regardless of the recentness of events, all these things are sacred and purposeful, if only to get you to understand them! Even the seeming unrelated attributes of life are trying to talk to you. The amazing thing is that when you start talking to your body, the discourse that you will discover as to what is going on will amaze you. It has to do with seeming unbiological things such as anger situations that you thought were only in your head. Would it shock you to know that all the cells knew of it? It has to do with jealousy and lack of self-worth. Your biology knows about it all—each cell, counting the days. The cells are there waiting, waiting for you to understand how to change them. They have heard this message tonight also. The difference is that they must wait for the spark of life that is your soul to make a choice. You make the choice—the biological equipment is ready to start the changes—and it WILL hear you.

And so the message has been put forward. This is what we want you to know: You have the choice to be balanced, healed, and peaceful about the future. In closing, we say again that in all love, don't you think we know what you've been through? This night, before you retire, we want you to know that you have some wonderful, loving entities that stand next to your bed. They are family. They have always been there, but perhaps you are not aware of it. They, like the abundance of cells in your body, are waiting for a CHOICE...of your intent...and your verbalization of it.

Oh, dear ones, some of you at this time will understand that a piece of home has come through this channel and touched you! Let the peace of God enter your heart at this time and know that you are dearly loved!

As so it is!

Kryon

Ascension II

Chapter Five

ear ones, when Kryon originally came, we spoke of planetary changes, and you have seen the weather patterns shift, and you have seen the Earth shake. You have seen many things that we predicted would take place. This is the love/Earth connection. For we are here in honor of you! The changing of the grid and the planetary shifts are as though the Earth were under repair. Think of it as "under construction..."

Kryon - Page 88

"Ascension II"
Channeled in
Portland, OR

The Kryon Writings, Inc.

PMB 422
1155 Camino Del Mar
Del Mar, California 92014
[www.kryonqtly.com]

"Ascension II"
Live Channeling
Portland, OR

These live channelings have been edited with additional words and thoughts to allow clarification and better understanding of the written word.

From the writer...

Discussions on the ascension process are some of the hottest metaphysical topics today. In Kryon Book Three, *Alchemy of the Human Spirit*, published in 1995, Chapter Eight dealt with ascension as channeled by Kryon. Now here it is again, but this time there is more—so it becomes Kryon's second installment on the popular subject (hence, the "II"). It is typical that as time moves forward in our New Age that the definition, concept, and eventual meaning of the ascension process, perhaps the most powerful New Age gift, will be revealed to us in greater detail.

Greetings, dear ones, I am Kryon of Magnetic Service. Hold this energy now, for this is a precious time. There is a difference here that has not been felt for some time. It is an energy that will support the message of this night, which is about great gifts for humans. But let us hold this for a moment. Oh, the love between Spirit and humanity is like a rose—delicate, cherished, aromatic. It must be kept and cared for. It's nothing that you can cast away and have it remain beautiful by itself. No. You must nurture it. Like a small child it is, this rose, and if cherished and if nurtured and if loved, it will bloom. And it is the bloom of this rose that we wish to speak of this night.

Oh, there are those in this place who truly do not believe what is taking place now. They are of the opinion that God stopped talking to mankind in this fashion years ago. We are here to tell you that it has never stopped, because the love of God never stopped! Why would it stop, when you are indeed the ones who carry such a precious task—honored and loved in this universe of entities? Who is it who told you that there was a time when you were not allowed to do this anymore? Whoever said that did a disservice to you, for it is the loving communication in this fashion that nurtures your very heart. But you're not the only one, for Spirit has love and has a heart, too. It's huge, and when we tell you we love you, we pass the information that we are IN LOVE with you!

We have told so many groups like this one that the words you are hearing and reading now represent the same kind of communication that was offered from the burning bush not so long ago. And I would not have said this so often to you as humans if it were not so. Now some of you are starting to realize why, for the example rings with a metaphor. You have heard the voice before and it has the same authority. It's the authority of LOVE, and it's the authority of HOME that comes before you this night. And it sits before you now and says, "*I have the authority to wash your feet and love you dearly.*" That's the authority of Spirit. Get used to it. For this is the channeled message of Spirit for you.

Oh, there is great energy tonight. Let me describe this energy in words that are different than I have used before. This is a time that's PRECIOUS. I have never used this word before in a channeling like this, and my partner translates it properly. Right now this energy is tender. It is because there are enough of you who truly understand what is before you right now—not a father figure, not an authoritarian—but a partner who says, "I want to take your hand. It's time, and I wish to show you something you have not realized before." The lesson of this night and within this energy has a preciousness and a tenderness that is powerful and potent! This is the second (and more expansive) message that we are going to speak of now. It is described by one word—a word that is inadequate for the attribute, but it's the only one you have. The word is ASCENSION. We are going to expound tonight on ascension in an energy that was not possible even a month ago. But it is now.

It's the assemblage of humans this night who sit in the chairs by appointment who have caused this to happen. Not just the integrity of those who are here, but the intensity of passion this night for those of you who sit in those chairs who are saying, "*I am ready to find out more.*" For some of you truly understand that it's no accident that you find yourself on this planet right now. Now, some of you are saying, "*I'm too old. Why couldn't this have happened years ago*" [referring to an enlightened under- standing of spiritual purpose]? Oh, dear ones, your age has nothing to do with it and everything to do with it. It represents the "now." It is a perfect time for you. So the ones who are in advanced years in this place have advanced wisdom. Feel it! Everything is appropriate. For had it been sooner, it would not have worked for you, and you know what I'm talking about. For those who are older in human years will need to hold the wisdom for the younger ones, who will come to them for advice. The younger ones will have the energy to go and do and BE!

Ascension. It's a poor word because you don't have another that actually means what it is. The closest word you have for what the true attribute of ascension is, is *graduation*, and even gradu- ation does not tell the entire story. Ascension by its very name indicates rise, and that is correct, for it represents the raising in vibration of everything. Everything! We will describe that as we continue. But it does not carry the meaning that you think. Some of you are anxious to get on with your own personal ascension, and you are saying, "I want to ascend into the clouds like some of the masters of old and be done with this place and be out of my biology."

We say to you, dear ones, that this is not what Spirit means by *ascension*. This is an anointed time, and the information passed here is going to give you insight into your gifts and into your power. Let me tell you what ascension is. Ascension is a graduation by design, and with permission, that is human enablement at its highest form. It is where humans have permission, EARNED by every one, to move into a status that has you REMAIN on the planet, living a very long time while actually moving into the next incarnation that you designed for yourselves—without ever having to experience death! That's *ascension*. Did you get that? You move forward into the next designed expression holding your biology, vibrating at a high enough level to allow for such a thing without death. Does this begin to reveal to you how long we want you to stay? Think about it.

Ah, but there's a timeline involved, and we're going to discuss that as well. Ascension is *marriage*. It is a partnership with the golden angel that sits on the throne in your life, which you call your Higher Self [as described earlier in this book]. It's a marriage with all the things that go with it, commitment, promise, and fidelity. It's marriage—that's what ascension is.

So, who are these that are going to take this status? As we proceed more in this explanation, you are going to understand the timeline that will be revealed. Do not misunderstand or be misinformed or have your feelings hurt when we tell you that not all of you will ascend. Again, we tell you that this status is not for everyone. But the process that leads to it, is. Now how can that be? The reason is this, dear ones: The process of beginning to ascend and beginning to raise your vibration as a human being is what you should be about right now—if you choose to do it. It is a question of how far you wish to take it. There are no rules that say that you must go a certain place, maintain a certain vibration, or say specific mantras all day. No. This process is extremely personal!

As we proceed, you'll understand a little more about why you would wish to stop and hold a certain vibration, serving the planet in this capacity and not going any further. Some of you may wish to go all the way, part of the way, or just begin the process. In each case, your request is an honored place, unique for each individual. It may not surprise you to know that this particular continent

(North America) is behind regarding ascension status. There are more humans involved in this process on other continents of this Earth than yours. They are understanding and taking this attribute in greater numbers. That is why the critical mass is being reached faster. This quest is worldwide, and it is taking place in a greater way on other continents than on this one. That is why Earth is changing so quickly.

Oh, you are a grand part of it, and this is as it should be. There is a channeling going on at this instant in another part of this planet that has this very message using these very words. I've never told you that, have I? You are receiving it at the same time, and that is often the way Spirit works. This message is not proprietary for one group. It is for all humans at the same time, and although I can tell you where this is, I choose not to. They are connecting with you, and you with them. They do not speak your language, but are of a fine lineage.

The Earth

Before we continue regarding ascension, let us speak about the Earth. Some of you might say, *"Kryon, why would you talk about the Earth when you're revealing ascension? Instead, talk about humans and what ascension means and what it feels like and what the gifts are."* No. We must talk about the Earth first. This will now marry to the information previously given this very day, within this place, and in another. I previously told you that "as the Earth goes, so humanity goes." This is why we are so interested in your planetary aspects. I speak to an elite group now that understands that the very dirt of this planet contains consciousness!

Dear ones, this is where the elements of your biology came from. For there are only a given amount of elements on your planet, and whether they are converted into carbon-based life energy or whether they remain as rock, they remain as the same quantity. Therefore, the elements in your body and your cells, and the life energy that surges through you are originally part of the Earth. It has a consciousness, this Earth of yours. Your Earth must shift before you are allowed to go further. Its consciousness must cooperate with what you are doing. This is not new news.

There are four kinds of shifts going on in the planet: Magnetic, meteorological, geological, and spiritual. The magnetics that we have spoken of often are the magnetics of your grid system, which, by the way, are influenced by your sun, which is the portal of communication that we have talked to you about before. It is the posturing of this grid that gives you the gifts of the New Age, because as the grid moves the veil (the spiritual aspect that is your duality), it starts to lift. The veil must lift a certain degree before you can have the gifts—and it is not done lifting yet. I will tell you when we get to the discussion of the timeline, what to expect. You have also seen magnetic north start to move. I told you of this exact shift when I first arrived in 1989—and now you can measure it yourself.

It was years ago that I also sat in front of groups like this and I told you about your current weather changes. Expect them to continue. It is like being in a house under construction, I said— irritating, uncomfortable, a work in progress. And it's happening on schedule—not because I told you it would, but because the elements are responding to your consciousness! It continues to happen, and we tell you that many of the new patterns, dear ones, will continue indefinitely. You will learn to work with them, and you will have to reconfigure the banks of the rivers and the dams that you build to allow for them. For many winters will continue to be cold and harsh, and there will continue to be flooding which wasn't an issue before 1989.

It is all part of the readjustment of the planet. The planet must change first to allow the humans who are on it to change next. Shift, Earth changes—it's all part of ascension. That's what it's about, dear ones. The end times are about *ascension*. It is not about fear, but there are those who do not understand ascension, who do not understand vibrating at a higher level. To them it can look frightening.

Let me tell you about the geological aspects of the planet. There is a measurement right now, a science measurement, which you call a resonance. It is a measurement of the standing-wave scenario between the surface of the Earth and the top of the ionosphere. In the past it has had a resonance as measured for eons as 7 in your vibrational units [Hertz]. Today it's at 10, moving toward 11!* Did you know that? The geology of the planet is changing for you, not just the weather, and what is said next is not meant to strike fear in the hearts of those of you who live in this area, but it is given in love and refers to the planet as a whole. You are about to see more of the insides of the Earth come out and visit you. Some of the events are going to happen in unlikely spots—not the expected ones, dear ones, not the expected ones.

Although there may be volcanic activity here [the Portland area], it is your duty if you so choose, to hold the energy in a spot like this that has potential for disaster—to clear it and never let it become a disaster here. Listen, dear ones, it was last year that the orbital mechanics were changed of an asteroid to allow for "a near miss." This asteroid carried an incredible amount of energy for YOU, given to this planet within its pass.** You see, it was the light workers, each one, and their meditations and their intent who allowed for the miss. It was the warriors of the light on your planet who actually changed the orbit of this astronomical body! Is it so astounding, therefore, to inform you that you can control your area and keep these overflows of the magma of Earth in check? It is not that difficult. Meditate on it. Keep your area safe, for it is precious and it is tender and it's yours to protect. Again, we tell you that human con-sciousness changes physics! They are re-lated, as we have revealed before. But you shall see this volcanic activity globally in unexpected areas. Watch for it—it will be with you soon.***(bottom, next page)

*See page 373 "The Science Chapter"
**See page 358 "The Science Chapter"

Spiritually, none who have studied what is taking place now on this planet could have missed this: The gifts for the planet and for you have been delivered here (by us) in many forms. The "near miss" last year of the asteroid, the comets that have visited you in the last two years, the gamma ray activity, and many other physical attributes that remain a mystery to you all have been spiritual gifts, presented in a real three-dimensional physical world for you to see. This energy, purposefully delivered to the planet was for ascension! Therefore we again tell you that the physical is related to the spiritual.

Let us speak now of the science that is being given to you. Now be careful, dear ones, for in these next few moments I'm going to give you information that is new. Be cautious in how you treat it, for some of you will wish to make it more sensational than it is, and it doesn't necessarily have to be. If there is any sensationalism, it is the fact that incredible love is being transmitted to your hearts now.

The timeline started in 1987, and on your planet, given in that year, was the ability to understand and finally implement *scaler-wave* technology. And you started your experiments in earnest about that time, and we invite you to validate what I'm going to tell you next. For you studied the inventions and the discoveries—the three-dimensional science from the one you call Tesla, and started experimenting in that year. But it was not on this continent. No. And if I can take you back to a time in 1987 on another continent

---

***Within three weeks of this channeling in Portland, volcanoes were reported in the Mexico City area, the British colony Montserrat and Jakarta. Earthquakes were reported near Japan, Indonesia, Chile and Taiwan.*

More magma soon?

you call Australia, in the middle of that continent were two towers, set up by this government (U.S.) in a place called Pine Gap. There were experiments then—experiments with scaler waves and the towers—transmittal of energy through the ground. But you see, there were mistakes made, dear ones. For you did not understand the complex phase relationships and resonance attributes with scaler. For they are enormous, and they build up and become exponential very quickly. Like too many soldiers in step on a bridge, the resonances create enormous wavelike properties. Had you known that, this experiment would not have caused the mantle of the Earth to shift on the other side of the planet like it did. Some of you will do some research and be astounded at this information. Humans caused an earthquake—the first human-made ones in history!

Now here you find yourselves again with the same technology except you're not dealing with the ground anymore. You've decided to aim it at the sky! Four of you in this audience will understand these words because there's a code in this sentence when I say, "*Here is some advice: Take AIM at this technology and expose it.*" * And that is the code I give you. We have told you this before. Oh, dear ones, there is science being given to the planet that is being used for healing, and as my partner explained this night, you are beginning to understand and address the SPIRITUAL aspects of your biology because of it. It is your privilege, and it is a gift that is given to you in all love, and it's happening everywhere. The technology that is represented in this room [speaking of Dr. Todd Ovokaitys in the audience**] is one of many. For the same kinds of attributes are presented. Make no mistake. There are ones in this room, dear ones, who will change the planet right here among you. There are warriors of science! There are warriors of intent! There are warriors of meditation

*See page 243 "The HAARP Update"
**See page 378 "The Science Chapter"

here, which are going to make this planet different than the way it is today—If they choose to. Choice! Intent! Are you starting to see a pattern here?

So the Earth has changed greatly to allow for human ascension, and the inventions that you have received are meant to expand and extend your life. That's the entire reason they're being given to you. But as with any science, some of the new knowledge is being used for other purposes as well, perhaps less honorable than the pursuit of spiritual awareness. In all our love, we say that these gifts are given to you for life extension—for peace. For they will marry with what you are being given personally, if you choose to use them for your graduation—for the thing we call ascension.

Let us speak of this timeline right now. The ascension timeline is a 24-year window. From the end of 1987 on, to about the beginning of 2012, is the window. Now those of you who are starting to see what happened in this window are understanding that the beginning was what we called and have described in other writings as the eleven-eleven (11:11). Do you remember what the eleven-eleven was? Let me remind you: It was a spiritual window—a gateway of human code change for your DNA. Permission was given at that time for humans to have an ascension potential. It was a result of the measurement you called the Harmonic Convergence. The year 1987 is when it all began. Then you experienced the twelve-twelve (12:12), which was the "passing of the torch" from many entities who were not human, holding the energy of the planet, now giving the responsibility wholly to you, finally allowing humans and the planet to be self-enabled. You are now holding more energy than you ever had before; you're able to carry your Higher Self around without help. Ascension, permission passed to you, permission to graduate, permission to move forward! Then there were the comets and asteroids and other items and attributes given to this planet for your energy—for you to "pull out" of storage within the planet Earth, spiritually, when needed.

First was Earth, the vehicle, the object you stand upon—the partner, the one who you share elements in your body with. The consciousness of Earth had to come first. Now it's your turn. What this means as you sit here is that you have time to continue this process of graduation. Spirit is not here looking at you and telling you that you must accomplish it overnight. Hardly! You can't. The energy has not been given that will allow for a full ascension yet. It is gradual, as you might imagine. Permission has been given, and the energy has been postured for a partial trip, and many of you are starting to take it now. More will come as you need it, and permission to continue has already been given.

There have been many instructions given to you about how many steps are involved in what you must do. So many of them have been given in wonderful intent and are accurate. Semantics sometimes fails, however, and because you are talking about an interdimensional aspect of humanity that is new, much hides within the instructions. Names and processes are often "labeled" as different, but they are the same. There are still yet-to-be channeled messages that will make more sense on a day-by-day basis with respect to what is before you. So you are being asked again to go slow. Understand that there are 14 years left [at the time of this message in 1997], and there will be energy passed along the way to allow for these things.

Humanity

So now we speak of humanity. Have you understood the gifts and tools that are being given to you for graduation? When I first came and I told you about the implant/release, I explained that it was a gift. I revealed a spiritual aspect you had before you within the New Age. I did not BRING it to you. YOU, within your work on the planet, allowed for it. It follows the Harmonic Convergence and the 11:11 and the 12:12. It is a gift that allows you to clear your karma and is an integral part of the ascension process. The gift is your honor and your privilege. You have earned it!

Evil and fear: Oh dear ones, such is the potential for the gifts of love that they would bring change to you, and some apprehension. For you feel the changes, and they surge within you. Some have felt the surge and do not understand them and have said, "This can't be right." Others of you have said, "I feel home visiting me again. I've felt this before!" You know where you felt it? Oh, we've told you, we've told you. So many of you in this precious, precious place have been brothers and sisters in that time we call Atlantis. And that is where you felt it before. My partner covers a part of his body that we're going to talk about before this message is over [Lee puts his hand on his chest], and it's not his heart.

The gifts and the tools that are given to you to allow for graduation and ascension will be ongoing throughout this 24-year window. And so far, you have earned and received many of the gifts already. Permission was one. The gift of karma clearing—the gift of healing yourself—the gift of great energy facilitation, and the most powerful one: the gift of INTENT. There is no greater gift than that which is given to humanity where they can INTEND something and have it carry enormous potential energy for them and others around them. Think of it, almost like magic—INTENT!

Emotionally what are you feeling (those of you who have decided to go to the next level to vibrate at a higher level)? Some have said, "*Dear God (Spirit), I don't know where I'm going, but I choose this first step of graduation and ascension.*" What is it you're feeling? Let me give you an emotion that may surprise you: SORROW! It's not what you think, not what you think. It is not sadness and sorrow for a poor life, or for things that may be happening around you. No, instead, you are feeling the disconnection with who you were, who you used to be. You see, you're becoming something else. We have spoken of this before, about the New Age humans becoming something else. Disconnection is what you are feeling.

There are some of you who have actually had visions and dreams of your own death, but let me tell you that there is no greater honor than within a vision like this. It does not mean that you're going to die, dear ones. It is metaphoric. It means that the old self, the one you came in with, is gone. And the new one that you've asked for with the higher vibration is surging through your body. Do you know what this does to US [entities on Kryon's side of the veil] to see you do this? You see, there's now incredible hope, tremendous hope, marvelous hope, that in 12 to 14 years we will see some astounding changes in this planet. When the critical mass is reached, there will be surprises all around. The emotion of disconnection is with many of you, and we wish to explain right now why you would feel such a thing. There's nothing wrong with you. You are moving into an area that so few have ever been, and YOU are the forerunners of this ascension process.

What about the family? What's going to happen to the family? Let me tell you that there are two parts to this answer. The first is astounding, since it deals with the "karmic family." Did you know about karmic groups? All of you know each other! I believe you know that, don't you? Brothers, sisters, cousins, mothers, fathers—you've been here before and you travel through your incarnations in groups, overlapping in age and death and life—in groups. You have a karmic connection with the person who sits next to you even though you may not know his or her name. I guarantee it. For the first time in human existence you are being allowed to step out of these groups on your own, while you are here, and claim your own island (persona) as a group. You have that much power! When we speak of family, then, we are saying *karmic family.* Is it no wonder you feel emotional sorrow, because you are saying good-bye to a large group that you have traveled with in an astral way for eons of time, and here you are saying good-bye because you have chosen to become something else.

With your karma clean and clear, you are moving into a graduation status and leaving them to do the same as they wish, or not. You, therefore, are no longer connected. The strand is broken, and you feel it.

What about HUMAN families? Oh, dear ones, it's important that you understand this: We have been in front of you many times, and we have told you that to take the karma-clearing gift that we called the *release* is going to make you a much better person. And we told you that those around will see it because it creates peace, less anxiety, and brings you to a realization of responsibility and reveals who you are. Mates will enjoy it. Children will enjoy it. Family and friends will enjoy it because you have the potential and permission to become a more peaceful human being. Now, let us turn the page in this new and expanded energy and say this: This is NOT necessarily what is facing you when we talk about vibrational shift and graduate ascension status.

Within the disconnection from the old self and the removal from karma, some will move into a vibration that will not be the one that your mate has. And this is why some of you may wish to remain where you are. Because for your life it might be better to stay there. It serves you. It serves the children and therefore serves the planet. Then, perhaps, later you might choose to move forward. These are things only YOU will know, and there is NO judgment around this! You will not be left in the dirt (so to speak)! Any human being who decides to vibrate at a higher level, even in the first stage of graduation, is honored and loved like every other. If all they do is go only that far and stay there, it is appropriate for them. The decision requires discernment and intuition for them, and they'll know what is proper. It's not a race. There's no competition here. There's only spiritual appropriateness and contract.

But here is an oddity, dear ones: For those of you who wish to go the route, to vibrate at a higher rate and stay current with the information and the energy that is being passed to this planet, there is a group of humans who will understand and be with you. Many will not be shocked to understand this realization and understand that these I speak of are the new children of this planet. For they will see what you're doing and will hold your hand and look at you. And in their own way their, very own cells will congratulate you for what you are doing for them, and many of them will do the same. For it will be easier for them than for you within this 24-year window, for they come in with new awareness and a feeling of purpose. Family! Karmic, biological, and a challenge—did you really expect anything else?*

What is this person in graduate status feeling like? Let me tell you. We have already told you that those of you who are vibrating higher are having different sleep patterns. You remember that, don't you [regarding the attribute of being awakened sometimes twice a night, with feelings that you are not alone]? We also told you that you are having different eating patterns. You remember that, too, don't you? We've also told you that there are some of you, because of your vibrational changes, who are closer to certain astral attributes and entities than you were before. And because of that you're starting to see, or think you are seeing, some of these entities around you—waking up in the middle of the night with a start, thinking that your room is full of entities. Ha ha! Well, YOU'RE RIGHT! We have talked about your support group before and how many of them there are. It would astound you. For every human being there is a legion of helpers. They know who you are, you know. You are actually becoming closer to their dimension when you decide to take the road to ascension.

What are you thinking, those of you who are in ascension status? Let me tell you. You are slow to anger, you are. You have a tolerance level you never thought possible before. Yes, you do. You have a new powerful love attribute, and you look at others differently. But here is the big one: You realize the goal! Discernment now comes from within. You have every single answer you ever wanted from the golden angel that sits on that throne you call your Higher Self. Yes. And so the discernment and the power of what to do next and where to go is coming from within. Not from

*See page 255 "The Indigo Children"

a guru or a channel. Not from a psychic, and not from this stage [speaking of the riser that Lee is on]. This [the channeling] is information, dear ones. The spiritual action comes from you. We are giving you information in love, and then you take it and act on it. What is being transmitted here is the LOVE of God, but what you do with it creates the changes for the planet. It's YOU who are doing the work.

Finally, let us talk about your biology. We have spoken of this before. There is much going on in your bodies at the cellular level (those who have chosen the ascension road). There will come a day when it will be a phenomenon to be studied and something that your medicine will wonder at—that so many have these "odd" attributes! What is it, they will say, that suddenly in this society has caused the reawakening of the organ you call the thymus? What caused it? It's INTENT! Intent to live a long time. INTENT to change your health—and INTENT to remain. You see, your bodies were designed to live over 900 years! Now here it comes: The methods that will internally support that notion start with a *reawakening of the thymus*. It starts with the DNA being changed by your own INTENT, live-essence substances and attributes [including magnetics as one of them], and facilitators. Do you doubt such a thing could happen? Oh, it could happen now! You don't have to wait 14 years. It is available today! There isn't a person in this room who can't walk from here healed and ready to move forward. If you want help, there are facilitators here, and there are substances here. My partner brings facilitation with him of a type perhaps you have not seen before, but that is appropriate for this room [speaking of the Kryon workers that are participating in the conference]. There are people here who will meet other people this night and live longer lives because of it! That's why you were brought here. That's why you sit in these chairs.

Finally, we tell you that something is also happening to your body clock [those who have given intent]. You are being slowed down, but it may not appear that way to you. Here's the key: If it appears as though the Earth is traveling around you faster, YOU are being slowed down. The body clock is going to operate slower, so it's going to count fewer pulses, and therefore last longer. That's what's happening.

Oh, dear ones, we have given you an insight as to the timeline. We have given you an insight as to what your biology is doing and what your emotions are doing. We have told you what to look for. We've given you information that everything is not all here yet and that you were honored for even beginning the journey without all the information. We have told you that some may go partway and that it's appropriate to stop—and that there is no judgment over this. We have also told you that some will go all the way. What's going to happen in 2012? Another measurement. And if, dear ones, that measurement is found to be a certain vibration, you are all going to see an entirely different planet—and that is what is going to trigger the mass landing. That. They cannot arrive in that manner until you are in their time frame, and that is why some of your ancient prophecies are showing the end of time as you know it in 2012. It's only the end of the attribute of time, however, that you have now as you move into another kind. A new clock is given to Earth at that time, if the measurement is found to be a certain way. Because it is relative, you may feel very little, but your astronomers will know. They will slowly see evidence within the cosmos of changes around them. Things that they used to look at that were spinning wildly will seem to slow down. It's you who are slowing down, bringing other anomalies into a better focus.

Love. There is no greater power in the Universe. Do you wonder where your guides are coming from? The master guides are arriving from where the energy is being transmitted. It's from the great central sun. It is from the source that is as far away as you can even imagine. That's where I'm from, and that's where you are from. It's the energy of home. Meanwhile, I'm here for the duration to love you—to sit at your feet in meetings like this and say that this is a precious time, to say that I am here to wash your feet with the tears of joy that we have for the humans sitting in this place [and reading these words]. There will never be another time just like this one, for the energy that is here tonight developed by exactly the humans here will never be repeated. And so it means that this is an anointed, unique place, and I want you to sit here just for a moment and think about that.

There are contracts between you and those around you that you have no concept of. You sit next to loved ones who you've agonized over who perished in the past—and you don't even know it. You don't see their names, and they don't look the same to you, for much is hidden from one incarnation to the next. But you're all family. Believe it! The words *tender* and *precious* are used again because that is what this energy is here tonight, different from other times—powerful and appropriate for this anointed message. Let everyone go from this place remembering something that we say so often, for it is so true: In perfect love, we know your names. We know what you've been through, and because of that…

You are dearly loved.

And so it is.

Kryon

"Humanity, the Vanishing Species"
Channeled in
Portsmouth, NH

The Kryon Writings, Inc.

PMB 422
1155 Camino Del Mar
Del Mar, California 92014
[www.kryonqtly.com]

"Humanity, the Vanishing Species"
Live Channeling
Portsmouth, NH

*These live channelings have been edited with additional
words and thoughts to allow clarification and better
understanding of the written word.*

From the writer...

Wow! The title sounds like we are headed for extinction. Is this
the case? Read on, and you'll find out. In one of the most practical
channels yet given (in New Hampshire). Right after this event, I went
to New York City, where again, Kryon channeled before the S.E.A.T.
at the United Nations (the next chapter). This East Coast visit was
one of the most memorable of my life.

Greetings, dear ones, for I am Kryon of Magnetic Service!
As you are getting used to the voice of my partner
speaking to you now, we're going to fill this room with
something very special. For we have told you before that the more
there are in the gathering, the more intense it is, depending upon
the consciousness of those here, and we're here this night to say
to each of you, "Oh, dear ones, we know who you are."

There are those who will now become used to hearing my
partner's voice, as the voice of the spiritual power of the burning
bush itself, as we press upon this assemblage with a cone of love.
Oh, dear ones, it is Spirit itself that has the privilege of walking
between the seats! Each and every one of you is known by name,
and not necessarily the names that you've chosen for yourself.
Indeed, there will be love presented this night, and if you let the
"pieces of God" that you are, radiate and invite us in, it will enhance
the experience for the others. For this night is poignant with

power! All of the things that you thought were impossible—perhaps the very reason you're here—can be gratified and resolved this very night. It is time, is it not? Oh, dear ones, feel the presence of the anointed ones, not just your guides, but all of those that Kryon brings tonight. For there are many who will flood this room at this time who you know oh so well, that will give you the feeling of love in your life and hug you and hold you in these few moments, and you will feel them. They're here to say one thing, *"You are dearly loved. Don't you think we know what you've been through?"* Those are the words that we're using for you this night.

We are going to suspend the learning series for this channel. And, instead, we are going to go into an overview, which we have not gone into for some time—an overview that will help explain some things. We're going to call this message, "Humanity, the Vanishing Species."

Now some of you will say, *"Oh, no, what do you mean by that, Kryon? Are we in trouble? Are we going to be terminated?"* We are here in great love to say, "No." Humanity as you know it will vanish as the ones who take the vibrational increase take over. Your humanness will become something else entirely, you see. It's the alchemy of the spirit that is taking place that will change you from humans to something else uniquely different from an old-energy human.

Now, in order to talk about this change, we would like to give you an overview of yourselves—and some of it is humorous to Spirit. But the humor comes from the fact that is appropriate that you have duality, and we'll talk of that in a moment.

Created Equal

Some have said that the Scriptures and some ancient sayings will tell you that all humans are created equal. Yet as you look around, you say, *"I don't truly believe that."* First of all, half of you are another gender. And each gender thinks (and is often very glad) that they are not the other [laughter]! In their deepest thoughts they say, "*Look at us...we are not equal—I'm glad I am not one of them*" [more laughter].

Created equal? Hardly (you might say)! What about abilities? You see those with wonderful abilities—and you don't have them. Some of you would say that the abilities of many supersede others on a scale that is grand. How could Spirit, therefore, say you're created equal? Do we even dare touch upon the appearance department [more laughter]? Hardly created equal, you might say.

No, dear ones. What this means is that each and every one of you arrives with the image of God, and the IMAGE is the equality that you carry. For it is the image that has the opportunity to change this planet. One by one! All the things that you do with this image can change the planet. We're talking about the fact that what you do as healers with your image of God, and what you do as humans walking this planet with your karma and with your challenges, has the ability to change another person. And those that you change will shock you in what they might do—and we always bring this up when we speak about your power.

Hiding in the great plan that you have no concept of are wonderful things—anointed things. Oh, healer! Oh, counselor! The next time the one stands in front of you that you have never seen before and asks you for healing, be aware that this could be the one! This could be the one who has unborn children who are going to literally explode into the world with the kind of energy that will make a difference! And you sit before them to counsel and heal—realizing that what you do at this point will make a difference for the planet's future, regardless of what they feel is happening or not happening. This is your Power! Unbelievable power you have—synchronistic power to change this planet through the act of everyday work, one at a time, one by one!

What if you are not a healer? Listen: When the one comes up and asks, "*What is it with you? You're different.*" You can shrink into the corner and say to yourself, *"They would never believe it...this New Age stuff,"* or you could answer and say, *"I have discovered something precious, now that you ask."* Then share with them what part you choose. You see, you can change a life this way, by planting the seeds and revealing the beautiful, anointed spirit of God in your life to them! In a simple way, you will find that it grows and resounds, and the reason is because the INTENT of the one asking creates a sacred moment, and the intent of the one replying creates POWER. And it's this power in stating your truth to the one that can change the many. Believe it! It changes lives. Each and every one of you can do this. Created equal? Yes, you are. Yes, you are!

The Duality

All humanity comes in with a duality. Humans are fun to look at. Oh, dear ones, precious are you who have come into this planet knowing full well that when you arrived, your piece of God would be disguised so completely that you would ask yourselves over and over, *"Who am I?"* Oh, we love you for this, this duality—this challenge that you willingly carry! Let's skip the discussion of the karma that you carry, and instead let us look at these other things that each and every one of you has when you arrive.

Preoccupation with Drama

This attribute is not logical! Not enlightened. Not positive. Yet you thrive on it. We have spoken of it before, but it is important to mention it again. It seems as though so many humans create their own drama, then delight in wallowing in it. Those who are somehow able to extract themselves momentarily from this situation find themselves suddenly free of it—then they go create some more. Oh, dear ones, this is a large part of the duality. The challenge is to choose to move through the drama—to realize that it is an old-energy concept and does not suit the peace of an enlightened, changing human.

Some of this drama is created with the intellect (remember us speaking of this before?). This is the part of the duality that wakes you up at three in the morning from a deep sleep and with a very clear voice announces, *"Isn't there something we can worry about?"* Even if you are a most positive person, enlightened in every way, it doesn't take long in your drowsiness and half-consciousness to agree with it! *"What shall we worry about now?"* and you go along with it. Oh, dear ones, it is a trick, this is. It's part of the challenge. It's the intellect part of you that wants to tell you that you are nothing, created in the perfectness of the duality.

Dwelling In The Past

Humans love to dwell in the past. Now, linear time is not something that Kryon is fond of, but it is what I deal with constantly when I'm here. It is amazing for me to see how humanity treats time, for they will select a portion of time that was meaningful to them, then they will worship it forever! And if that's not strange enough, there are others who will take their most horrible time, wrap themselves around it, and never come out! Preoccupation with the past—energy spent in a circle, in another circle, then in another circle. It perpetuates itself and promotes a closed human—one who will keep oneself from finding out who one really is.

[stopping]

There is healing taking place now. And we give this a moment, for there are those of you who have finally realized things in this moment. It's the third language taking place during this lesson that is touching the hearts of some of those in this room right now. The teaching from this channel is one thing in the English language, but it is this third language that Kryon speaks, and the entourage is passing to you, which is changing lives right now.

Ego

All humans have ego, and it is one of the greatest mysteries to those of us who have never experienced duality. Make no mistake, ego is the antithesis of love, and many of you know this. It is the balance of this ego with love that is critical. All of these duality attributes are appropriate, given to you in love, imprinted upon your very biology. It is what you do with it that is so honored. Ego, tempered with love, becomes appropriate. It is in its raw, untempered form that it becomes the enemy of love. Think about it. Isn't it odd that a poison becomes a healing substance when love is added? That's the way it is with ego.

We have given you the four attributes of love, and if you will study raw ego, you will see that all of the attributes are opposite.

Love Attributes Revisited [see Chapter one].

(1) The first attribute of love is that love is quiet. Ego is not. Ego will shout from the highest tops, *"Here I am!"* Love will not.

(2) Love has no agenda. Ego does. *"If you will do this, I will do that,"* says Ego. And then I will win. An agenda in every step.

(3) Love does not puff itself up. That's all Ego does most of the time!

(4) And finally, love has the wisdom to use the other three. Ego does not know it's a fool. Remember that.

Yet these ego attributes are among you, and they are part of you when you come in. Mothers see these things in their children and wonder where they came from! They were designed by Spirit, and planned by yourselves to disguise the God within.

Amount of People

Let's speak about the numbers of humans on the planet now. We tell you something just in case you didn't realize it: Did you know, dear ones, that almost every single human who had a past life since the time of humanity began—is alive and walking the planet right now? Did you know that? Is it any wonder we call it "family"? Did you ever think of that? And those who are rich in past-expression experience are the ones who will sit before these family groups and be the forerunners of the New Age, because they have been there, and they know the plan, and they stood in line to be here at this time!

You have far many more humans alive at this time than you have ever had in any time on the planet. You might ask, *"Even if we took all those who have ever lived in history, and all of their past lives and placed them here now, there are sill more alive now. Where did the others come from?* "And we say, you are correct. Some are new ones and come from different places. They have agreed to come in for the first time, and you know who they are, since you can spot a first-timer. These are the ones who seemingly have no idea about the way Earth works. When you say something to them that would normally elicit a response expected from a regular human being, they look at you with a blank stare. They don't react like you expect. They also have other attributes that we will not discuss now. Theses are the first-timers. Oh, love them, each one. They are pure. They come in with attributes that are different from yours, each one loved just as you are.

The Other Guys (Who Help Us)

What about other entities on the planet? There aren't just humans. What about the support group, Kryon? You know you have guides and angels—oh, yes, we have talked about that. But let us now discuss the ones that we have not talked much about—the placeholders, the devas, the ones in the gardens, the ones in the oceans that breathe air. The ones that hold the place of sacredness, waiting for their part later. The animals, the entities that cannot be seen in the rocks and in the very dirt—and the energy that is present in the sky. All of these are here—for your service—and that of humanity. When my partner told you earlier that the Earth will change as you change, he was accurate. For the very dirt of this planet will vibrate differently as the consciousness of the planet's humans change. It's happening now. This is simple cause and effect. You move, and the Earth moves. It is this way. And so the next time you feel fearful regarding these Earth changes, understand that Earth is *under construction*, and it's responding to you! Look at it in love and appropriateness. Each time it may surprise you, fearful as it may seem. We have revealed this before in some detail.

Biology (see page 152)

Let us talk about human biology, one of the favorite things that Kryon loves to speak about. I know you might ask, "*Why would Kryon want to talk about human biology? Kryon is the magnetic master—the grid specialist.*" And we say, oh, dear ones, the grid is being postured and changed and moved and adjusted for only one reason. And that is so the magnetic imprint that is part of your DNA will see the other side of the veil more clearly. It is the biology that is being addressed with the grid change, and as your biology changes, so does the planet. So although Kryon and the entourage are planetary workers, they're also working with you personally. That is what is happening.

Let us speak more of this. As we have said before, your scientists will never find what they call "the missing link," you know. It doesn't exist here. That part of you which was given that contains the spark of the soul, the spiritual self, the Higher Self, the Merkabah, the imprint, and that which supplies karmic lessons—is the biology that was given to you by others from another place in your own galaxy. Science will never find the final jump that caused humanity to exist, and so the metaphor of Adam and Eve has credibility. It was handed to you in this fashion and you multiplied in the fashion as described, although it was handed to you in many places at the same time on your planet. Seed biology—given to you from afar in all appropriateness and with great spiritual intent.

Let me tell you more about this biology. Its instruction sets are magnetic, and all the things that go into its construction and its workings are postured by magnetics. This is why we tell you to be careful when you use magnetic healing. This is why we tell you to be careful that you balance yourselves and do no more with the magnets than that. Do not use the magnets as you would use a mattress or as you would use a chair—that is to say, do not use the power of magnetic healing as though it were to be applied without thought or intent for the rest of your days! It will not balance you when used in this fashion. It will eventually unbalance you! Use it only long enough to create the balance that you feel is appropriate for your biology—then put it away. After the healing is finished, do you still continue to take the potent treatments? No. Understand that the human being is a self-balancing entity, did you know this? If it is unbalanced, then facilitate it back to balance, then leave it alone to do its perfect work.

Your biology is designed to last forever, rejuvenating and balancing if left alone, but the fact is that it isn't left alone, for you have instruction sets in your very cells within the DNA, that count the days as you age. The instructions release the chemistry that allows for your death, to inhibit the rejuvenation, and allow for aging and disease to enter. *"Oh what kind of a trick is this?"* you might ask—in a body designed to last forever, which rejuvenates itself, which contains the seeds of its early demise. We say this: By divine design it is, dear ones! It facilitates the engine of karma, creating short lifetime after lifetime. Life and death is the cycle and the engine of learning for the planet—**until now**.

In this new energy, you have the privilege as light beings of this planet to change this attribute, and again we say, we want you to stay! Gone are the old-energy concepts that require you to come and go to facilitate the planet! And for that reason in these next years, you will be given rejuvenation processes, some using machinery and some not, some with chemistry and some without. Some just using the very life force within, allowing you to change your imprint attributes, stop the release of the aging chemistry, and live a very long time. Isn't it about time? And know this: This new arrangement is not a gift from Spirit. Oh, dear ones, this is a **right** you earned! It's because you worked it out. It is because in these last years you have chosen on your own to move together and meditate in high places for high reasons and high aspirations. For you have seen the God within, and you've followed the light. Your bodies have increased their vibrations slowly, and each time you reach another plateau, we're going to give you new tools. You'll be able to go to the next vibratory level faster and easier.

Here is a fact of biology we have not discussed before in public channel, and although some of these messages seem cryptic, they will be less so when the discoveries are made. Then you can say, *"I remember when Kryon talked about that."* Originally there was a process within your cells that was meant to keep you healthy. Kryon will call it *"the sequestering of the proteins into a hidden clump that disguised itself as something else."* This devious device holding the proteins easily passes across the cell membrane into other cells. Although you have seen it many times in your close examinations, you have not yet identified what it is—the sequestered proteins. The reason for it is to take the healthy proteins and make sure that they are passed to other cells intact, keeping the other cells healthy, even if other proteins in the cell are not. It was, therefore, a method of sustaining health. Now it has turned into a method of transmitting disease! For the new viruses that you have in your cells now quickly attack proteins. The proteins are then spoiled, sequestered, hidden, and passed through the membrane to another cell. So what was once a protection against disease has now become a hidden transmitter of a virus that was never expected to occur, but was released [see the United Nations channel regarding AIDS]. Look for it. When found, it will help you to understand why cells infect each other in this new energy.

There is a magnetic imprint on every single DNA strand, but it's very possible that your science, even the enlightened science, may never see it. It's appropriate that it never be disturbed, *but you may see its shadow*, and we're here to tell you that there will be those scientists who are able, through the experimenting on another process, to accidentally discover the shadow of the magnetic imprint. We will have more on that later in a more grand discussion of biology.

Vibrating at a Higher Level

Some of you are moving into new higher vibrations, and we know this and we are honoring you for this. This is why we say that much of the human species is changing into something else, for your vibration is increasing, and every time it does, you turn into nothing less than a stellar being on its way to becoming something that does not resemble the old-energy human, but something that is closer to your Higher Self—a vibration and a meld that is far closer to those spiritual beings who are around you now. Let me explain.

If you think you are one of these persons who is moving into a higher vibration, let me ask you if you have these attributes:

(1) Some of you are actually seeing and feeling the entities around you. You awaken from a sleep at night absolutely sure that there are numbers of people in your room! You look around and you see nothing, but they're there, and you know they are, and you absolutely feel them! Some of you have felt them touch you, and you awaken with a start to find no one there. Some of you are frightened by this, thinking that you are being abducted, but nothing happens, and you become worried about the next time it might happen. Oh, dear ones, let me tell you that this is a clear sign of a higher vibration in you, and it will not stop. In fact, it may intensify, and the reason is because you are vibrating at a higher level, closer to the entities that are here on this planet to support you. They are the guides, the ones in the dirt, and the ones in the very planet itself. And there are numbers of them for every one of

you. Don't be surprised if you sense them. Those of you who work with the dirt already do. It's the ones who walk around on the planet in your regular culture who are not used to seeing them every day. More awareness of the entities around you is a gift!

(2) The next is the awareness of the dirt. Some of you are actually experiencing for the first time the alliance with the dirt of this planet. As you walk around, you can sense what the ancients and the natives sensed here in the very land where we are. You can feel that there is power and purpose and energy in the very directions of north, east, south, and west. Imagine such a thing — that the directions themselves would have a personality! They do! Imagine such a thing—that the atmosphere has life force.! It does! And that the dirt of the Earth has consciousness. It does, indeed! Don't be surprised if it speaks to you some day, and you start to feel it. It's a wonderful experience, for deep in there (the dirt of the planet) churns the love machine, dear ones—the honor that the planet has for the humans who walk on it. It's an alliance, you see. The Earth is not a thing that you walk on. It's a partner that you are here with in lesson and in love. Start to understand the alliance.

(3) Some of you are finding out that you are eating less, and it doesn't seem to make any difference to your energy. Whatever your metabolism is, and whether you like it or not, you're finding that you're eating less and are satisfied sooner. This is another attribute of higher vibration. I tell you this, and it may sound astounding to you as it does to my partner, but there will come a day when you will not have to eat at all—such is the power of the vanishing human species!

(4) There are some of you who are experiencing what Kryon calls the "triad of Sleep." Three spots of sleep, interrupted twice, and you call it insomnia. It's part of the new vibration, dear ones, and it is anointed. It's given in love, and when it takes place, do not worry. Thank your guides for the triad of Sleep. Take the moments you are awake that otherwise bothered you, and honor yourself by saying, "*I am dearly loved. I am moving into a new vibration.*"

These sleep states will then become normal for you. *"Kryon, is it going to get better?"* you might ask. "No." Never ask to return to the old vibration. First of all, you can't. Second of all, understand that the new attributes are part of the "new you," and they are here with great purpose and love. Get used to them. They are part of the metamorphosis, and they are part of the alchemy. They represent the vanishing of the human species.

Questions about What's Next

Finally, let us discuss some of the biggest questions you have, and we will group them. Here are two:

"Kryon, what will happen in the future, and what am I supposed to do about it?"

There is a timeline present, dear ones, which anyone who is familiar with the energy of the numbers could have predicted easily. The Kryon entourage will be finished with the magnetic grid alignments in 2002. After that, the new grid is in place, and the changes for your enablement are complete. The next year will, therefore, be a year representing change (the completion), and that will be the year of 2003—a *five* year (2+0+0+3), and the year to mark the end of the alignments. It will take time for you to adjust to the new alignments as they settle into your DNA instructions and allow for more enablement, as the grids themselves transmit the energies of the cosmos that we have sent you to allow for your new times.

The next *five* year after 2003 is 2012 (2+0+1+2), and that, dear ones, is a **major marker**. For the year 2012, if you believe your ancient history and also the ones that foretold about time itself, is when your time apparently ends! What could that mean? Some have said that it means the end of the planet—termination. However, it really means change, dear ones. Have we ever told you this? That as the vibration of humanity increases and the humans become less of what they were in the old energy, and as the Earth vibrates at a different rate, your time frame will react! Yes, we have. [See the previous channel on page 173—Ascension II]. We spoke often about how the physics will react to the love energy (new consciousness), and the very atoms themselves will change, creating a new time frame for the planet. If you have followed the physics information of Kryon, dear ones, this will now begin to make sense.

Like all other spiritual things, this is not going to happen instantly on January 1, 2012, so don't get out your devices to record it. It is only a marker of the beginning of an appropriate future for you, and we give you this information knowing full well that you have the ability to move into it or not, as you choose. You have the ability and power to reach the critical mass and move forward to allow for this facilitation or not, as you choose. We are fully aware that these predictions are based upon the consciousness of the planet right now, and of the acceleration at this very moment.

The year 2012 will then be what you would call a marker that will meld slowly into a new time, as the humans become more adjusted to their permission to change the time frame. So look at your Mayan calendar and find out what it says about 2012. Look into the past to see what the spiritual historians have said about 2012, and you will see an alignment of information between those in the past and the ones who are currently studying the new signs and the mathematics of the circles. What is it? IT'S PERMISSION TO CHANGE. It's permission to move into another time frame, for true enlightened beings are not in your time frame. When you raise your vibration to match theirs, your time frame will change to a closer match with theirs.

"What am I supposed to do about it?" you may ask. "Kryon, where is my part in all this?" We'll give you information that has not changed since the beginning of this channel. Take care of YOURSELF. That's all we ask you to do. **The one will change the many**. Are you listening? **The one will change the many!**

Regardless of what you think is taking place within your life and on the Earth, the plan is far grander than that—far grander than that! You are so important in your work. Even if you only sit before one human at a time, understand the scope of the fact that your one-at-a-time work changes many down the line. Healers, you have no idea of the synchronicity involved in this! Continue on. Raise your own vibration. Be circumspect, and use your discernment in all of these things.

Channeling

"*What am I supposed to do with channeled works?*" you might ask. "*How do I behave with channeled information?*"

Here is something we have mentioned before: Dear ones, use channeled information as you would any resource book. Glean what you wish from it, then shut the book, and put it on the shelf, because it is YOU who is enabled, not the channel. You don't need a constant channeler, and you don't need a guru, and you don't need a leader. You are the shepherd! Move forward with the power you have in your own heart. Use the information as a resource to raise your vibration and power as a light worker. You will do the work for the planet—not the channel [also on page 28].

Those You Are Going to Meet

Here is a question that is filled with energy: "*Kryon, you said we're going to meet others. When are they going to be here, and what are we supposed to do with them?*" [Channeled again at the United Nations—the next chapter in this book and page 26.]

Let me give you a hint, and we have given others this metaphor in channel before. When you travel, you come from the desolate country and travel into the heart of the city to meet friends of your choice who wait for you. They are sophisticated and knowledgeable and echo your consciousness. On the way, you are going to pass through other areas of the city first, which are the outskirts, and you're going to meet those along the way which do not represent the ones in the middle of the city whom you are expecting

That's where you are as a planet right now. You see, you are being poked and prodded and tickled by all sorts of entities from the outskirts for all sorts of reasons. They are not the ones you are scheduled to meet, for the ones you're to meet are the ones who are aware of who you are, and are waiting for you. Oh, dear ones, you speak of mass landings? Let me tell you this—that when your vibration and time frame matches theirs, they will meet you—and not before! That's what this is all about, because when you arrive at that place of high vibration, that is when you will show up on their "radar screen," and not before. Discern the fact that the ones who are showing up now are absolutely not the ones you are scheduled to meet, and as we have said before: (a) They do not have permission to take you anywhere, and (b) they wish to deceive you as to their real purpose. Don't trust them!

"What am I going to do when it (the final meeting) happens?" you might ask.

Dear ones, you'll know what to do. You'll know. A fearful event? No—only to those remaining in the old energy might it appear frightening. Perhaps you will have to take some of those under your arm and comfort them and bring them along. Not a fearful event, dear ones...an event of great spiritual significance.

There is so much love in all of this! To think that you have arrived at this place astounds the very heart of Spirit itself. To think that this message could be given to a group of humans saying, "You're changing and you're moving forward and you have a future that is promising and amazingly profound," is something that even those in my entourage thought was impossible. This planet of free choice has allowed you to move in any direction you wished to go, and you've decided on your own to move upwards.

Where Am I Supposed to Be Now?

"Kryon, right now, where am I supposed to be?"

There are some of you who are going to be called to other areas of this great land and this great planet. We tell you to look for the synchronicity in this. You may say, *"I love it here. I don't want to move."* And we say to you that we honor this feeling. No one will be taken anywhere unless they have a passion to go there. This is the promise we have for you. Spirit is not going to pluck you from one place and take you to a place that you do not enjoy being in. Some of you may have the privilege of going somewhere temporarily until you get to the right place, so never think that the place you're taken to is the final place, either. There is a constantly changing master plan at work, and it can only work efficiently when you say, *"Tell me what you want me to know."* Then look for the signs. Someone may come up to you and tell you of a place that you have wondered about for some time, and then a week later you get the same inquiry from another person. Look at this, because it represents the way Spirit works with synchronicity. Here's why it is important. You are needed in certain places on this planet. All of the enlightened will want to be in the portals, believe me, but this is not correct, for it ignores the rest of the Earth! So many will be called and given a passion to move to places in order to "hold the energy."

For instance, I have requested that my partner stay where he lives because it needs the energy he has. We are indeed gathering light workers there, and high science of the New Age there, and healers there to hold the energy in that spot. It isn't a portal at all, but rather a place that needs to have the energy held there by those of high vibration. This is the way you serve the Earth.

And so it is that you might have a passion and a synchronicity to be drawn or called to a specific place, and you might say, *"This is not an enlightened place you're calling me to,"* and we're saying it's the place where we need you to be, and if you go there

you'll be honored—honored with good work and good relationships and good feelings. Good moods, health, healing, and a sense
of purpose.

That's what "being in the right place" is. It's being in that
"sweet spot" of contract. Be open for this, dear ones, for it is the
workers we need to have say, "*All right, I'll go there, and I will
honor the process that draws me there as well.*"

What Can I Do?

Finally, the question is this: "*Kryon, what can I do right now?*"

Dear ones, don't you think we know who you are? Don't you
think we know what you're going through—or what is going on in
your body right now? These are the things that have been given
to you for lesson. There are some very dark secrets that you carry
that you've told no one about. Don't you think we know this? For
those of you who feel helpless with the disease ravaging your body,
don't you think we know this? We'll give you some statements that
should send chills up your spine:

There is nothing that you have that is not curable!

*There is no situation that you are in that cannot be
resolved—and everyone involved can win!*

This has to do with permission. It has to do with self-worth and
comes from your absolute knowledge that YOU ARE A PIECE OF
GOD! It starts in your inner being, and so we invite you to "sit in
that golden chair of knowledge" [see Chapter One, "Sitting in The
Chair"]. The chair that Wo was invited to sit in when he was taken
on the metaphoric trip to the rooms of lesson [Kryon parable].
When he went into the room of gold and he saw that this was the
room his guides could not go into, he didn't realize at the time that
this was the room of his own self-essence. This is the room that
asks him to feel, "*I'm worthy of being on Earth.*" And as we have
told countless humans since we have been here, this is the room

that we invite you to sit in now—in the chair made of gold! And your place in that chair will beget all of the other rooms: the room of abundance, the room of peace, the room of health, and the room of appropriate contract. It doesn't matter what you are faced with, oh dear ones. We absolutely know what some of you are going through. There is a win-win scenario within that horrible puzzle you have, where your co-creation in this particular situation will change another's life, and things will be remarkably positive. There is a light at the end of that tunnel you currently see blackness in, if you will simply understand and accept self-worth.

Verbalize daily. "*I am a child of God and am worthy of being in this place called Earth. In the name of Spirit, I co-create my healing and expect my vibration to change. God, what is it you want me to know?*" Then be silent. How many of you have ever been in love with God? Perhaps you've had this wonderful outpouring of love for an entity of some kind, a great master? It's time for you to take that energy and turn it inward and love yourself! This is not ego. This is loving yourself in a way that is correct, since it is the love of the piece of God in you. It is, therefore, the love of God turned inward. Stand tall! It's time you took your place!

This is the message of Kryon. It is about human enablement, and as long as I am here, which will be a very, very long time, I will carry this message. And when enough of you hear it and give intent to move into your power, the human being of today will cease to exist forever, and in its place will be the being of light that you are becoming!

Remarkable, each one of you!

We love you, dear ones, each and every one.

And so it is.

Kryon

The United Nations Channelings

Chapter Six

"*Just one or two enlightened workers giving energy toward a focus can change reality. That is how much power you have! The vibrational change of your biology and your enlightenment means so much to this planet! The things that you do here in this room will affect the things that happen in the big room, not too far away from here (referring to the General Assembly).*"

Kryon at the United Nations—1995

"The United Nations Channeling 1995"
Channeled in
New York, NY

The Kryon Writings, Inc.

PMB 422
1155 Camino Del Mar
Del Mar, California 92014
[www.kryonqtly.com]

"The United Nations Channeling 1995"
Live Channeling
New York, NY

From the writer...

It was my first trip to the Big Apple - Tuesday November 21, 1995, numerologically an "11" day (1+1+2+1+1+9+9+5=29) (2+9=11). After a wild twenty-minute trip in a cab through the endless cement and glass canyons of Manhattan island, the familiar UN complex with its multicolored flags in front seemed a welcome sight for this Southern California boy. I was told that the flags don't go up unless the countries they represent are working that day, and all the flags were in full flight.

I was seated next to my partner, Jan, and Zehra Boccia, our delightful New York host and Kryon advocate who had opened her home on the upper West Side to us for the four-day stay we needed to accomplish our work.

I was on my way to speak at the Society for Enlightenment and Transformation (S.E.A.T.) at the United Nations, and was reflecting on all the circumstances that had brought us here to present Kryon to delegates, workers, and guests of such a prestigious organization.

The Enlightenment Society is one of the fifty member clubs of the United Nations Staff Recreation Council. It was founded in 1975, and its objective is to provide divine service to United Nations staff, delegates, mission staff and guests. Every month a speaker is invited to enlighten, transform, inspire and entertain an audience of about 40-50 people. The five members of the executive committee of the Society are hard working staff members of the United Nations who organize these events in their spare time and offer them during the lunch period. The deepest purpose of the Society matches that of the United Nations - to bring peace to our planet. Under the fine direction of Mohammad Ramadan in1995, Kryon was only the third channeled entity to be invited in the past few years for these meetings and it was going to happen in just a few moments.

We had been briefed on the protocol, and we were dressed accordingly. Jan was wearing one of her normal high-fashion silk outfits, with a vest of her own design. She had chosen forest green, a conservative color to honor the formality of the day. I was in a basic black suit with a silk brown shirt and matching tie. Never had we presented Kryon in such a formal way, but this was different, and we could feel the energy around the event as soon as we arrived at 10:30 a.m.

We walked calmly into the building where we needed to pass through metal detectors, under the watchful eyes of highly trained, uniformed United Nations security officers, but our minds were anything but calm. Although not nervous, I was surging with the honor of how Kryon had orchestrated such a marvelous thing as this. I turned to look at Jan and realized she was almost at the point of tears. Both of us looked around and realized that we were representing light workers around the globe in perhaps the only venue that would ever allow governments to speak together of such things as spiritual enlightenment and extraterrestrials. The moment was not lost on either of us, and we gently passed through security, our passports ready.

We met up with Mohammad, our gracious S.E.A.T. host, who quickly led us past the places the tourists see, into the areas where the work is done. We walked past original Picassos and unbelievable murals given to the UN by member countries in the past. I wont forget the wall of portraits of past UN Secretary Generals. Each man had a five-foot-high oil portrait arranged in order of the dates of service, but with no nameplates of any kind. The men and women who walked these corridors knew exactly who these men were, and of their enormous commitment to a peaceful planetary coexistence.

We passed the Security Council chambers and the large popular General Assembly meeting room. Then came the word that in Dayton, at 10:30 a.m., a few moments ago, a peace treaty had been signed settling the Bosnian crisis. I reflected on the fact that we had walked into the building at that exact moment. A sense of history in the making was beginning to creep up on me.

After a lunch at the UN cafeteria where we met some of Mohammed's guests, we reviewed the rules on audio or video could be commercially recorded, but a cassette could be used for transcription later. After the meal, we made our way to Conference Room 6. We were told that the conference rooms were constantly in use, and ours would be no different. There was a group just leaving as we entered, and we knew that another meeting of some kind was scheduled minutes after we were to finish.

Scheduled to begin at exactly 1:15, we were to end at 2:45 or before. Within the 90 minutes, I was to lecture for 30, then handle questions and answers for 30. Jan was to direct a meditation and toning for 10 minutes, and Kryon was to channel for 20 or less. We had never conducted such a strict agenda, or had Kryon boxed into such a short time, but we both knew that it would be no problem. Both of us were feeling the presence of Spirit in a way that we had never felt before, and we both nodded in understanding that this was one of those moments where you meet your contract head-on. Jan and I both knew we were standing in the right place at the right time, and that all would go well. This was the "sweet spot" that Kryon had told us about so many times. Everything around us dimmed in perspective to this, and we both felt loved by Spirit at that moment.

We had five minutes to get our group in place, but Jan and I stopped to warmly hug the sole United Nations guard that had found a Kryon book months ago and never stopped his quest until he got it to someone important at the S.E.A.T. It was this man who was responsible for igniting the interest, causing us to be standing where we were now. As the story goes, the word spread about Kryon, and we were visited and "checked out" by S.E.A.T. officers during a workshop in Indianapolis, Indiana. Our invitation to speak followed thereafter.

As we looked over the room, we were told that it was here that Iran and Iraq signed their treaty over ten years ago - again the sense of world history and lineage was upon me. The blond tables and chairs looked like they were from my mother's house in the '50s, but I quickly realized that the decor was undoubtedly representative of a conservative generic consciousness, and rather old at that. The main room was basically a rectangle of tables facing inward, with microphones on the tables at almost each chair. Layered behind the tables and chairs were theater-type seats on slightly higher tiered levels. Each chair or seat had an earpiece. This was used to either amplify what was being said, or for translations into the six authorized UN languages (Arabic, Chinese, English, French, Russian, and Spanish). In our case, there were no translators present, but the dark slanted glass along one full wall signaled where the translators would have sat if they had been used. Within the rectangle of tables, there were other smaller tables, the use of which still escapes me.

We were immediately seated at the head of the table, and a permanent nameplate in front of me had the word Chairman. Everything became quiet. In the room there were both men and women of all ages, and it was obvious we were in the presence of several cultures. Most of the men had gray or black business suits, and one had his note pad out. The room quickly filled, the doors closed, and it became very quiet. All eyes were on us, and without any ceremony at all, our host began speaking at 1:15 on the dot.

"Good afternoon, ladies and gentlemen. For those who do not know me, my name is Mohammad Ramadan, and I wish to welcome you all to this rare presentation by Lee Carroll and his wife, Jan Tober. As you know, Lee humbly likes to call himself 'the translator' of the invisible master Kryon, who appears in times of great changes. Meanwhile, Kryon himself gratefully calls Carroll 'my partner.' So today we will be meeting a real trinity, Lee and his two partners!

"Carroll was a successful businessman, but also a skeptic. He was totally unaware of his new mission, which had been long predicted by his wife Jan. Carroll's other partner is the metaphysical surprise of the '90s. His wisdom has revolutionized past and present

mystical knowledge. His message of tremendous love and hope has swept the world in less than two years. His forecasts about the mysterious explosive comets, gamma-ray bursts, and the double bursts of radio emission have been validated by puzzled astronomers and physicists and have added more credibility to the inevitable marriage of science, spirituality, and metaphysics.

"Today Carroll will give a quick review of his life with Kryon, followed by a segment of questions and answers. After a short meditation by his wife, Jan, the other partner, Kryon, will take over and give a special message to the audience, and possibly to the rest of the UN family and the world.

"Please give a big hand to Kryon and his two partners in their first visit ever to New York."

It began. Although I felt slightly overanimated for the conservative crowd, I tried my best to give them a 30-minute synopsis of what had happened to me and what Kryon was all about. At 1:45 precisely, we went into questions and answers. This lasted exactly the 30 minutes prescribed, and then it was Jan's turn. She gave a wonderful meditation (as is her style), then led the group in a very conservative toning sequence. At 2:20 on the nose, I felt the warmth of Kryon in the room, and uttered those words that always announce his presence...

The United Nations Channel (#1)

Greetings, dear ones, I am Kryon of Magnetic Service! It is no accident that we sit in this sacred place. Now, some of you are surprised to hear me through my partner, since you have not before. He is a translator—a verifier—for he remains conscious in his body, and I feed him the thought groups of love for each of you. We speak now to each of you as you sit in your seat and not to any group that is here, and we say before we begin that even if you do not believe what you are hearing is real, it is. It is from the same source that spoke to Moses from the Burning Bush. We know you by name and it is not a name, that even you are aware of.

We sit at your feet in awe! You are the ones who have made the difference on this planet; for you to even be here means that you are interested in the energy that is happening now, oh dear ones. This is the energy of love! Make no mistake. Let no one tell you differently—this New Age that you have created has a power, which is the power of love. There is no negative thing or negative entity that you cannot change, for you are completely in control in every single way with the new gifts of Spirit. We ask you to look around to see what you have done—and when we say "you," we mean you!...those who sit here...those who read these words. You may not think that you have contributed to the whole, but oh, you have! Just one or two enlightened workers giving energy toward a focus can change reality. That is how much power you have. The vibrational change of your biology and your enlightenment means so much to this planet! There have been so few who have done so much already, and it's going to increase even more. The things that you do here in this room will affect the things that happen in the big room, not too far away from here (referring to the General Assembly).

You have had prophets tell you that there are areas of the Middle East right now that should be running red with the blood of battle but in these very areas what is happening instead is that these "would-be" enemies are discussing how to share their water! You have leaders of countries right now who not too many years ago were in the dark dungeons and the prisons within their very own countries—now they sit in the high seats of leadership. What kind of global consciousness change does this tell you about? You have made such a difference in all of these things. Look around you—the specter of country against country has lessened greatly in these past years. Did you think this was an accident? And when the political walls came tumbling down and all the changes happened, did you think it was a mistake that they happened simultaneously with the changes of your consciousness—and the New Age messages and the channelings? No! For you have watched physical occurrences and political occurrences that *shook hands* with the simultaneous enlightenment of humanity. Now we tell you that the battles that you see now on this planet are tribe against tribe. They will all be tribal, and they all are, even as you look at them now. These energies from eons that have developed between these tribes and these races must be settled, and now is the time for the settlement. You will watch the few that remain settle themselves, and you will also help them to be settled. And although you may not know why you are helping to settle them, I'll tell you, and that is because you are moving quickly to a place that will represent the "tribe of Earth." For there will come a time when the spokesmen from this place will represent the tribe of Earth to others that are not from here!

Now, we have told you that the focus of your energies is critical, and that a few rooms full of enlightened workers with purpose and intent can change the planet. So we give you now some admonitions and some energies and some things for focus. I would not be Kryon if I did not tell you these things at this time. There are four of them, and they are presented in love.

(1) The first is: We beg you, dear ones, to give energy and focus toward the solution of something that is taking place right now. For on your planet currently, there are scientists working on energy transmission through the ground (and the air). Now this is a valid science and will indeed work. It is not new and has been done before—almost one hundred years ago. But oh, you have such power now in your current machines, and we ask you to slow down! For you do not yet understand the resonance factors of the crust and the mantle of Earth. When one resonates, so will another. Therefore, unless you slow down with these experiments

and push less energy into the ground, you may actually cause the earthquakes that you fear the most! We tell you that there is tremendous damage potential in these experiments, and although we are not asking you to stop them, we advise you to **go slowly and be careful of your home**.

(2) Here is another: There is a disease which is ravaging your planet, which even now as we speak you have no control over. It attacks your immune system, and all of you have noticed the virility of it—how it changes so often—how it mutates sporadically—how it is unstoppable and how damaging and sorrowful it is. We tell you, dear ones, that this is simply a forerunner of many like it unless you **stop defoliating this planet**. For this disease is of the forest, and it came from the forest and manifested itself into humanity. The balance of the forest was changed by humans, allowing for a biological imbalance to take place within a system that otherwise would have kept it in check. There are other diseases waiting to emerge that may never show themselves if they remain balanced—where they belong and have always been— deep within the balanced foliage of the forest! Oh, keep them there, hear this! Give energy to this! Focus on this in your meditations, and the humans that make the decisions will feel it. Yes, they will!

(3) Here is another admonition: We speak now of giving energy to the governments of this planet to start informing their people of the truth about those who have visited from another place. For this is real, ongoing, and it will lead eventually to a time where you will know these visitors by name and will speak to them personally. We give admonishment to the governments of this planet before it is too late, before they appear foolish and lose control. We say, "**Tell your people what you know**! Share with them the news—not in fear, but in enlightenment and in honesty—as to what has taken place. Tell them of the conversations you have already had with these others, and the communications that you know about. Put this truth on the table so humanity can see it! It is time.

(4) And here is the fourth. It is for those in this room and those of this enlightened society: It is time you told metaphysical workers all over the planet that there is a room in this United Nations where you can meditate and channel and feel the love of Spirit! If you want this energy to soar and make a difference within this organization, you're going to have to tell more people about it. Oh, not so that they will come, or not so there will be any kind of negative reaction, but so they can sit quietly in places where they live and speak the name of this organization to give it power! That's why. So we ask you to open the lid. Do not hide this group. Be courageous, for you will be honored with results!

Dear ones, there is a small parable that has already been published and known to those who read the messages of Spirit within the Kryon Writings. It has never been given publicly, however, and we had asked that it remain private until now. For we knew of the potential of this meeting years ago, and now it is time to speak it. The parable is short, but it is filled with power. It is the "Story of the Tar Pit."

It seems that all humanity was hindered by tar to the degree that it was difficult to walk from one place to another. The tar would stick to the humans wherever they walked. But this was the way of the world, for all humans shared this attribute. Everywhere they walked, the tar would stick. It would cling to their clothing and make them dirty, and many times (depending upon how thick it was) it would actually stop them. Other times it would only slow them down, but this was the way of the things for all and was accepted.

One human discovered through his enlightenment, a gift from God. He gave intent to be different in the New Age and claimed this gift. When he did so, the tar receded from him. And so everywhere he walked, the tar moved away as he walked into it! It no longer stuck to him. His clothes were always clean and everywhere he went, he did so easily—gliding from place to place. There were no more stoppages and no more difficulties.

Now, he was not evangelistic about this gift, and he kept it to himself. He told himself that even though the gift was available to everyone, it was very personal. So he decided it was not appropriate to mention it to the others. Before long, however, those around him noticed that he was not in any way hampered by the tar. So it wasn't long before they asked him, "What has happened? How did this take place? You look so free—so peaceful! Your clothes are always clean, and you're able to move so quickly past us!"

So he willingly told them about his personal gift from God, and many of them also gave intent for it as well. Each person to whatever degree that they asked, received the gift, and soon many were walking around without the tar sticking to them. And so it was that over a period of time, there was a large group of enlightened humans who had changed themselves, yet it had started with only one— concerned only to improve himself. So we say to you, the one who changed himself also made a difference for many—even though there was no conscious effort on his part to do so.

So this is the way of it as you sit in the chair now. For what you do with yourself **personally**, right now, will make a difference in the future to many, including those in the big room not far from here. Your personal intent to change yourself can change the reality of the entire planet!

So it is with love we have come to you in these few moments, in this linear time to fill this room with love. And even though there are those here who may not feel a difference at the moment, or may not even believe what has happened here is real, they will be changed. For the seeds of truth have been planted firmly in each mind that is here...and they will remember when it is time.

AND SO IT IS!"

Kryon

From the writer...

The time was 2:43. Kryon had finished with two minutes to spare. It was all over so quickly, and it seemed there was so much more to say. We wanted to meet everyone, and managed to hug a few men in suits (a strange feeling for me...my culture only supports hugging men in aloha shirts [ha ha].) Then we were quickly ushered out of the room and back into the cafeteria where many questions were answered.

Later that day we were treated to a VIP tour of the UN facilities, and then on to an apartment on the 11th floor of a 32-story building about five blocks from the UN for a potluck dinner with some of those who had attended. More questions ensued, and a fine time of sharing was had while the evening wore on.

It's funny the things you remember in retrospect. Later that night, we spent a moment on the roof of the 32-story apartment building. I had never seen such a sight! Downtown Manhattan at that height looked like millions of sparkling crystals in a sea of darkness. You really couldn't see the street, and there were other buildings towering above ours. It was a surreal feeling of floating in a vertical spaceship made of glass and stone.

Somehow it struck a remembrance in me. Had I been here before? Perhaps there was something else that looked like this that was hidden from me at a cellular level? Why did this scene grab me so much? With all I had been through this day, why did this view hold my attention?

I looked to Kryon for an answer, and as he does so many times, he gave me the warmth of love that is now such a familiar feeling...and a huge "wink." It was Kryon's way of saying, "Someday all these things will be known to you. For now, be still, and do the work."

That was good enough for me. I lingered there for a while trying to figure it out. Neither Jan nor I slept much that night. A week later, back in Del Mar, we got a letter from Mohammad.

"We express our deepest gratitude for your most illuminating and uplifting presentation at the UN. The impact could be measured not by the reactions expressed verbally as much as by the energy raised and the peace and oneness felt that day. True, the lecture was, as our Public Relations Officer from Spain described it: 'an earthquake,' but it was also as gentle as a 'family reunion,' as some put it."

Thanks to many of you for your incredible focus of energy on this day for Jan and myself.

Offered in Love,

Lee Carroll

"It's about individual hearts, you know. It's about what you can do for yourself, which will then change the atmosphere around you. And as you do this, dear ones, the ones around you will change as well. So again we have the instruction that the change in one will facilitate the change in many, and therefore the power of just a few enlightened ones will affect the whole. Planetary change is 'in the works' here in this room..."

Kryon at the United Nations—1996

"The United Nations Channeling 1996"
Channeled in
New York, NY

The Kryon Writings, Inc.

PMB 422
1155 Camino Del Mar
Del Mar, California 92014
[www.kryonqtly.com]

"The United Nations Channeling 1996"
Live Channeling
New York, NY

From the writer...

Tuesday, November 26, 1996 seemed to be like any other day, except I knew it wasn't. I awoke and looked out the window. There stretched in front of me was New York's Central Park as seen from the twelfth floor of my hotel room. I saw Wollman skating rink, and part of the pond, and farther down I could even see the roof of the Museum of Art. It was beautiful, flanking Central Park West and Eighth Avenues with an unending line of towering cement and glass buildings, like a giant regal chess set, just waiting for a game to be started within the trees. In just two days, the Macy's Day Parade would wind its way along the park, watched by millions, including Jan and me. There was so much history here! ... From George Washington to John Lennon... and I was looking at it realizing that in my own way I was going to contribute to it in just a few short hours... no more than a quarter mile away on the banks of the East River at the United Nations building.

I remembered last year at this time, what I was thinking. It was a similar story. Kryon had been invited to bring the Society of Enlightenment and Transformation (S.E.A.T.) a channeled message at the United Nations. That's when I learned that there was actually an organization within the UN that meditated together and spoke of extraterrestrials and other metaphysical subjects! And they did so in the very areas of the building, not too far from the General Assembly chamber, in an area reserved for delegates and guests only - not the part that tourists see.

Whatever you think of the United Nations, and believe me, there are many who don't think much of it, I would invite you to also look at the overview. There is far more going on within that building than the assignment of blue helmeted policemen of the world that don't make peace very well, or the reported conspiratorial attempts at creating a controlling world government. Instead, there are thousands of workers who report to this building each day and toil on world hunger, disease control, and saving the children of the planet from cultures that can't house or feed them. The humanitarians outnumber the politicians, and you can feel the energy of this when you enter. It's the only place like it in on the Earth where the world can come together regularly. Right in the middle of it is the S.E.A.T., meditating for world peace, and bringing love and enlightenment into the very rooms where treaties are signed, and where governments decide how to work with each other.

Again I knew that I would enter this building and channel Kryon to the delegates who were interested enough to come to this closed meeting of the S.E.A.T., a member of the United Nations Staff Recreation Council, and a bright spot in this building of political powers. After many years of service as president of the S.E.A.T., Mohammad Ramadan, my host of last year, had deservedly retired. Now Cristine Arismendy had taken the post and was scheduled to meet us and walk Jan and me through the high security checkpoint with metal detectors and very strict United Nations security officers, as we did last year on our way into the secured areas where business is done.

Again we were met and chaperoned by our gracious friend Zehra Boccia, who was instrumental in bringing Kryon to the United Nations both times. We honor you, Zehra, for your part in all this! It was also Zehra who showed me that I didn't have to pray out loud in the back seat in order to survive the New York taxi trip down to First and E 43rd streets where the UN building is. I just watched how calm she was and figured that she knew something I didn't. How do the cabs drive like that and survive? Perhaps it's that so few of them speak English that they don't know what the traffic signs say? Maybe they have some kind of cab Angels that protect all humans going 50 miles an hour at the same time, seemingly occupying exactly the same physical space. Oh, well, I again survived the cab ride. I think I was so happy to be alive when I stepped out that the thought of presenting Kryon again at the UN was now going to be the easiest part of my day.

This second UN Kryon visit was different. In the past year, the Kryon work had grown considerably with the addition of a fourth Kryon book, foreign rights for many languages, taking Kryon international, the premiere of the Kryon Quarterly Magazine, and lots of scientific validation - enough so that MD's and researchers were becoming regular attendees at Kryon seminars. Jan and I went alone last year, but this time we had some of our "Kryon family" of workers with us, also. We were allowed six guests, so we included Geoff Hoppe and Linda Benyo (now representing the *Crimson Circle*), Rob Harris (from the Kryon E-magazine), Dr. Todd Ovokaitys (M.D. science researcher), and Steve and Barbara Rother (Now responsible for *Planetlightworker* on the net). Rob's wife, Barbara Harris (a partner in the graphics firm that does the Kryon website), had to stay home and attend to clients... and we missed her.

At the appointed area, we met a very gracious S.E.A.T. president, Cristine Arismendy, and again I was struck by how Spirit finds the exact perfect person for the important spiritual jobs on this planet! Even though we hadn't personally met, she felt immediately like family and made us feel extremely welcome. We proceeded past the checkpoints, had coffee together, then went directly to Conference Room 7, where the channeling was to take place. These meetings assemble and move along quickly, and again I felt the formality and protocol of the event. Unlike the informality that I try to create at the Kryon seminars, this group moved quickly to their seats, were quiet and ready, and the meeting began immediately.

As we were introduced by Cristine, I looked around the room. I could see that my friends had taken up seats, not together, but in groups that formed a triangle when you added the two of us. They had formed what I call the "flying wedge" energy protection, using what we had learned about sacred geometry and the energy created therein. Cristine was almost finished, and I mused at the eclectic group in front of us - representing so many places, so many cultures, and so many belief systems. Kryon came to me at that moment and whispered, "Remember they are just like you: They are greatly loved by Spirit and deserve to be here. They are in the right place at the right time. Honor this moment! For the real work for the planet is done individually one by one by those such as these." I knew right then that Kryon's message would be personal as well as planetary - very much like Kryon always is. He has championed the idea that planetary change is done one heart at a time.

Cristine finished her introduction. I spoke briefly about some of the things I had on my mind personally, then I turned it over to Jan. She did a wonderful meditation, leading the room gracefully through a self-empowering exercise and visualization. As Jan finished, I glanced at my watch. Kryon had 30 minutes - no more. We had to leave the room promptly to allow for the next UN committee. I smiled to myself, knowing that I didn't have to worry about the clock. Kryon knows what time it is. Then he spoke, and I felt the love wash that always accompanies his message, and the feeling of appropriateness that he always brings, and I felt the entourage of angels and guides that are always present when groups gather to hear the words of Kryon.

The United Nations Channel (#2)

Greetings dear ones, I am Kryon of Magnetic Service. This room is filled with the love of Spirit! Let's get right to it! Perhaps some of you have been coming to a place like this [the UN] to feel you can make changes. We are here to say INDEED! That through your heart and your consciousness and the "Piece of God" that each one of you carries with you—this very group has the power to change the planet! But it must start individually with each of you. It is an often-stated Kryon theme that says that your "Piece of God" must radiate self-worth to your own mind. You must understand who you are, and believe indeed that you are here for a purpose. This is the beginning of your vibrational change.

Each one of you sitting in your chair has reason to be, and perhaps that reason is to combine with others through the thoughts as generated in today's meditation, to change the planet—even while sitting here in a place like this. For the energy here is great with purpose and intent, and you are not here by accident.

Let us now speak briefly about something potent, and I speak to all who are seeing and hearing this message: There is nothing in your individual life that cannot be changed right now if you choose to change it. Although Kryon may speak of planetary issues, and in a moment the Kryon may speak of non-earthly things, for now let me address a message to your heart: Perhaps you are carrying something in your body that you feel is inappropriate for your life. Perhaps it is a secret only known by you? Perhaps there are situations around you that are uncomfortable? Perhaps you are despondent or depressed, saying, "Nothing can ever make this better." We say this to you: Oh, dear one, you are so dearly loved! That "Piece of God" within you has the power to change all of the things around you—even the attributes you fear the most! There is nothing too difficult for the miracle of spiritual physics to change! And your guides stand poised as the room increases in the love energy—right now.

It's about individual hearts, you know. It's about what you can do for yourself, which will then change the atmosphere around you. And as you do this, dear ones, the ones around you will change as well. So again we have the instruction that the change in one will facilitate the change in many, and therefore the power of just a few enlightened ones will affect the whole. Make no mistake! This power is the power of love and higher vibration.

Planetary change is "in the works" here in this room. So we encourage you to continue what you are doing here [the S.E.A.T.].

Dear ones, we have four items to address in the short time we have. Now we speak to the assemblage—not just those in this room, but also the ones who will read these messages [like you, right now]. Even though there are only a few hearing these words, the real energy of this message is going through this entire building, and the items presented today will facilitate thoughts in others not here now—perhaps even to those who meet in the big room not far from here (the General Assembly). Such is the way Spirit works that the *now* time frame supersedes the past and future.

(1) Let me tell you a story of Joe. Joe was a man who lived in a house with others, and this house had many rooms. Each person who lived in the house had a room of their own, and Joe loved the room he lived in. All the rooms were special, and he had seen many of the other rooms and felt they were beautiful, too. But Joe had one of the larger rooms, which had more resources than the others. He kept a close watch on all the parts of it and kept it as peaceful and beautiful as he could.

He would get together with the others occasionally and discuss how to collectively beautify the whole, but he felt his room was the most special, as did each of the others about their own space.

Joe found that by painting the walls certain colors, he could create specific moods and attitudes—creating certain protections he needed, and a great deal of beauty. So he did, and he used his room's resources and kept his room to his liking through his lifetime. And as so it came to be that Joe's technical resources also increased with time, since he had one of the larger rooms. Joe eventually looked up at his ceiling and noted that it needed repair. Using his new technology, he could now reach his ceiling, so Joe increased the strength of his ceiling structure and beautified it at the same time—something he had not been able to do previously.

Now it wasn't long before Joe also reached out and said, "With my technology, I can also improve the roof that is over my room. I know I can make it better for my space. I will do these things." So it was that Joe used his technology to beautify his roof and make it better for his purposes. But in the process of doing so, he made an error, for he did not understand the concept of the collectiveness of the roof and that it was a part of the other rooms.

Those in the other rooms said nothing about Joe's efforts, since they did not understand what Joe was trying to do, and in fact, Joe did not fully understand his technology either. His intent was good, but his wisdom fell short, and a mistake happened. Due to his incomplete knowledge, the roof over Joe's room became unstable and failed. But that was not all that happened. Since the roof was collective, and existed not in pieces above each room, but as a total system, it also was affected. In time, Joe's efforts regarding his own roof gradually changed the entire roof, endangering the whole house. Joe realized that the ignorance he had shown within his own room had indeed caused chaos and danger for the whole house, and he was ashamed.

Now this parable is not lost on any of you! We tell you that your technology on this continent is so powerful at this point in time that the experiments within the confines of the skies of your country will absolutely affect all countries! So we again say to you: Slow down until you understand fully what you are doing! Do not undertake these kinds of powerful experiments without seeking the advice of the others on the planet who share your same atmosphere. You cannot do this and feel you are isolated and alone on the planet. Gather in places like this [the UN] and speak of these things! Bring up the subject in the "big room." This is why this building exists! We challenge you! It is time.

(2) Now we have a question for you: If you were to build an organization of nations such as this from the beginning again, would it make sense to you in these new times, with the millennium approaching, to have the wisdom of the planet's ancients present

in your planning? Could you use their collective ideas, or perhaps their secrets, previously hidden? I think you would say, "*Yes! That is an excellent idea.*"

Why is it, then, that there is no place in this vast organization for that very wisdom? Did you forget that it is available? Do you discount that it would be valuable? Even on this continent there are the native ancestors of the ancients that still carry the understanding of the old Spiritual Earth ways. They understand the spiritual nature of the land, and of peace. They understand co-existence with the elements, and the energy of the west, east, north, and south.

Those ancients who founded the tropical islands of the entire Earth fully understood their own star ancestry! And their human ancestors still teach it to this day in an unwritten language and know how it all fits together with the energy of Earth.

Those on the other side of the planet from you right now that are today building fires with sticks for warmth and gathering around in a primitive fashion may understand better than any wise person in this building how things actually work! There are ancestors of ancients on every continent, and their knowledge fits together—did you know that? For the truth of the planet never changes, but the basics are often lost to the modern ones.

Yet none of these wise ones are represented in this building, since they do not own the land they are on. They carry the greatest wisdom that this planet has to offer humanity today—but because they are not politically powerful, they are ignored.

And so we say that it is time to consider a council of elders, of the spiritual wise, to advise the rest of you—validated by their planetary lineage and not their governmental credentials. If you do this, it will indeed bring results for you—all of you! There is no greater time than this for such an idea. Perhaps it will now occur—in the big room down the hall.

(3) Here is the third issue for today: It is about what you call extraterrestrials. Dear ones, you have not yet met the ones you expect to meet. When your planet is of a vibrational intent that matches that of the others, it will be as a beacon to them to come. They will bring you great news and wonderful help. But the beacon is not yet in place [see pp26 & 208].

The ones you are meeting now are not forerunners of the others. They are outsiders—peripheral entities that absolutely do not represent the vibration of those who are waiting.

Did you know that the universe is teeming with life? Even subsequent to my last visit in this very building, you have discovered over nine planets not in your solar system! So almost overnight your science is saying, *"Indeed there are other planets other than the ones attached to our sun!"* It won't be long before they will also be saying, *"Indeed there is other life besides that which is attached to our sun."* It is only a matter of time. Here is news, something never channeled before: There is a far greater chance of intelligent life within solar systems with twin suns than just one sun. There are reasons for this, and your own science will someday validate why this is so. The incidence of dual stars supporting a group of planets is greater than that which you have here—which is of only one sun. You might say, *"We have intelligent life, and we have only one sun. Why is that?"* And we say that we have hidden you well—very well!

We have advised you before on this subject. Listen! Nations of this Earth, pool what you know with the others so you will understand the intent of the messengers! Each of you has a piece, but none of you has the whole. You are being given a great deal of misinformation by those who are the "peripherals." They will trick you into doing things that otherwise you would not if you had the whole knowledge. They have an agenda that is not commensurate with the raising of the planet's vibration, and this agenda is filled with lies. When you reveal what you know, there can be no secrets! There is great irony that by keeping these extraterrestrial activities a secret, you are perpetuating their very agenda, and it is not in your interest! Do not trust those who are physically here now! They do not represent the ones to come.

Oh, they are amazing. Their technology is beyond yours, and their presence is being sequestered by powerful humans—in a way that is inappropriate for planetary growth and enlightenment. SHARE THE KNOWLEDGE!

(4) Finally, we have a message for you that may appear cryptic. But those who understand the overview will quickly understand what is being asked. You, as the planet Earth, have moved far beyond where we thought you would be at this linear time. You have chosen peace repeatedly when given the challenge. Oh, you may see the strife around you and the suffering of many, and the many tribal wars. These are but a residue of the old energy. But the overview is this dear ones: PEACE IS NO LONGER AN OPTION. IT IS A NECESSITY. Those who are moving into a higher vibration totally understand this. This planet cannot exist in the vibratory state it is moving toward and also sustain war. This is why your very organization [UN] is still sustained—even with all those who are trying to eliminate it!

Look around you. All of the predictions of the ancient doom sayers are void! You have broken the prediction paradigm that said you would not make it this far! Your Armageddon didn't happen when it was supposed to—did anyone notice? Your old energy of war is not acceptable, and the new millennium promises a time of peace and tolerance...and love. It's up to you to take it there, however. You are on the right track, and the timetable that many predicted for your demise simply has vanished. Even the timetables from New Age channels have been changed. Your future is changing almost daily, due to the vibratory change in the dirt of the Earth itself! Did you notice?

There is one major challenge left, dear ones, and it is an important one: MAKE PEACE WITH THE DRAGON—we will leave this message alone for now.

All of you are dearly loved. We know the names of each of you here. We know what you are going through and what brought you to this place to sit in these chairs and hear these words. We say to you, there is a grand plan for your life! We sit before you and plant the seeds of truth and love. We sprinkle you with the essence of "home," and hope you recognize the God force that is here now. If you are in your contract right now, you can feel the love that is being sent to you. If you don't understand these words, we tell you that the seeds are still being planted. It's about free choice and intent. It's about honor for humanity. Someday you might allow the seeds to grow, and it will change the way you view everything! You will finally understand that you are actually an anointed being—with the very essence of God within each of you— appropriate for your time here, honored for being where you now sit!

We love you dearly.

And so it is!

Kryon

From Lee:

As these last words from Kryon echoed in the room, Steve Rother, one of the Kryon team, looked at the large clock in back of me and above my head. The second-hand was hitting the mark on the hour exactly when we were instructed to finish. Kryon had paced the message exactly, and made certain Steve saw it—another validation that defied coincidence within the ongoing work of Kryon.

As I now look back on the channeling, I again see the familiar Kryon pattern. First the singular, then the whole. He begins with love for the individual, then he speaks of the whole, then he returns to the single person again. His message for the UN was not timid. I interpreted portions of his message in a loud fashion when appropriate, but the love always shone through. Even in the midst of his most potent admonition for the nations of the world, Kryon's countenance continued to shout the word HONOR for humanity.

He tells us that we are special and that we have the power to get to the finish line! He admires our achievements and speaks of obtaining the "critical mass" of human consciousness. He addresses the fact that the planet is responding to our work, and invites us to see it—and now at the United Nations he again gives advice to the masses.

When finished, Kryon gently addressed the individual human who he sees is in fear and pain. With a feeling of honor he says, "*Isn't it time you healed yourself?*" Then he offers to wash their feet! Such is the continuing caring energy of that entity that I channel, the one who is the magnetic master, and also one of the Angels of the New Age.

PS: Thanks to Miguel Gonzalez, a S.E.A.T. member who attended this meeting at the UN, for being the only one in the room whose recorder worked! My digital unit's new batteries drained in ten minutes, and many others had difficulty as well. His cassette allowed this transcription. The energy in the room that day was indeed charged.

HAARP
An Update

From the Writer...

When the United Nations channeling was finished in 1995, I had no idea about the high-energy experiments that were going on that Kryon spoke of. Even as I write this, things are being revealed that are changing even what I thought Kryon meant back then. Here is what I know: There are two major experiments being run by the United States government, one in Alaska, and one in Australia, both of which use tremendous new technology originally developed by Nikola Tesla (inventor of the radio and alternating current—what—you didn't know that? That's a subject for another book).

When I found out about the High Frequency Active Auroral Research Program (HAARP) a month after the 1995 UN channel, (one of the two high energy-experiments) I absolutely knew that this was what Kryon was speaking of. Scientists in Alaska at a "hush-hush" project site were planning on building an atmospheric heating station using Tesla technology. It promised potentially astounding solutions to some very basic defense problems in our country—perhaps the *Holy Grail* for all branches of the military, and a cheap solution to heretofore very expensive weapons systems. For less than the cost of one nuclear sub, this experiment is thought to be the scientist's finest hour since the Los Alamos project brought us the ability to split the atom. It's that important.

HAARP represents a plan to pump more than a gigawatt (that's one billion watts, folks) directed through the use of scalar waves (a Tesla term) into the ionosphere in an experimental way that will begin by blowing a 30-mile-wide hole. What follows is a story I wrote for the *Sedona Journal of Emergence* that dramatizes and explains in layman's terms what HAARP is about. Keep reading. Even among this frightening news there is hope and wonderful new information.

The HAARP Project

U nlike most office doors, this one closed with a dull "thump," since it was of those heavy ones for sound-proofing. The shapely secretary entered, was briefly eyed by the few men who were seated at the tables, and then was ignored as she took her place and prepared to transcribe the meeting.

It was the mid-eighties somewhere in Virginia. Scientists from ARCO Production Technologies Corp. were meeting with high Navy and Air Force officials in a private security office. No uniforms were present, since long ago they had learned that the press watches the comings and goings of highly ranked brass; therefore, business suits were the order of the day—no stars of the Air Force generals or wide stripes of the admirals in sight. The highly ranked officers were slightly uncomfortable out of uniform and were shifting in their seats.

The men from ARCO were preparing some slides and graphics. "Let's get right to the point," said one of the scientists. "You all know from previous contacts that we have developed the Eastlund and Tesla patents to a workable system." All eyes were on the scientists, since some of the military brass hadn't really heard the entire story until today. One of them yawned, expecting another boring meeting.

"Gentlemen," the scientist continued, "what if I told you that we had it within our power to kill any missile in flight toward the United States at a range of four thousand miles from our shore without firing a shot?" The Air Force generals smiled.

"In addition, what if I told you that using the same technology, we could communicate with any submarine at any depth immediately in real time without the cumbersome underwater 'wake-up bell' one-letter-at-a-time system you have now?" The admiral at the table maintained a poker face, a testament to years of experience sitting across from those who wanted something.

"That's not all, gentlemen," continued the scientist in a business as usual manner. "We believe that this technology can also give us the ability to see up to several kilometers into the ground, depending on geological makeup, showing us nuclear bunkers, silos—like an x-ray of the enemy's entire topography... there's more."

The scientist rose from his chair and approached the overhead projector. "Within this same new technology, we firmly believe, based on our experiments, that we can eventually manipulate weather over any battlefield on Earth." No one blinked much at this point, and all were digesting this last statement. The admiral, still hearing the words about sub communication ringing in his ears, spoke first.

"At what cost?"

The scientist was ready for this question. "Admiral," he said, "our entire program for the next ten years will cost us less than half the cost of one nuclear submarine, and..." he paused for effect, "the funding from Congress is already in place for initial experiments."

"This is doable?" asked the admiral in a skeptical tone.

"Absolutely...and already patented." replied the scientist.

"What's the technology?" the admiral asked.

"We are going to inject high-frequency radio energy into the ionosphere to create huge low frequency (ELF) virtual antennas. Then we can focus the energy from this 'ionosphere mirror' to disrupt incoming missiles—in fact any electronics at all. We do this by heating regions of the lower and upper ionosphere—literally boiling it—to create a kind of electronic lens. This is where the focus ability comes to communicate deep into the water for the subs, or to knock down the incomings." He continued without waiting for a reply.

"Selective heating of the atmosphere is also what can change the weather. We could potentially create floods, droughts—very useful to our military." The scientists now waited for reaction.

"You still haven't told me what the technology is," stated the admiral.

"We are using proprietary phased-array transmitting, steering, and pulsing techniques," said the man from ARCO. "You see—"

"Scalar technology," interrupted one of the high-ranking Air Force men. "right out of the Tesla days. We were on the wrong side of it when the Soviet Union was up and running. Their secret 'Woodpecker' system was just a variation of this—and it drove our communications crazy. At this point, gentlemen, it appears to be the 'Holy Grail' of defense technology for all of us—in any branch of service."

The admiral spoke again. "All right, what's the down side? How fast can we get it, and what about secrecy?" The room lights dimmed as if on cue, and the overhead projector snapped on. "Take at look at this, gentlemen." The screen showed a facility surrounded by a fence. Within it there were a few innocent shacks, and 36 spindly clothesline-like antennas—hardly the ominous weapon the military men had imagined. Snow and ice were everywhere, and a lone man in a parka stood on the steps of one of the shacks as if posing for the camera.

"Gentlemen, take a look at what the public will know as **HAARP: The High-Frequency Active Auroral Research Program**. Its appearance to the public is a small science experiment in the black spruce forest in central Alaska—far from any population." The slide changed to an illustrated graphic of the Earth's ionosphere.

"Eventually we will have 360 antennae. When the project is fully operational in early 1997, we'll start by heating or exciting

30-mile-wide holes directly above the experiment—kind of like a giant microwave oven. We'll punch a hole and measure the results. Punch another…etc. We expect it will take about three months for each hole to close, and the data will begin to tell us more about how to focus our eventual virtual mirror." There was a moment of silence, then the admiral spoke.

"What about the environment?" he asked. "Didn't you have to get environmental impact statements? We moved a barracks last year and had to measure the effect on earthworms! How did you get this thing through?"

The ARCO man reached into a small briefcase and drew out a thick report, tossing it on the table so it slid and stopped right in front of the admiral. He looked at the cover.

"This statement was filed by the Air Force!" exploded the admiral. "Sorry, admiral" said the Air Force general. We had a 'heads up' about a year ago." The admiral gave the general a long stare.

He opened the environmental impact statement and read *"…the normally upward directed ionospheric research instrument (IRI) transmissions can raise the internal body temperature of nearby people; ignite road flares in the trunks of cars; detonate aerial munitions used in electronic fuses; and scramble aircraft communications, navigation, and flight-control systems."*

"Unbelievable!" exclaimed the admiral, closing the report. "I don't know how you got this thing through. What about the unknown effects of this? How about the ozone? Could we do damage that is not repairable to our own atmosphere?"

"We don't know," said the ARCO man as he turned around to continue the presentation. "But we're going to find out."

The report of this meeting is a fictitious depiction of a compilation of numerous meetings like it over the period of several years in the mid to late 1980s. All the players and facts are accurate—even the environmental impact statement as filed by the Air Force is quoted correctly, and the PROJECT IS REAL.

HAARP is perhaps the most dangerous, outrageous experiment undertaken for our country's defense with the exception of the first explosion of the atomic bomb at Los Alamos. Prior to that event, the physicists were asked what they thought would happen when it went off. There was wild speculation from "fizzle" to "lighting the Earth's atmosphere on fire." They simply didn't know—but they did it anyway!

Popular Science magazine of September '95 reported on HAARP. This normally optimistic and entertaining magazine was very strong in their condemnation of what is being built in Alaska. They reported that HAARP is being managed by the USAF Phillips Laboratory and the Office of Naval Research. Equipment is supplied by Advanced Power Technologies, a Washington, D.C. based subsidiary of E-Systems of Dallas, longtime maker of electronics used in ultra-secret projects such as the president's E-4B "doomsday plane."

They go on to report that Richard Williams, a physical chemist and consultant to the Sarnoff Laboratory at Princeton University, is worried and states: "Speculation and controversy surround the question of whether HAARP's 1.7 gigawatts (1.7 billion watts) of effective radiated power in the 1.8 to 10MHz frequency range might cause lasting damage to Earth's upper atmosphere. HAARP will dump enormous amounts of energy into the upper atmosphere, and we don't know what will happen. With experiments on this scale, irreparable damage could be done in a short time. The immediate need is for open discussion. To do otherwise would be an act of global vandalism."

What does Alaska think? Again, according to *Popular Science* (Sept. '95): *"State Rep. Jeanette James, whose district surrounds the HAARP site, has repeatedly asked Air Force officials about the project and has been told 'not to worry.' She says, 'My gut feeling is that it is frightening. I'm skeptical. I don't think they know what they are doing.'"*

This is not a technical explanation, and I won't dwell on the technical attributes of this military project under the guise of simple research. This is a plea for all who are reading this to find out more about HAARP for yourselves so you understand the reality and scope of it. A recently published book that represents good solid research into the technical aspects of this experiment is *Angels Don't Play This HAARP,* by Jeane Manning and Dr. Nick Begich. It is available by calling 907-249-9111. It's a "must read" for anyone interested in the subject.

The Miracle of Synchronicity

It was Christmas, 1996, one month after the last United Nations Kryon channeling, that we had a Kryon event in Laguna Hills, California. In a crowd of 500 people there was one who would hear of HAARP and have a profound reaction. Paula Randol Smith, a Los Angeles resident, was startled by the information, and it "rang" within her.

Paula was in the "right place at the right time," and recognized that this HAARP subject was somehow related to her contract. She could not ignore the "calling" that she felt. What could one woman do to make the planet more aware of this dangerous experiment? Was this political outrage or spiritual appropriateness?

Within a few weeks of the channel, Paula had sorted it all out. She was not a show business personality, nor was she wealthy. Paula was a single woman in LA who was starting to vibrate with "why she was here." She realized that her job was indeed to make the planet aware! How? What could she do?

Exemplified in Kryon's parable of the missing bridge, Paula did not "think like a human." She sat in the presence of Spirit and gave INTENT to follow her passion—that of somehow changing the consciousness of our country by informing an entire population about HAARP. How could she do something that the TV show *20/20* had refused to do? How could one woman with no background in science carry such a load? Was it dangerous? Where would she start?

Paula started at the beginning.

"Paula, don't think like a human!" I could hear Kryon saying.

On her own, she located an award-winning documentary film producer/director named Wendy Robbins. After hearing Paula's concerns and doing some study, Wendy agreed to participate in a big way, sacrificing normal remuneration protocol. She became a committed partner in the production, eventually traveling all over the country with Paula, toting cameras, tapes, and gear everywhere.

There was no time for a funding program, and besides—how does one organize such a project immediately, and by oneself? So she sold her land and business! With her regular income and assets now gone, Paula was heading toward the "missing bridge" in the Kryon parable.

"Keep going, Paula. You are loved, and there are gifts for you along the way!" I continued to hear Kryon saying.

To hear Paula tell it, there was synchronicity everywhere. Doors were opened in her quest to interview and photograph that were closed almost the instant she was finished—never being granted to another. She met with and filmed Dr. Nick Begich, co-writer of *Angels Don't Play This HAARP*, and then was granted access and permission to film and interview John Heckscher, director of the HAARP project. Many scientists and authors who represent both sides of the discussion were also included before she and Wendy were finished. She discovered things she didn't want to know—enough for another documentary!

She was followed in black cars, had her phone tapped, and was surveyed by folks who she will probably never meet—yet she continued. All through it, integrity and fairness were paramount in her quest to present something that would tell its own story without her having to generate sensationalism through clever editing or script writing.

One year later, the results of paula's work are in her hand. In Breckenridge, Colorado, during the summer of 96, I stood proudly among a group of enlightened humans who were there to view and celebrate a rough-cut presentation of the new documentary *Holes in Heaven*, the first-class one-hour documentary film on HARRP to be syndicated nationally in 1998. At this writing, she is still trusting Spirit for the balance of the funding in order to complete the project. I know that it will happen.

It was a very moving time for me. I welled up with emotion to think about what she had been through—what the results of her efforts would contribute to the planet! Make no mistake: This was not a fairy tale. This took work, the conquering of fear, and lots of co-creation on Paula's part, along with Wendy and others (many in the Kryon seminars) who worked and helped fund the project after the initial monies were gone. But while racing toward the chasm of the "missing bridge," Paula found all the pieces and parts of the new bridge, and at this writing, is moving over the precipice (metaphorically) with a professional production in her hand that will inform literally millions of people on this continent about HAARP.

Holes in Heaven is a fair presentation, with scientific argument and discussion, about the basic issue of HAARP. It is not fear-based or sensational. It is factual and unbiased, but potent in its revelation of what the project is, and the potential results of it. If you are interested in obtaining the tape, see page 242. Perhaps you might consider helping with the next project? Here is the address: Holes in Heaven Project; PO Box 91655, Pasadena, CA 91101-1655. One year ago, as I wrote this, there was nothing, now take a look at page 388 (published in 1999). Does this show you what CONTRACT is all about?

Thank you, Paula!

Now, there is one more to do, and perhaps there is still more synchronicity for us to see. When in Portland, Oregon, a couple of months before the 1997 Kryon tour of Australia, Kryon started channeling about the other high-energy experiment he had mentioned in 1995.

Pine Gap is the name of still another dangerous experiment using (what else?) more attributes of New Age Tesla technology. The facility is deep within the Australian continent. Somehow with the use of scalar technology, energy is being transmitted through the ground. According to Kryon, it has already caused earthquakes, and he advises us to expose this work as well. There is already an organization in Australia that is publicizing it—perhaps a good starting point toward reaching the mainstream here.

Does Kryon want to stop HAARP and PINE GAP? Are we supposed to get militant and march on these facilities? NO.

In both United Nations channelings, Kryon advised that we (1) get informed, and (2) slow down. We, as human beings, can't "un-invent" any technology. We can, however, be responsible for how we develop anything that is so new that it might shake the very foundation or ceiling of our "house" if we are not careful. GO SLOWLY! BE RESPONSIBLE! are the words of Kryon.

As meditators with great INTENT, you, as readers of this book, can do something even on this very day: Give visualization to these things, and meditate on them. The year-long effort to do so on the Internet with meditations led by **Steve Rother*** of San Diego involved many people all over the country who gathered around their computers to read Steve's words and give energy and INTENT to somehow bringing HAARP into public consciousness. Their efforts, under Steve's tireless direction, and those of meditators like you, have paid off—and a woman who was *scheduled* to be sitting in a chair in Laguna Beach at a Kryon seminar in December 1996, arrived on schedule and felt the tug of love that she came for. It changed her life, and will change the awareness of millions.

Do you start to understand how "family" makes a difference here? Do you ever feel that you can't make a difference? As Kryon states, "Your INTENT is everything!" Start using your collective power, and watch things happen! I have seen this *up close and personal*. It still astonishes me to watch the *reality* of it.

Lee Carroll

---

* Interested in Steve Rother's online meditations?
  See [http://www.lightworker.com]

The Indigo Children

Chapter Seven

"The Indigo Children"
A Report

From the writer...

Kryon has channeled pieces and parts of information regarding the "indigo" children, and it is now time to reveal a composite of what is before us regarding this subject. There is yet to be a concise Kryon channeling that is totally about this subject, so I will bring you a synopsis of both what Kryon has said and what I have discovered in my travels regarding indigos. I believe that some of what follows will help to explain much about today's kids to many parents reading this.

Before I begin, it's time to finally get something correct. The study of "life colors" was originally channeled and brought to us some years ago by a woman named Nancy Ann Tappe. Her book, *Understanding Your Life Through Color,** was the first to expose this concept to our modern metaphysics. Others emulated it shortly after it was published, and some actually benefited financially from her work without permission. I want to honor her in these pages for being first, and for being so accurate!

Life colors are like spiritual auric color overlays that define similar personality traits within color groups. Nancy's inspired work correctly identified the attributes of the groups and then went on to apply them to everyday life. Much like the science of astrology, which is able to group personality attributes from our magnetic birth imprints, so our color overlay also carries certain similar human traits that are very noticeable when you know what to look for.

---

* *Understanding Your Life Through Color*
Nancy Ann Tappe - ISBN 0-940399-00-8
Awakenings Book Store (CA) (949) 457-0797
Mind, Body, Soul Book Store (IN) (317) 889-3612
Credit Cards Accepted in both stores

Nancy continues to give her color workshops around the country, and I can tell you from personal experience that they are a hoot! It's really fun to see your own personal attributes exposed this way, and also a bit weird! In a "violet" workshop I attended, since I am mostly a violet life color, Nancy was able to accurately predict almost exactly how the group of attending "violet folks" were going to walk, talk, and solve problems during the tests that followed. She was right, and we laughed at ourselves all day long! Nancy also gives private sessions and is generally able to identify your life color almost instantly (*see her address at the bottom of the last page*).

Like viewing auras and other spiritual attributes, not everyone can "see" a color overlay, but after reading Nancy's book, you can correlate a person's color from the list of attributes identified as belonging to the group. This knowledge is not only helpful for self-examination (as in astrology), but also beneficial to enable a facilitator to better help a person. Okay, it's also fun, too!

The indigo color is just one attribute of the new children coming onto the planet now, but it is a consistent one, so Kryon has referred to them as "the indigo children." This is one more validation for Nancy's work (as if she needed it). Although the information presented here is from Kryon and my own personal experience, it "shakes hands" with Nancy's work—another validation that accurate New Age knowledge will find its way into several venues simultaneously. Spirit works that way, you know. Here is my information regarding the indigos. I also recommend that you get Nancy's information to have an even better idea of the fascinating work regarding all the life colors.

The Indigo Children

One of the most amazing attributes of the New Age is going to come right out of the cribs of thousands of homes all over the world. The new children of the "indigo" color have arrived en masse and are already among us. Sometimes I think this is what has been predicted as "the mass landing"(only kidding)!

Although Kryon has foretold these children as early as 1989 (when he arrived), it has only been recently that he has channeled specific information regarding some of their attributes and how we might benefit in our interactions with them.

As sensational as it might sound, Kryon tells us that we have earned the right to start changing our actual biology. This will be necessary to take us into the new millennium at a higher vibration, heading toward a time in the not-too-distant future where the planet will be given permission to change in an even greater way. With many humans in a vibration state that is much higher than we are experiencing now, the planet will be given permission to slowly evolve into a new dimension, and a new vibration of its own. Kryon isn't alone in this prediction, and you can find it not only in other current channels, but also in the calendars of the ancients.

With new gifts and spiritual tools from Spirit, Kryon tells us in multiple channels about how we are able to begin our own transformations. Through all of this, however, Kryon has also given us information about the new children *coming in* now. Evidently these new ones are being given a different kind of duality consciousness, and some even have some physical attributes that are unique.

When Kryon began to give some specifics, day-care workers in each seminar would shake their heads in agreement, verifying indeed that the children have been much different in the last few years. Many of these workers have been caring for children for over fifteen years and are keenly aware of some remarkable changes in attitude over the last five.

The New Kids

Spiritual consciousness: Be aware that these new children have an overlay of knowledge of **who they are** that is far different from what we had as children. At the cellular level, they "know" that they are creatures of the Universe, with incredible purpose (not lesson) on the planet. The duality of their consciousness is therefore different from ours. The result is multifold: First, they are positioned to be able to change into a new vibration if they choose to, far easier than we can. If and when the moment in any of them arrives for self-discovery during their lives, they will have far less trouble with self-worth issues, fear, or past-life residue. They often carry no lessons with them at all from former lives! Their transition into a new vibration will be effortless, and they will completely grasp some very complex issues about vibrational changes and how these work with the very dirt of the planet. Some will come in with no karma at all.

This doesn't automatically mean that the new children will all become New Age enlightened beings—hardly. They will still have the same free choice we have for self-discovery, but if the discovery is made, they have better equipment to carry out the work than we did. It would be like having the attributes of Babe Ruth hiding in all of us. Some of us won't even pick up a bat, but those who do will have a great ability to hit the ball. The other side of the coin is that their "special" attributes are ripe for problems within their personalities if we don't recognize who they are.

Kryon told mothers and fathers that indigos would have to be recognized and be treated differently. The worst thing parents can do is to belittle or shame one of these children in order to get them to behave. Now, this fact has been true even for regular children in past years, so what's the difference? Kryon says that in the past, a child who was told that he wasn't worth much might be affected in an adverse way. It would come out in later life, and this person might have to undergo counseling as an adult for worthiness issues. So what's new?

Kryon now says that because of the new awareness, the child will instead experience a total breach of trust if told they are worthless, since they absolutely know better! He or she will know that they are being lied to! The result will be withdrawal and lack of trust. The child cannot be convinced that he is anything but deserving of all that is! He intuitively knows who he is at the cellular level. This "Kingship" and "Queenship" is the difference in how they feel. Many adults are seeing this attribute and calling the kids "headstrong" and "difficult." Instead, the children can have good, solid self-worth, and cellular information that they absolutely belong here right now! They asked for it, and here they are.

This can be both a blessing and a disaster, depending on what the setting is that the child finds himself in. If, for instance, the child is the only indigo among many older-consciousness children (like we were), he is going to look like a misfit. Inside, the child will be shouting, *"Why doesn't anyone recognize me? Why don't the other kids get it? Why are they acting this way? They are all stupid!"* An indigo child has subtle remembrances about the other side that gradually taper off by the time they are ten years old.

At a *Kryon at Home* meeting, I met a day-care worker who told us all of a story regarding a very angry and frustrated little three-year-old girl. She was not getting the reaction from the other children that she expected. They didn't have any of the concepts that she came in with. They were slow, didn't listen, didn't want to participate in the things she wanted, and were starting to obviously reject her. In great rage and tears she stomped over to the woman in charge and screamed at her, *"I'm so sorry I came back"* [true story]!

I met a family at a Kryon gathering that brought their two indigo children to the seminar! Both children (six and eight), were delightful to speak to. I asked the boy, *"What did they call you before you got here?"* Obviously I wanted to see if he had any remembrance of a past life. Much to my shock, he did! *"They called me Daddy,"* he replied, as if it were no big deal. The parents absolutely glowed. They were a united family in Spirit, with children they respected and were able to honor in an entirely different way than the old paradigm. Subsequently, this has happened two more times, with parents bringing their indigos to a gathering of adults for a seven-hour event! No video games or cartoons—just channeling and lecture. The children were awesome in their attention.

Speaking of attention, there is an anomaly that has seemingly *popped up* in the last few years that is almost always indigo related. What would happen to you if you came into a world knowing who you were, with a feeling of family belonging—then nobody recognized you, and instead treated you like you were an outcast instead of a creature of royalty? In addition, what if you were a child experiencing this and couldn't do anything about it? Your intellect couldn't figure out what was wrong! The answer, I am sorry to say, is *Attention Deficit Disorder* and *Attention Deficit Hyperactive Disorder* (ADD and ADHD). These kids will either "check out" of reality, sliding into their own out-of-body world in order to exist, or just the opposite— bouncing off the walls in order to distract the real issue in their lives, and hopefully attract help.

Many parents have to use drugs on their indigos, since there simply doesn't seem to be any other way to create normalcy for the household, or to allow the child to develop. This will change. Already, energy facilitators are having great luck with ADD and ADHD, but must work with the parents, also. Changing the child's environment also sometimes works, but there is no guarantee that the new situation will be any better. Some have found that the food *blue-green algae* makes a large difference in behavior—almost like the child's biology balances itself with the intake of this new material.

By the way, if you try the *blue-green algae*, parents report the best results are obtained from the material that was naturally grown at Klamath Lake in Oregon (I don't sell it, even if it sounds like it. But I do eat it. It's food, not a supplement, and fits into the Kryon category of live-essence substances that pack a "whallop" by balancing the biology quickly and naturally).

Some things just don't work anymore with the indigo kids. Guilt will not work as it did when we were young. "*Wait till your dad gets home*" is a phrase that simply won't bring about the results it used to. Instead, the child will not seem to react at all, and the desired fear of dad finding out simply won't work. The child's inner knowing of "who he is" short-circuits many of the old tricks of discipline.

"*What can we do*?" the parents ask.

Attitude: Kryon told us that the New Age children would act differently, and the day-care specialists again are seeing this. Here is an example: The New Age children will not stand in a line (cue up) when told to. (Oh no! What's going to happen at Disneyland?). Instead, the day-care folks are giving the children the goals that standing in line will bring, and then giving them a time frame to work it out for themselves. Therefore, instead of saying, "*Okay, kids, get in line right now to receive your lunch,*" the workers are saying, "*Okay, kids, it's lunchtime, and you have three minutes to prepare the line.*" Suddenly it becomes a group effort to figure out who is going to stand in line first, and where the line will begin. The children solve the puzzle themselves (gasp!), and take responsibility for the action to bring about the result. It's a new way of thinking both for the kids and the adults who watch over them. Seemingly the choice prompts responsible action (not in my day!).

You can already see that this new method, as well as many others, centers on giving the kids more information at younger ages to allow them to figure it out for themselves. Take responsibility at age five? Figure out a social issue (compromise on who gets to stand in line first)? Does this sound like some New Age principles for adults or for kids? It's for both, and that's the whole point. These children are far more aware of how things work, and you can't fool them!

So what should parents do about control and discipline? The answer is that they should first explain to children (no matter how young—even those who cannot speak yet) why they are being asked to do something, and then give them a choice (if old enough). I was in the home of a three-year-old indigo child. You could look into his eyes and see what an old soul he was. His parents knew who he was and were very successful in the task of getting him to interface in a meaningful way with the family. At dinner, instead of being told to "sit down," he was asked to choose "where to sit" (the parents had thoughtfully prepared a couple of options). Therefore, an uncaring command became a loving request to choose. In both cases, the overview was that dinner was being served, and an expected action was required. The child looked at the situation, and you could actually see that he was taking responsibility for deciding which chair to sit on. The idea of rejecting "coming to dinner" was never there.

I also saw the child object once or twice later in the evening (he was tired and crabby like all children get), and he was firmly disciplined appropriately with stern words and an accompanying action. The difference? He was treated correctly with respect, but he still tried to push himself past his appropriate place (as all children do to test their power). Then came the expected disciplinary action, with a logical, calm explanation. The difference here was not in the way the child was disciplined as much as in the way he was treated up to and during the problem. Through all of this, the child gets the point: "*We treat you with respect, and you do the same with us.*"

Make no mistake: This is not spoiling the child. Instead, this is a method of everyday treatment that is different from how it used to be. This isn't "walking on eggs" with the kid. It's honoring the child with choice, Instead of "*Do what you are told, and stop asking questions!*" Kryon tells parents to make friends with their children very early, and try to drop the old parent/child relationship that **we** all knew as children.

Parents have also brought indigo infants to the seminars. In Breckenridge, Colorado, a newly adopted orphan from overseas was being carried on the mother's back. The child was absolutely captivating, and you could look into her eyes and see so much wisdom. (You could also predict that this kid was going to be a handful! She will demand attention, but not from ego. This attribute comes from a covert knowledge of her cellular lineage. Parents don't have to bow down, just honor who the children are, and expect it in return.) When I was at the lectern speaking about indigo children, I told the folks that one was in attendance and was in the back with her mother. Hundreds of people turned to look. The reaction of the child? She cocked her head, recognized that folks were honoring her—and waved—as if to say, *"Yep, that's me!"* It was a precious moment, and we all laughed and laughed.

Parents will discover extremely early that their children will respond to being honored, and indeed can have a far different relationship than we ever had as children with our parents. The children will be far wiser, and will shock us with the self-discipline they will develop (self-responsibility). They will recognize social issues faster and be far more concerned with "grown-up" things at a much earlier age—and yes, they will become our friends early on. Good-bye, generation gap. It's an old-energy paradigm. I have seen this!

Three times this year we had indigo teenagers attend a Kryon seminar. In one case, the boy demanded that his parents bring him (he had found the Kryon books by himself). In the second case, one came as a total equal with his parents, absorbing all the information, meditation, toning, and channeling as the adults did (seven hours worth). In the third case, the boy read the Kryon books and resounded greatly to them. He received permission from his parents in Alaska to come alone to a Kryon seminar!

In each case, I spent time with these precious ones. Okay, so they were still teenagers, and spoke and acted like teenagers. (Can you remember your teen years? I honor the growing-up process and pray to Spirit that I will never forget what it was like. I believe it has helped me to relate to young people.) The difference in these young ones was in the wisdom factor. They asked extremely potent questions about life and their teenage role in it. We often discussed much, and as I watched them leave, I thought to myself, *There goes an entirely new breed of human!*

So if you didn't already get it, here are some suggestions until some enlightened day-care worker or teacher writes the coming bestselling book on the *new children* (are you listening—there's a book to write, here)!

(1) From birth, treat the child like he or she is a young adult—especially using your tone of voice. Use this method to honor his or her life force. The child expects this, and will react negatively if you don't. Always expect to be honored in return. At first, the child won't seem to understand your request for reciprocation, but verbally begin the request, anyway. Mom, your INTENT to honor and be honored is the key (remember the channelings about INTENT?). Set up the agreement early. Nothing you do can create it, and you have to earn it with your actions. Do this verbally. The indigo responds to cellular responsibility. Often it is the only lesson he or she comes in with and needs this kind of input!

(2) Tell the children from birth verbally what is going on. Explain everything. Okay, there is eye-rolling going on from moms every-where. Really—do it! The children can sense at a cellular level what you are doing. Moms, I want you to remember something that may have happened at the birth of your child. Remember the very first time you were able to hold that infant and look into those wide eyes for a long time? Did the child look back to yours? Yes it did. What did you feel during the first "eye lock"? Was there communication? YES! Every mom I have spoken to remembers that moment—because of the internal communication!

INTENT is the power of communication, and it works from the day these children arrive in the hospital. They will know if you want it, don't want it, or even if you are a new mom! They are wise in many areas that you were not, so expect many mature things seemingly beyond their age.

(3) As soon as possible, give the children choices over absolutely everything you can! Prepare scenarios for eating, sleeping, and playing that they can **choose** from. Remember, it suits the children's "royalty" to be asked which choice they would like. They will respond to the "royal family" by giving you a maturity you did not expect. They don't look at you as nonroyalty. They understand the lineage, and will return the gift of honor as they grow. If they are royal, they also believe that you must be, too! When you understand this mind-set, you will fare far better in your everyday relationship with them.

(4) Discipline them as you would with any children, but do it with less emotion than you might otherwise. Raw emotion for effect will not work with the these kids any more than guilt does. Yelling won't bring about change in them, and will make you look weak. If you "lose it," they win. Whereas my generation would cower at the strong voice of an angry, out-of-control parent, the indigos might actually smile! Oops, you just lost!

A good quick, quiet disciplinary action, which was what you said would happen, delivered on schedule at the appropriate time, is what works best—yep, even in the supermarket. Don't worry about the other shoppers—they don't have to go home with the kid! Be consistent with this (I know it's hard). The indigos' maturity at an early age will create understanding sooner about what happens when they test you. The worst thing you can do with an indigo child is to let them "run over" you. They will, if you let them. Then it's hard to recover their respect. According to Nancy AnnTappe, these children actually *respond* to your emotional state. This is different than *reacting* to it. Love, resolve, integrity—remember that these are all emotions too. These children are very intuitive!

(5) Watch for signs of incredible frustration when they start interacting with other children. Some of this is normal. It's the deep depression and "clamming up" that is the telltale sign of deep frustration or depression. Later, this might explode into an overactive performance, as I spoke of earlier. Both are defense mechanisms that are borne from feeling absolutely alone, even with other children to play with.

Since these kids don't have a "brand" on them that says *New Age Indigo kid,* there will be some trial and error to find other children they relate to. From a metaphysical standpoint, you are probably more apt to find other indigo children faster that are children of *light workers* than by changing schools and simply hoping for a better group. If that's the case and you find some children of your metaphysical friends to be indigos, then get the kids together regularly. It will be a good balance for all the children and will go a long way to help them tolerate the ones that don't understand them at school. Why might the children of light workers be indigos? FAMILY! Kryon speaks of it often. We incarnate into spiritual groups around the planet. "Family" is less likely to be biological and far more likely to be spiritual.

Don't be afraid to get help! Look to facilitators and those who work with children professionally as soon as you recognize a problem that you feel is beyond your ability. Call them if you simply need guidance. Many professionals dealing with these children effectively are not New Age, but they do have a wonderful grasp on practical answers, anyway. These helpers have recognized the symptoms, developed some answers, and are having good results. It's not that hard to see the "indigo experience" happening in our society, and there are many good educators and psychologists who have tackled the issue, without any spiritual significance being assigned to the situation. They are being honored with good answers, for Spirit is not proprietary (as I have said before). Their INTENT to help the children is as powerful and valuable as that given from any light worker. It is their passion, remember, that has placed them in the right place at the right time to help indigos all over the planet.

Not all children being born right now are indigos, but as time goes on, more and more will be. It all started about 1970 with a small percentage of indigos arriving, and now it's up to about 80 percent or slightly higher as this book is being written. At that rate, I believe that the children will be able to find like-minded infant friends more easily. It's the 3- to 6-year-olds who are searching right now (as I write in 1998). They came from a group where only about 30 percent or less were indigos. Shortly, they all will be. Their message to us?

"Here we come, ready or not!"

Offered in love,

Lee Carroll

For more information, see page 254

Intent and Co-creation

Chapter Eight

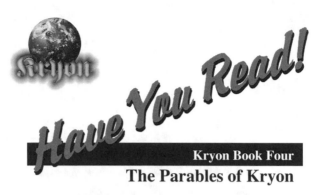

Kryon Book Four
The Parables of Kryon

"For anyone who is ready for the next evolutionary step, this information from Kryon is invaluable. It is both self-healing and planetary healing...Kryon really lets us know that all is well and we have work to do"

■ **Louise L. Hay** - Best-Selling Author

Books and tapes can be purchased in retail stores, or on our Internet store
~ Credit cards welcome ~
1-800-352-6657 - www.kryon.com

"Co-Creation in the New Age"
Channeled in
Portland, OR

The Kryon Writings, Inc.

PMB 422
1155 Camino Del Mar
Del Mar, California 92014
[www.kryonqtly.com]

"Co-Creation in the New Age"
Live Channeling
Portland, OR

*These live channelings have been edited with additional
words and thoughts to allow clarification and better
understanding of the written word.*

From the writer...

The live channel that follows is about co-creation. It is actually
only a portion of a live channel given in Portland Oregon, and
contains one of my favorite parables. It is also one of the only
channels in this book that also has an audiocassette available
(although the cassette is not as complete due to the ever-present
process of rechannel that Kryon offers as I edit the live channels for
publication—allowing new thoughts and updated information).

Before I present this information, I want to discuss from my point
of view one of the most powerful new gifts of Spirit (God) in this New
Age. Although Kryon gives it great emphasis, I wish to give it even
more. The gift is the power of INTENT, and I wish to expand on it
from a human point of view.

In the Kryon seminars, I lecture about the fact that Kryon has
told us that **consciousness changes physics**! This theme, simply
stated, is that we as a human race are constantly changing everything from our future to our everyday lives through our consciousness. The tool of change is INTENT.

I point out in the lecture series that it is astounding to look at the
overview of the planet since the Harmonic Convergence, and since
the "new" tools and gifts started arriving, enabling humans to have
personal power in a greater manner than ever. The overview shows
a remarkable positive change!

From the fall of communism almost overnight a few years back,
there is a string of events that goes against almost everything we
were taught in the last 25 years that would happen on the planet.

None of the old doom-and-gloom information is on schedule, and although I will not go into all the details here (come to a Kryon seminar in your area), I will tell you that the predictions of the great and very accurate Nostradamus are now way off track, as well as the New Age predictors and prophets Sheldon Nidle and Michael Gordon Scallion. In the case of the last two, it's running 0 for 0 on all counts. Even the Christian end times expert Hall Lindsey (*The Late Great Planet Earth*) is finding that his Armageddon timetable is behind, based on his first writings (see the Chapter Ten in this book for more).

Kryon tells us that all these doom-and-gloom scenarios (including *Revelations*) are old-energy predictions, and that we, collectively as humans, have changed the planet. The same energy that is creating a situation where all the conflicts of the world are now tribal (as Kryon predicted), is also responsible for the sudden resolution in 1997 of a 30-year Guatemalan civil war (where 90,000 citizens were killed). There is a growing wisdom of peace within humanity, even within those who have had their families murdered by their enemies—enemies who are now sitting at the table across from them, with the new consciousness of tolerance and change.

Resolution and the will for peace are slowly beginning to win, over eons of hatred and feelings of "revenge at any cost." Even the Middle East is beginning to show the contradiction. The idea of peace is beginning to win over the idea of victory or revenge or hatred, or the fact that something is deserved by lineage or promise. Ordinary citizens of that area are tired of conflict, and are ready to settle or compromise 3,000 year-old arguments, looking for ways of doing so with honor, but also fairness. Part of the conflict and bloodshed we watch exemplifies this very fact. There are still factions that hate, but they are at odds with their very own leadership.

From those I have spoken to who actually live in those areas, moms and dads in those fine countries have INTENT to raise healthy children in an atmosphere of peace and appropriate worship according to their lineage, no matter what ancient tongue they speak. Both sides want this! Poll the ordinary population and see. Among themselves they have tolerance that has not yet hit the halls of their own governmental seats. The INTENT of the people who live there, and consciousness of this New Age, will eventually win this battle. In the process, it will dash the Armageddon scenario to bits, and many religious scholars worldwide will try to find answers as to what the "delay" is.

Human consciousness is changing worldwide. Angel shops are springing up all over our continent. Alternate healing (even astrology) has been featured on the covers of major mainstream magazines such as *Time* and *Life* in the past years. Our television, besides giving us doom-and-gloom prediction programs, is also giving us prime time angel specials and even regular programming with angelic themes and spiritual overtones.* Many of our theatrical releases are broaching New Age themes and are becoming more metaphysical within their messages.

The wealthiest men and women on Earth are suddenly deciding to share their wealth with "no strings attached" for the humanitarian efforts of the United Nations and other worldwide humane efforts. I just want to mention that this absolutely flies in the face of sensational information given to us, as New Age believers, that the super-wealthy were part of a closely kept and very secret "control the world" conspiracy. If so, their actions are not showing it.

The TV lineup for Fall 1997: *Nothing Sacred* (ABC) A priest struggles with his flock and faith. *Good News* (UPN) A new pastor arrives to preach, teach and sing the gospel. *Soul Man* (ABC) A motorcycle-riding minister is also a single dad. *Teen Angel* (ABC) A dead kid comes back as his best buddy's guardian angel. *Touched by an Angel* (CBS) Angels visit troubled humans and tell them to trust God.

"In a March 97 *TV Guide* poll 61% of the respondents wanted more references to God in prime time." 1 (next page)

> "Universal Television is developing a sitcom for gospel singer Kirk Franklin, CBS will devote four hours this spring to a *Celestine Prophecy* miniseries. James martin, of the Catholic magazine *America',* postulates that all this activity is reflective of a general trend toward spirituality." [1]

The overview is important, rather than just what you are seeing on your local news programs. In a venue where sensationalism and bad news drives media subject matter, it is sometimes hard to get a good grasp of the overall changes that are occurring. From the lowest crime rate in New York's history, to a constant stream of stories about alternate medicine wings being included in hospital construction programs, there is definitely a consciousness shift taking place within our continent, and the planet, and it is due to the INTENT of human beings, and a critical mass that is slowly being achieved.

I ask you to check out the science chapter of this book (Chapter Ten). Find out what scientists are reporting regarding the power of the human mind. I don't mind revealing what my contention is regarding the "missing link" in physics. It is *human consciousness!* I believe that LOVE has the power to change matter and I'm not alone. More and more New Age scholars, progressive thinkers, and yes, even quantum physics researchers are agreeing that there is "something there" regarding the power of consciousness on physical matter. A 1997 address given on C-SPAN by Deepak Chopra basically echoes this same exact theme!

Fear-based scenarios are sensational, even if false. Good news does not sell like bad news. Even today, there are metaphysical newspapers (I call them *metatabs*—metaphysical tabloids) that are feeding us the most negative scenarios imaginable about our

---

[1] *Time* magazine, September 22 1997, "The God Squad".

future. From covert governmental enslaving programs with alien cooperation, to the Earth tilting on its axis soon, they spit out their fear-based messages in the name of the New Age. Monthly, themes are given that we, as humanity, are headed metaphorically into the dumper. And monthly, seeming "proof" is trotted out using hearsay and opinion by "experts" and "eye-witnesses." These are the same kinds of experts and eye-witnesses who gave us spectacular unbelievable scenarios regarding the Hale-Bopp comet in 1997, remember? These metatabs told us that something four times the size of Earth was accompanying the comet, and that a worldwide conspiracy of all telescope owners (amateur and all observatories) kept us (the regular folk) from seeing it. Evidently, as the story went, we would be too afraid if we knew the "truth." Aliens were going to be disgorged from this huge object and invade, or at the very least, they were going to pass by and give us messages and wave a lot. Thirty-nine people in my town believed all of this, by the way, and are now dead by their own hand. During all this hubbub, the co-discoverer of the Hale-Bopp comet, Alan Hale, was contacted regarding this spectacular information. Using documented photographs, Mr. Hale proved that it wasn't so. Instead of people all over the planet breathing a sigh of relief, Mr. Hale got hate mail! It seemed that the truth just wasn't spectacular enough. Not enough drama. Not enough conspiracy. Not enough fear.

INTENT is extremely powerful these days, and perhaps we ought to stop a moment and look carefully at what we are doing in our everyday lives to use it. Those who understand the new concept of "Partnering with God" understand that INTENT, plus partnering with the Higher Self, can "co-create" personal miracles, basically creating our own reality within the scope of walking through life. In addition, it seems that it helps those around us as well (back to the "Parable of the Tar Pit" as given in the transcription of the 1995 Kryon United Nations channel in Chapter Six). INTENT can also give us total discernment over what is true and untrue, creating peace over fear, and dispelling bogus fear-based information. To accept and believe all that is being fed to you by the fear-based messengers is to **totally give away your new power**. Is that what you had in mind for your life?

The following Kryon channel is going to give you some information regarding this co-creation gift, and some of its attributes, but I want to also discuss the literalness of it as well. Humans are powerful. As discussed in past books and articles, the 11:11 time-window a few years ago gave our human DNA permission to accept new power and changes. This was the beginning of the power we now are receiving regarding INTENT. Our intent is absolutely awesome in its effect on our lives, and we should be aware of what this means—not only when we use it when *partnering* with our Higher Selves—but also for those using it unwittingly *without* partnering.

Here is an example of what I mean. Let's say you are faced with an upcoming challenge. There is the potential of losing your home, job, business, or some other major issue that seemingly is totally out of your control. These situations, by the way, are exactly the ones that Spirit invites us to change, through "partnering and co-creative intent." It's the "*co*," however, that is critical. Instead of turning to our new gifts of Spirit, some people go right into fear reactions at challenges such as this. They verbalize out loud, "*I'm so afraid! Nothing ever goes right for me! This will be still another horrible thing in my life!*"**Bingo!** Their biology, the planet, and all the elements around them hear their powerful request through human INTENT. Let's see now, the INTENT was that it *should not go right*, and that *still another horrible thing will happen*. That's the intent as verbalized, and the physical universe (not the spiritual Higher Self part) will do everything to allow for the completion of that powerful human's intent. *Lee, are you saying that we can verbalize our own demise?* Absolutely! Your power is that great. Be careful what you say. Be careful what your intent is for yourself! Want to see what Kryon says about this exact thing? Go to page 328 in Chapter Nine.

The next time you have a major challenge—one that makes your palms sweat with fear—try this: (1) Immediately look at why it might be happening from a metaphysical point of view. What is the lesson? Why now? What does it mean metaphorically (there is almost always an obvious answer). (2) Meditate and co-create PEACE over the fear. Do this first. Don't start working the problem yet, or trying to create the solution. Get peaceful first! This gift of peace is yours for the asking and can be created! (3) Wait at least three days before you do anything about the actual problem. (4) Take responsibility for it. Understand that sometime when you had the "mind of God," you helped plan this test. Your Higher Self wanted this experience, and now here it is on schedule. With the planning of the test, you also (from the depth of your interdimensional wisdom) created the solution! (5) Finally, face off with your divine "partner," and start co-creating the solution you designed. When you do, don't tell your "partner—Higher Self"—how to solve it. Instead, visualize it being solved and gone, with a win-win solution for all parties.

Just as 1997 started coming to an end, and right before we gave this book to the printer, Kryon started channeling about the *golden platter*. He has given us yet another visualization regarding our problems on the Earth. Go back and read the "Parable of the Missing Bridge" in Kryon Book IV, *The Parables of Kryon*. This parable is the story of Henry speeding toward a chasm where a bridge was removed. He is told to "*keep going*," but is very fearful since the bridge is gone. Just as he is about to soar into space where the old bridge used to be, he is instead waved onto a new road where a brand-new bridge has been constructed out of sight of the old road Henry used day after day. Henry had never realized the new bridge was under construction, and is amazed by its beauty and size as he speeds over it. His problem is instantly over! He also realizes something else—construction on the new bridge was started long before the old one was removed, and long before he had started co-creating a solution for his own problem. Think about it.

Kryon tells us that there is a "golden platter" held by the "golden angel" (see Chapter One) that has all the solutions of every problem and test you will ever encounter on the planet! Just as when you were in school, the answers to every test you took were known in advance by those giving the lessons. So it is that the answers and solutions to your life's challenges are known by your Higher Self long before you ask!

How does it make you feel to know that you don't have to force solutions to the problems before you? How does it make you feel to know that perfect Divine solutions are available now and have been designed by you, just like the challenges were?

Amazing? You bet. Too weird to be true? Too many New Age people are discovering these Divine solutions for them to be flukes. It's real, and it's all part of the love of God. INTENT is the key, and intent while "Partnering with God" will unlock that golden platter and present amazing solutions to everyday issues.

Perhaps this should be the theme of the next Kryon book.

It's that important.

Lee Carroll

Kryon Channeling...

Greetings, dear ones, we wish to tell you something that is on many minds about co-creation. We would like to give you some information on the hows and whys of this powerful new gift..

What is it? First, we say that co-creation is that process whereby you as human beings can interact with your Higher Self, that piece of God that resides in each of you, to change the reality of your life. Big words—big concepts. **But the biggest hurdle is the actual belief that this process can exist.** Some of you have said, *"Oh, what a marvelous new gift. How long has it been around?"* We say, "About two thousand years!" For the great master of love himself was the one who first reported it to you. He said, *"All of you can be like me—as a child of God!"* He was the one who invited Peter to walk on the water, and Peter did. That's co-creation. But in this New Age, as you approach the millennium and the end of the Mayan calendar, these gifts of yours have been intensified far beyond those you had in the days when the great master of love walked the planet. So now the information comes forward as to how to actually make the gifts work, as well as some of the attributes around them. These will be explained so that there are few human assumptions in your thinking.

Rules. *"What are the rules around co-creation?"* you might ask. There are not very many of them, but one of the chief ones is often misunderstood, so we will now clear it up for you.

You can only co-create reality for yourself. Oh, there have been those who have asked, *"Kryon, does this mean we cannot pray for others? What about the energy of a group together praying for the healing of those who need it the most?"* Let us give you an example, and again, we're going to use our favorite example of a train.

It is like this: There are two trains sitting on a track. One is yours and one belongs to another human being. Each one of you is allowed to do anything you wish energy-wise to the other train that might enhance it and make it better. The engine sits there chugging and ready to move forward. You are permitted to address the other engine, to give it oil, to scrub it clean, to paint it and make it beautiful, to make it feel peaceful, to quiet the noise, if you will. You are allowed everything, except one thing: You cannot stoke its engine. You may do nothing to make it move forward.

As you look at your own train, you are allowed everything, including to stoke its engine, and put the coal in the fire to move it forward. So the speed and direction of your engine is *your* decision, and *yours* alone. Only *you* may move your own engine.

So are we saying that you cannot pray for others? No. What you may do is to give wonderful energy for their peacefulness, for their preparation, and for their healing. But oh, dear ones, they are the only ones who can make their lives move forward and balance themselves with their own INTENT! Healers, listen to this, for we have said this before and it has to do with co-creation (and many of you already understand this fully). Some facilitators among you have those who lay on your tables come back over and over and over again, asking you to do the same healing for them. You prepare them, you balance the energy around them, and you make healing available for them (you make things ready for them to stoke their engine). You move the boulders out of their path, and when they get up off that table, they are again ready for Divine potential, and they are peaceful.

It is *their* process, dear ones, if they choose, to stoke the engine of their path with intent or not. They may indeed choose to simply come back and be prepared over and over and over. There is nothing you can do as a healer to move them forward besides what you are doing. Realize, however, that the facilitators are honored greatly because there are many humans that need the balance before they can stoke their engine and move forward with intent. Therefore, **the facilitator is often the catalyst for human empowerment**, and balances energy and prepares humans to move forward on their own. When it is time to move your personal engine forward on your path, it is done on your own, taking no one with you. We hope this clears up how it is that you can pray for others, but you can only co-create for yourself with your own intent. Only you can move yourself into your own contract.

Let us speak more about this INTENT. We have told you that intent is extremely powerful, for it contains the wisdom of Spirit itself. Think for a moment what the "*co*" of co-creation means. This is the mechanics of the new tool and the new gift of Spirit, for "*co*" means "*you and Spirit*." In this case, "Spirit" is your Higher Self, the piece of God, and the piece of love that is from the Great Central Source that you all carry with you.

Create negativity for others? Some of you have said, "*Oh, this is a dangerous thing, this co-creation. Humans could create bad things for other people. If I'm not careful, I could even create bad things for myself.*" And we say, "Oh, dear ones, release your fear!" Remember the axioms: (1) You only create for yourself (not others), and (2) the word *co-creation* is speaking of a partnership with God! You don't understand the anointed spot that spiritual intent creates! You don't understand the "*co*'" yet. **For when you give intent to have any kind of a cooperative hand-hold with the Spirit of God, there is no evil or dark thing that can come into your life.** Evil is defined as an essence that totally lacks the love of God. As you stand with a hand-hold of spiritual co-creation, you are co-creating with God. You cannot create something bad for anyone, for it simply is not possible within the scheme of a pure heart, or within the scope of the gift. It is not in the agenda. It is not in the consciousness of love, so stop worrying. Let your intent be pure, and you will move forward in your co-creation.

It is impossible to give pure intent while holding the hand of your Higher Self and cause negativity in your own life. Listen to me when I tell you this, for it is pure truth. The co-creative process is a miracle of the human/God partnership and contains the seeds for all to benefit around you! It is the fear-based consciousness of your duality that tells you otherwise. As for harming yourself, the only thing that can do that is the **use of intent without the partnership**, by negative verbalization, instead of co-creation. Even though the "*co*" is missing, your human power of intent is still very active and potent. When you fully understand this concept, you will understand how you can instruct your body and consciousness into fear, unrest, victimization, and lack of self-worth. It "listens" to everything you tell it.

To exemplify the spiritual co-creative process, we are going to give you a story. There is going to be much told in the cracks and crannies of this tale about the attributes of co-creation. We want you to listen carefully, and put yourself in the place of Timothy as we tell you his story. We have learned long ago that humans respond to parables and remember them far longer than just facts. And so it is with great joy that we bring you the story of *Timothy and His Co-Creative Power*.

Timothy and His Co-Creative Power

Timothy was an enlightened human being. He lived in a grand town—a town with a beautiful river running through it, and he loved this place. Now Timothy had a passion. You see, all of his life he wanted to be a researcher—a doctor of research—one who would study humanity and make great medical changes to help all. And so it was that much of Timothy's life was spent obtaining this research degree. And he was indeed pleased that his life was going well, for he graduated with honors and he was a man of great intellect. Balancing his intellect was his spirituality, because Timothy was also a meditator.

Now, Timothy knew about co-creation. He also knew about the gift of Spirit that would allow him to void his karma. So he gave INTENT for his karma to be cleared so that he might move forward on his path. At the same time, Timothy decided to co-create what he wanted most in life. Timothy came into the Earth plane with a passion. Ever since he saw one, he wanted to know what the miracle was regarding the *autistic child*. For Timothy had a feeling that ran up and down his spine when he saw one such as this. He said to himself, "Even though some people find this tragic,

I feel there is a miracle there. I just know there is! Research is missing something—something important." *Now within the confines of this story of Timothy and co-creation, dear ones, there is scientific truth. For indeed there is a miracle in the autistic child waiting to be discovered—something that will help not only them, but humanity. And we invite you to find it.*

And so it was that Timothy decided to sit down and co-create his reality, for he understood about this New Age, and knew the process could be done. So he decided to co-create a situation where he would work with autistic children, and he would do it with colleagues who were meant to do it with him in a funded program within the city he loved. A big order, perhaps, but that's what his passion was. So Timothy held ceremony around his co-creation, and on his knees he said, *"Oh, Spirit, in the name of love, and all that is in this New Age that is given to me as a gift, I claim the power of co-creation. I co-create that I would have this vision, my passion, of working with the autistic child in this beautiful city of mine with others of like mind."* Now Timothy was also a wise, enlightened man, so he also said, *"But there are also things I know I am not aware of, so my prayer is that I be allowed to be in my contract, whatever it is."* But there was still part of Timothy that said quickly and softly after every meditation, *"Oh, but please let it be here, with the autistic child research"* [audience laughter].

Three months went by and nothing happened regarding his request, but Timothy continued his co-creative verbalization. It was an honoring of Spirit each time he said it, and he said it as often as he could: *"I co-create in the name of Spirit to be in my contract—right where I should be."*

Two more months went by and nothing happened. Now Timothy was not discouraged, but he was impatient. *"Why has nothing happened?"* he wondered. *"Ah, I know. I probably have to do something to move it along.* And so Timothy took his impressive credentials and he spread them around to the adjacent cities, saying to himself, "Perhaps this will motivate the process. This will start the funding, and this will create the interest." Timothy was right, **for Spirit was indeed waiting for Timothy to take the first step,** and he realized as he did that he had forgotten to physically *participate* in the work of the co-creation miracle.

Almost immediately, Timothy got a letter that bore a medical return address. As he opened it, he felt the tingle go up and down his spine that seemed to indicate something special was happening. Timothy said out loud, *"Oh, this is a window of opportunity. Thank you, Guides. I recognize the signs. Whatever is part of this letter is part of what I am to do."* Again, Timothy was correct, for after the letter was carefully opened, he read with great joy the offer that he was given within the words of the letter. He was being asked to come and join colleagues of like mind—other researchers who were studying the attributes of humanism. But his heart sank when he saw where the offer was from, for it was 300 miles to the north in a place that he never considered living. Worse than that, the study was not about children at all. Appropriately, but disheartening to Timothy, it was the study of the aged, and the diseases that set upon them in his society.

Now Timothy knew that this is not what he exactly wanted, but it was so close! He longed to be in the presence of those who felt the same about research and human studies. Just think of it—a small group of researchers whom he could study with and make a difference for the planet! He had the chills, and he knew this was the window of opportunity he had created, and so Timothy took it.

He arrived in a town 300 miles to the north and began his life there, and an odd thing happened almost immediately. Like a small miracle taking place, he received a house to live in that he was shortly able to purchase. Through anomalies of the financial system and a good-hearted person, Timothy owned this home within three weeks of his arrival. This is something he never thought would be possible so quickly in his life, and it was significant to him. Although the house was bigger than he needed, it represented something that was important in his culture, and also set him up for something yet to be revealed. Timothy thanked Spirit for this miracle, and knew that this was a strong validation along his path indicating that he was at the right place at the right time.

Timothy moved on to start work with his colleagues. There were seven of them, Timothy being the eighth one. And the more he worked with them, the more he enjoyed them. He got to know them, each one, and spent time in their homes and with their families. Not all of them had Timothy's New Age belief system. In fact, some of them had the old-energy religious beliefs, and were of the tribes of David, but they were all princes and princesses in Timothy's mind. For he shared the love of humanity with them, and the love of the work and the compassion of research with them, and he never judged them for their beliefs or their heritage.

Ever mindful of his real passion, Timothy would go home and write letters to all those he knew who were working on autistic children's problems and ask, "*This is my opinion; what do you think?*" Therefore, he kept alive his hope about working with the autistic children. Timothy kept up with autistic developments even though he was not yet in the actual field. He felt good about the way things were working out, but then there was a change.

Ah, dear ones, something happened to Timothy. There were times when he started to sigh a lot. He stuttered often. Timothy found himself looking at his shoes, and he found himself staring at a certain wall for hours on end. He wasn't sleeping very well either. Timothy's chemistry was changing, and he knew it. Timothy was experiencing what humans call a *temporary insanity*! You see, Timothy had fallen in love [audience laughter]!

Oh, she was beautiful, this white-coated doctor he was working with—the one he could barely speak to without going into a stupor. What was she thinking about him? Timothy had never been interested in a relationship. All he had was his passion for work with the autistic children. He hadn't been with women much, and he did not know how to go about approaching a relationship. Timothy felt he was not worthy, and then a miracle happened in his life, for the beautiful one in the white coat looked at him one day and said, *"Timothy, I love you."* Oh! Then he really was insane for a while [more laughter]!

And so it was that Timothy met the one he was supposed to meet, you see, at the right time and the right place—something that he had no idea about back in the city 300 miles to the south— something that he didn't even seem to need or want. *A woman would get in the way of a career*, Timothy had thought. Oh, but not this precious one, for she loved what he loved. This one appreciated what he appreciated. This one meditated with him; she understood the New Age, and as they got to know each other, he realized that she had given intent using her co-creation to also be in the right place at the right time! Does this really surprise any of you?

And so the love of God had struck, guiding Timothy 300 miles to a place where he did not want to go, and involving him in research that he did not want to do, for the purpose of combining him with his life's partner. Timothy celebrated, as he partnered with this one, and they indeed married in that city. And then the big miracle house was just the right size, you see.

Timothy moved forward in his work, and great things were accomplished. With Sarah's help and the help of those colleagues with him, they found many things about the diseases of the aged. In fact, their project was scheduled to end. They had done all they could. Three years went by, and they came to the end of the time of their research. Timothy did not have any idea what was going to happen at that time. Long ago he had stopped co-creating in his mind. Timothy had thought mistakenly that God was done— that perhaps he wasn't supposed to have his passion—that what he had was *okay* and *good enough*. After all, look what he had! Look at the happiness he enjoyed. Look at the joy he possessed daily. What could be better than this?

It was when the other letter came at the end of the project and he held it in his hands that he recognized the name on the letter and again felt the chills. It was from the one that he had been corresponding with regarding the autistic work. Timothy put the letter on the table and looked at it. He said, *"Oh, I don't even want to open this! Its energy is amazing!"* As he looked at the letter, all the verbalization in his meditations came flooding back to him. He used to say, *"Oh, Spirit, I co-create that I be in my sweet spot—in the right place at the right time."* Timothy couldn't stand the suspense and opened the letter.

The letter read, *"Dear Timothy: We have an opportunity for you to work in the city in which you were born, and the funding is in place for the study of the autistic child. Would it be possible for you to assemble a team of colleagues and come home?"* Timothy dropped the letter in disbelief! He realized the overview of the planning and the appropriateness of it all. Timothy celebrated with his wife the fact that Spirit had never forgotten in the years that had gone by what his original request was—*"I want to be in the right place at the right time,"* he had said. *"I want to be everything I said I'd be."*

And so it was that Timothy took the colleagues whom he had worked with so successfully in the town 300 miles to the north, and returned to his home and started work with the very ones whom he had come to know. And they did great things, indeed, and they participated in Timothy's sweet spot!

Now there is great love connected with this story of Timothy, and we might start analyzing it, you and I, so that you may apply it to your life. But you see, the story isn't over yet. No. There is one thing more. It is a glorious thing. It is something precious—filled with love, ceremony, and honor. For Timothy's wife, Sarah, gave birth to a son they called John. And, dear ones, as soon as it could be determined, the son was found to be autistic. Sarah and Timothy went to their altar, and because of their overview of life, and because of their enlightenment and wisdom in Spirit, they celebrated that moment! And they brought their son with them and they sat him on the floor in front of them. He looked at them with wide eyes—this precious gifted one. And they said to him, *"John, we know you don't understand us, but you ARE in the right place at the right time"* [enthusiastic audience applause]!

You see, the appropriateness of Spirit and the love of God had been given again, and what some would think of as a tragedy was an honored blessing for Timothy and Sarah, and these enlightened human parents knew it. Indeed, there could have been no greater parents than these for John.

As we analyze this story, dear ones, we ask you to look back and see what happened. Timothy gave intent for what he wanted and what he needed. The first thing that happened was nothing at all. Until Timothy moved accordingly and decided he would take the first step, nothing happened. Timothy realized he was part of the *"co"*—Spirit and human. That's when he sent out the letters. Timothy was impatient, but Spirit was not. From the time he partially got what he asked for, three years had gone by and he found himself in another city doing things that he had no idea needed to be done. Although it wasn't exactly what he had asked for, Timothy was blessed at every point. He was given validations when it was necessary. His guides gave him chills to know where the windows of opportunities were, even after Timothy had stopped co-creating. He felt things were *good enough*, but Spirit fulfilled the contract when the timing was correct to do so! Then he and Sarah received the final gift at the end—one that Timothy could never had known would be appropriate, but was.

Do you see the overview of timing? Do you understand that all is not what it seems? Do you understand that a great part of co-creating with spirit is patience and faith? Timothy did, and he was honored with his contract. Did you also notice that those around him were helped and blessed by his patience and his faith? Again, we bring you to see the fact that when you are in your contract, those around you win with you! Often, even though you create for yourself only, those around you are also changed in the process.

We gave you this story so that you could see that all things are possible in your life! We know that some of you are in the process of co-creating. The first thing we wish to tell you is this: YOU ARE WORTHY OF THIS GIFT! If you do not think so and cannot bring it to your own consciousness that you are, then you should get facilitation that will help you polarize yourself—balance yourself so that you may move forward and stoke that engine of worthiness, for you are indeed worthy.

Do not be afraid to create abundance in your life, dear ones. Don't you think you deserve it? In the most abundant society of the planet, don't you think you deserve it? We speak about the abundance of the essence of Spirit itself, and of the abundance of peace in your life.

And so it is this night that we leave you. We leave you in a state of love, and as you exit this place and return home, before you retire this night, know this: Those entities around you that are assigned to you and are part of your aura, regularly celebrate your life! They are waiting to spring into action at your words and your INTENT. They are part of the bridge between you and your Higher Self. You are never alone! That piece of God which is your Higher Self is waiting to take you to the place that you came in for—the passion that is your contract—the part of *home* you always carry with you—the *remembrance* of who you are, and why you are here!

And so it is.   *Kryon*

Most-Asked Questions

Chapter Nine

Most-Asked Questions
Chapter Nine

From the writer...

Within the last two years, questions were gathered on a regular basis from readers all over the country. Many of these were published in various journals, and in the *Kryon Quarterly* (now, don't you wish you had a subscription?). I have tried to include some of the most-asked questions about metaphysics and life in general in these next few pages. Some of the answers may surprise you, and some are what you might have always suspected or hoped would be the case. Some difficult questions regarding controversial subjects have also been included. Here is the list of categories that will be covered by Kryon in this chapter.

```
Animals/Mammals
Ascension
Contracts/Sweet spot
Death
Devas and Little People
Guides
Homosexuality
Human Soul
Human Vibrational Shift
Implant/Release
Light Workers/ Warriors
Live Essence Medicines
Magnetic Mattresses
Meditation
Music
Negativity and Fear
Ouiji Boards
Relationships
Soulmates/ Twin Flames
Walk-Ins
World Financial Collapse
```

Animals and Mammals

Question: Are animals on the planet also dearly loved (as you say we are)? What is their role? Do they have souls? What about the mammals in the sea? I have trouble understanding why many innocent creatures suffer so greatly at the hands of man.

Answer: When we say "you are dearly loved," we are speaking of the fact that you and I know each other, and that your human soul is at a cosmic energy level that is that same as ours is, with a Merkabah that is like ours. It has what you call a soul, which is an actual piece of God! That soul is here in lesson on this planet for great purpose.

The animals are not here in lesson experience as you are, but in service to make your goal possible. They are entities that do not carry the same lesson or piece of God that you do, but that indeed are "dearly loved" and play a great part in Earth's plan.

The animals are here for several reasons, and some of the reasons will make absolute sense to many of you and shock the rest. Many animals on the planet are here for energy balance. There is much to tell you here, but for now let us say that the energy you all feel around the mammals of the sea is real, for they are here for an inspired and anointed purpose that will show itself in the future. For now, they hold a specific balance for the planet that is indeed spiritual! Many large animals of the forest are also here for planetary balance. Other animals are here just for your comfort and company. Many of you have already felt the love they carry for humans, and you know of what I speak. They also hold energy and respond to your thoughts. They know intuitively things you cannot and will never "see." They are here in order to help balance humans as you live your lives on this planet.

Finally, there are many that are here for you to eat [gasp!]. They come in service to humanity to allow for your sustenance and health. Their entire purpose is to feed humanity in certain parts of the planet. Without them, it would be impossible to sustain humanity above five billion souls. For those who doubt that this is so we invite you to study the ancient ones, and how they regularly "called" an animal into their village for sustenance. Ceremony resulted in a normally fierce animal coming by agreement into the village in a docile way where it was honored and eaten. This was by agreement between animal and human—and was well understood. This is not to say that all humans should eat meat. Many of you regularly do not eat meat and balance your bodies without it. This is an honored process and will result in good health, but it should not be looked at as something you are doing for the animals. Do it for yourself.

You also asked about the suffering of animals at the hands of humans. It is your choice to honor these creatures or not to—no matter what their specific purpose is. The ones that are to be consumed should be honored as much as the ones that keep you company—perhaps even more so! What you do with them is your karma and shows your enlightenment. The animals know why they are here, and humans should be respectful of all entities on the planet (and there are many) who have agreed to come in to service this great planet of free choice. Those of you who work with the animals to make their lives better while they are here are truly doing something that counts! Yes, they are dearly loved.

Ascension (see Chapter Five in this book)

Question: *I've heard a lot about "ascension" lately. Everyone seems to have a different idea about what it is. Some think it means being taken off by ETs. Others say our physical bodies will become invisible, and some say nothing will happen to us physically but that we will just move into our next lifetime in this body. Could you help me understand the ascension process?*

Answer: Ascension is the invitation to each human being to move into the next dimensions slowly through the process of learning and enlightened techniques, while remaining on the planet. It is a great vibratory change, and it isn't for everyone. Indeed, it allows you to remain in biology and move into the next incarnation without death (hence, the meaning of the word *ascension*).

It is imperative that you stay here if you wish to change the planet, but there is no judgment or penalty for those who wish to leave after they are into the higher vibrations. Each individual will discern what is best, and there are reasons that you are not aware of for many of these kinds of individual decisions. Some have to do with energy balance on the planet, or unfinished galactic plans for a specific entity. When you begin this trek, you begin to move into the energy of the God part of you, and it can be intense. Not all of you are asked to do this, however, and there is no "right" or "wrong" about your decision to wait, or not do it at all. Many will remain in a lower vibration (when compared to ascension status, but high when compared to your existing vibration) that needs to hold certain grounding attributes for the planet itself. This will be clearer over time as you create the "bed" for the new graduate Earth to exist.

As we have discussed before, on the 12:12 it was necessary for at least 144,000 to intend this status, and we have told you before that this indeed happened. It probably will not surprise you to learn that most of the humans who took this vibrational increase were already prepared, and were not on the continent you call America. All this is appropriate and does not detract from your goal within your culture. Those who took this status are very aware that the target for vibrational change has no political or continental boundaries, and they count on you to continue to help the planet.

It will be necessary for many on your continent to also take this step in order for the vibration of the planet to respond accordingly, and to take you into the next millennium toward your "null time" of 2012. Training for this is already being brought to you. In 2012 (or thereabouts), the entire planet (the very dirt itself) will enjoy the potential of shifting to another dimension, and will slowly move toward that goal—not an abrupt change, but permission for a slow change. Along the way you will also have help, since your dimensional and vibrational shift will actually be a beacon to those who stand by, ready to show you more about the cosmos (what you have called the ETs). New science will be required to make spiritual shifts (surprise!), and you will benefit greatly from this help.

It's up to you, however, to make the preparations. This is what is happening all over the globe by intent of the current light workers. Your work in this year will be far greater than it was last year, but the speed at which you change your global vibration and consciousness will indeed affect both the timetable for your Earth change and the timetable for those you are scheduled to meet.

Contracts—Sweet Spot (See Chapter Eight in this book)
Question: How do I know if I'm in my contract? What exactly is a contract?

Answer: Have you taken responsibility for the conditions you find yourself in? How is your life going? Do you have peace? Do you feel victimized? Is there tolerance for other humans and conditions around you? What action have you taken spiritually to improve your life and lift your frequency? All of these things relate to your quest of finding that "sweet spot" we call your contract.

There has been more channeled on this subject than any other, for it relates to your ability for peace and self-healing. It is also the first step to what you call an "ascended status" on this planet (see the last question).

The *mind* of Spirit is sometimes confusing and is hidden from you while you are here. This, of course, is the duality of your entity. Many have tried to analyze it, but the intellect fails completely when it comes to understanding or explaining the incredible purity of the love energy that emanates from the planning you created for yourself.

There is no greater element of awe that we have for you than within the fact that you would stand in line to be here at this time! Figuratively, you sat in a grand place where you "contracted" your windows of opportunity with the others around you for the next few lives. Without any kind of predestination, you contracted with the others to play out the drama of the events you find yourself in. Are you male or female? Were you abused? Is there anger and hate in your life? Does abundance feel completely out of reach while you see it all around you for others? Are there those around you who regularly irritate and stir you up? All of these things were planned by you, and the others around you, and represent the mind of God— YOU, when you were not here!

The task is to recognize the contract. Accept the new gifts of Spirit! Take responsibility for what is happening to you, since you planned it. Then put on the mantle of Spirit and take action to co-create your passion...and your sweet spot in life. There is no problem that you cannot solve! Peace and healing can be yours if you own these principles. Then you can get on with what you planned for yourself over this and the next incarnation (while you remain in your biology), which we call your contract and your passion.

When you finally realize that by moving your karma aside and increasing your vibration, you can indeed claim the contract of this and the next incarnation, a whole new perspective will open up for you as to what can be accomplished.

We applaud you in your efforts and continue to love you unconditionally for your quest to raise your frequency—and the vibration of Earth itself!

Question: In Book III, you stress that each of us is fully responsible for everything in our lives, and that by acknowledging this we gain more control over things. It would appear that there is a new "Golden Rule" for the New Age, according to Kryon and friends, which states, "Whatever is done unto you, you are fully responsible for; you set it up yourself for your lesson," and conversely, "Whatever I do unto you is merely a fulfillment of a role you set up

for me to fulfill in your lesson." Whatever happened to the responsibility of the doer—the rapist, the mugger, the killer?

Answer: The very question and the tone of it betrays the duality
you live in, and what hides from you in the way things work. You
accurately present much of what Spirit wants you to know about
the way things work—then in your misunderstanding, you become
angry about it.

This is a complex subject, and it would be difficult even if you
had the consciousness of God, which is not possible while you are
here. It is this Divine understanding that tested the man Job—with
his permission—yet humans shrink in horror when they read what
happened to his family. Done in love? Yes. This is what we
absolutely cannot explain to you. The overview of lesson is foreign
to the human mind, as it should be to disguise it appropriately—
otherwise there is no lesson at all.

What you have to remember about this subject is that nothing
is predestined! You live on the PLANET OF FREE CHOICE, and
therefore may change any attribute you wish when you realize that
you indeed have that power (an enlightened consciousness).

Remember that when you arrive here there are several
imprints and gifts at your disposal. (1) You have a karmic overlay
that helps to "set up" agreements with others around you. This is
the area you discussed in your question—where seemingly negative things take place that we ask you to recognize as part of the
setup—but this attribute does not stand alone. (2) You have the
ability to change this setup at any time you wish and void your
karma! This is one of the New Age gifts and may be done at any
time, thereby allowing you the ability to avoid ever becoming the
victim, the rapist, or the killer. (3) The setups are only potentials
and agreements of lesson creation. They are not predestined and
don't necessarily have to happen at all. When they do, however,
we ask you to see how the "potentials" have played out, with your
permission, and invite you to recognize why they happened. Left

without any enlightenment or discovery of self, the potentials are more than likely to play out as planned. Remember my comment in a past channel?: "Don't be surprised if the one sent to Earth representing the hammer...is someday later in life surrounded by nails." The predispositions of karma naturally attract their counterparts, and play out the potential lessons—if left to do so.

Many of you will recognize this entire scenario and change to a higher vibration before even one karmic attribute takes place. This is where your victory really shines in the New Age! This is the prime example of responsibility, and karma voiding. Others of you find yourselves at the tail end of a heavy karmic attribute and now have the chance after the fact to take responsibility as either the doer or the victim. This responsibility after the fact is therefore also a victory. There was never intent by Spirit for any human to somehow recognize the spiritual aspects of a difficult plan and carry it out anyway. This would be a gross misrepresentation of what happens to people when they discover enlightenment, but understandable for humans to inquire about. It shows that many truly do not yet understand the light within, what it represents, or how it works.

When you truly recognize light, there isn't one of you who will chose the dark instead. If it seems that this takes place, then the light was never actually seen. The God within you, or "Higher Self," will always guide you to the truth. Your entire reason for being here is to discover this, and once it is before you, there isn't one of you that won't step into the light of home. Exposure to a higher vibration carries the attribute of severing the desire for a lower one. It is the physics of love.

Question: Dear Kryon, I am still having trouble understanding my contract. It's hard to ask to be in it when I am not aware that I can change my contract if I don't like it (that is, getting a fatal disease). Yet without knowing what It Is, how can I change it before it happens?

Question: Dear Kryon, in The Kryon Quarterly Issue #3, you state, "Will you walk into your fears in order to quickly get past them and move into your contract (the reason you came here)?" Must we move through all fear to get into our contract? Are there no fears or anxieties when we are in our contract? Is this the way to know?

Question: Dear Kryon, I have taken the "release," and it has been, as Kryon said, wonderful! With taking the "release," are the old contracts I set up now void?

Answer: It is human assumption that makes you think you only have ONE contract. It is true that Spirit uses the word *contract* as singular, and often asks you to find your "contract." Therefore you would naturally think that you only have one. Let me explain.

First, you have multiple contracts! (more on this in a moment). The reason Spirit only uses the singular word is because in the "now" of time as we are in, you are only aware of the current contract—whichever that would be. This communication anomaly is common with everything we do in channeling. There is simply no past or future for us, and often the "tense" of the language is odd, and now you get to see where plural and singular explanations are also unusual. The closer you get to the "now" time that we are in, the more you will understand. This is also why some human visionaries and seers that have an extremely clear vision of Earth changes, have returned from their visions to report on something they think is a spectacular upcoming event—only to be told by the geologists of your planet (gently) that what they clearly saw was the ancient past! It is therefore difficult for any of you to sort out what is current, gone, or coming, when you sit in the energy that we are in (it takes a great deal of practice in "not thinking like a human").

You pen contracts for yourselves long before you arrive. The basic ones are imprinted into your DNA first, and deal with karmic overlay. They are designed to complement and fulfill your karma, and you all have a potential to follow them. We have told you before that there is no predestination, but as we discussed in the second answer of this series, these overlays are like a magnet to your soul, and many of you go right down the path, as though you had no choice (which is not so).

When human karma is voided either by walking through it (the old method) or using the new release gift that is now yours (the new way), the next layer of contracts begin to activate. These are far more sacred and deal directly with you helping the planet's vibration (light working), instead of indirectly (working through personal karma and drama). Even those who are light workers have multiple possibilities for contracts, but I'm not necessarily speaking of which contract you choose from. Contracts are fulfilled in a linear fashion because you are in a linear time frame. Not too long ago, we gave you a parable of a man who lived his life doing many things well but felt he never found his contract. When he arrived on the other side of the veil, much to his surprise he found that he had stepped through multiple contracts in a linear fashion one at a time, helping many wherever he went and whatever he did! He had found them all, but was preoccupied looking for "it" while he was accomplishing "them."

Fear is common to all contracts—yes, even when you are vibrating at a high level. This is because it is the great tester of the soul and is the grand phantom of lesson. There is no time, even when in ascension (graduation) vibration, that fear does not come up to you and test you. In the old energy, it can create disease and death—such is its strength. As a light worker, it can be simply an irritant, but it is there, nevertheless. We have asked you to walk into the main human fear within the old energy (that of voiding your karma and vibrating at a higher level) in order to move on to your refined contracts. The fear is real! It's the fear of ridicule and even of death. It is often the "seed fear" of enlightenment that we have spoken of before. Once this initial fear is disarmed, however, the remaining fears are far more current, and arise only circumstantially instead of being ones that are with you always.

Ask my partner what he felt in April of this year when the main communication and news venue for his city asked him to go before thousands and explain the New Age! Ask him if he was afraid! YES! Such fear was real, but disabled in a moment by calling on the love source—but the fear was there. Ask him how he disarmed it and what he felt afterwards. It is a model of what is possible, and we give it willingly to Lee for him to experience it, and give you his solutions—one human to another. Even the channel, therefore, is poked and prodded by the same attributes as all the rest of you.

Do not expect your problems to disappear because you stand within your contract. The test of the planet is for you to realize who you are, and yet still interface with all the circumstances around you. It is by doing this that others around you will see how you deal with life. It is your peace and understanding in the face of real human drama that will make the highest impression on the others. You get to "feel" the fear as it arises, but you also get to recognize and experience the phantom it represents. Others will watch and learn from your peace.

If you search the channels of the past year, you will also discover something hiding—information that relates to how the Higher Self of each of you remains with the mind of God on the other side of the veil. It is in a place with others, continuing to plan your potentials, to allow for change as you engage in powerful spiritual intent. Therefore, your contract is always "current." This is more of a cosmic joke than you know!

Finally, remember this: It is the old-energy karmic contract that has you moving through disease and death, trouble and tribulation. These are things that have always been your "setups" to facilitate the planet. New contracts as light workers are about vibrational shift, helping the planet through meditation and healing, and STAYING ON THE PLANET FOR A VERY LONG TIME! We have spoken of this often in direct channel. We want you to stay! You have to, in order to accomplish what is before you!

Death

Question: I recently lost a loved one. His death was accidental, and the grief is overwhelming. Intellectually, I know he has gone to his true "homecoming," but emotionally, it is tearing me apart. How can I learn to understand and accept death?

Answer: Dear one, what you call synchronicity is at work here in this publication, for one of the channels that was selected for this book is about the *seven love connections* (page 77). One of those is the understanding of death.

I will not repeat what is given in that channel, but will ask that you read it. The true answer in your case is as follows: (1) Grieve for this one, and do not let anyone tell you not to. It is absolutely normal and is an honoring for his life. You will never forget him, and that is also appropriate. (2) Gradually understand and feel the truth that his passing was something that the two of you worked out together before you ever got here. Therefore, it is a "love gift" from him to you, one that is given for your growth and enlightenment. No greater gift can be given than this, and he asks you to "own it," for you helped in its creation. Then decide what it is you will do to honor his gift that will change you in a positive way for the rest of your life. Whatever that is will be your reciprocation to his gift.

Many take this special time for self-realization, and a move to the next enlightenment level. (3) As time goes on, move the knowledge of your INTELLECT that believes he has gone to his "homecoming" to your HEART. Know that only part of him has gone anywhere, and that his love energy remains with you! You can feel him and speak to him and communicate anytime you wish. If he chooses to, he might even give you communication back in your dreams. This is also common, and very real.

Do you think we can't understand the hurt of the heart? WE *ARE* LOVE! We know fully that there is perhaps no greater pain for the human being than that of the heart. You can carry this loved one's energy with you daily. Therefore, be free to feel him around you, and absorb the love. He is not gone at all and will accompany you for the rest of your life. We honor you all so greatly! Our love overflows with congratulations for the work you have done. Great, indeed, is this planet of free choice. Someday you will completely understand.

Devas and the Little People

Question: You told us that the 12:12 was significant because many of the unseen entities would be leaving Earth and passing their power to us. I regularly work with the devas of my garden. Are they leaving, too? They seem so present!

Answer: Let it be clear that there are many classes of entities that exist with you on this planet. You already know about humanity and that it is the focal point of the entire planetary existence. Next there is all the other life that you can see all around you that is also biological. Finally, there are all the entities that are balancing the planet in so many ways that you cannot see—and there are many more of them than there are of you! We do not itemize them for you, for it would be distracting—a situation where you would spend a great time looking for them, rather than the lessons and experience you came for.

Within the scope of these entities, there were many who held energy specifically for you as humans. You did not have the ability to hold any more of the energy of the Higher Self than a certain amount until things began changing some years ago (part of my job). Now we have told you that you are taking much of this energy away from these placeholding entities by agreement as you move toward graduation and ascension status. We have also told you that the energy level of the planet is always the same, but that the vibration is what is changing. In order to keep the energy the same, as you take on your power, the placeholders must therefore leave.

Many of you have experienced this, saying good-bye to many ancient ones in the forests and plains all around the Earth, and know of what I speak. Many times they had names, or their groups had names. There are tens of thousands of them that are now gone, and many that will leave in the future. Some of them lived within special areas that gave you special feelings when you walked there—and now you realize that indeed the specialness is gone in those areas. This is because they have departed in order to give you the power of the planet in a spiritual sense.

There are many, many more entities, however, that reside *in* the Earth that give the planet the life that we have spoken about. These are the ones that keep the balance of nature, as you call it, and respond directly to humans that work with the Earth. Some are called "Devas" and the *little ones* are the entities that made sacred spots in the forest. The "Devas" you speak about in your question are the ones that will always be with you until the very end of the existence of the planet. They are needed and extremely necessary for the "life within the dirt," as we have spoken before. They are necessary for a "living planet" that responds to the consciousness of humanity. You are the ones who have named them—therefore, the confusion. The ones you know are going to stay!

Your garden friends will be with you forever, and indeed respond to your efforts. On a grander scale, these are also the ones that hold the energy of the forests of the planet, the rocks of the desert, and the very air you breathe. There is so much here that would astound you! Give honor to the Earth, for it will give you honor back!

Guides

Question: How can I learn to communicate with my guides? How do I know if it's not just my own thoughts?

Answer: There is a communication with my partner within these very pages that will give you insight into this, for it was my honor to give you this information just recently.

It's impossible for your biology alone to give what you call precognition, or a "knowing" of something you believe you have seen before—but have not. Also, it can't easily give you an emotional "hit" on something you instantly see. Your intellect isn't fast enough to play a part in these things, and that's why your guides can give you these "pokes" before your intellect can analyze it away.

For years you have called this intuition, gut feeling, or *déjà vu*. Now you know what it really is. This is guide communication at its best, and uses emotion as its conduit. Therefore you can see that those who let themselves "feel" will be those that acknowledge the guidance of Spirit.

Give yourself permission to recognize these emotional attributes, and in your most quiet times, verbally acknowledge them. Tell the guides out loud that you love them—then stand back for action. Too simple? It is the human way of things to say you must work hard for any good thing. It is Spirit's message, however, that says you have deserved gifts waiting for you—simply for the asking, and that your work is in being here at all! The gifts, then, will enhance the real work of raising the frequency of the planet.

Homosexuality

Question: Dear Kryon, I am gay, and an enlightened man. I live in an American society that barely tolerates me, and actually has some laws against my way of life. The church I used to belong to cast me out as being evil and anti-God. I don't feel that I am violating some human ethic. My love is as true as any heterosexual, and I am a light worker. Tell me what I should know.

Answer: Dear one, less than two generations from now, there will be those who find this book and laugh at the quaintness of this very question. Before I answer, let me ask you and those reading this to examine a phenomenon about human society and "God."

Thirty years ago, interracial marriage was considered to be wrong by the laws of God. Now your society finds it common. The spiritual objections around it were either dropped or "rewritten" by those Divinely inspired and authorized to do so. Therefore, your actual interpretations of the instructions from God changed with your society's tolerance level—an interesting thing, indeed, how the interpretations of God seem to change regularly to match a changing culture!

The truth, of course, is that you find yourself in a situation that is known to create a test for you. Right now, in this time, you have agreed to come into your culture with an attribute that may alienate you from friends and religious followers. You have faced fear of rejection and have had to "swim upstream," so to speak, just as an everyday life occurrence. Your contract, therefore, has been set up well, and you are in the middle of it. Additionally, like so many like you, you have a Divine interest in yourselves! You feel part of the spiritual family. What a dichotomy indeed, to be judged as evil by those who are the high spiritual leaders—interpreting God for today's culture.

Now I say this: What is your **intent**? Is it to walk with love for all those around you and become an enlightened human being in this New Age? Is it to forgive those who see you as a spiritual blight on society? Can you have the kind of tolerance for them that they seem not to have for you? Can you overlook the fact that they freely quote the New Age master of love in order to condemn you, yet they don't seem to have the love tolerance that is the cornerstone of the master's message?

If the answer is yes, then there is nothing else you must do. Your INTENT is everything, and your life will be honored with peace over those who would cause unrest, and tolerance for the intolerable. Your sexual attributes are simply chemistry and setups within your DNA. They are given by agreement as gifts for you to experience in this life. Look on them in this fashion, and be comfortable with that fact that you are a perfect spiritual creation under God—loved beyond measure—just like all humans. But then you know that, don't you?

Human Soul

Question: Tell us more about our human soul. What is it? What are the particulars?

Answer: You have asked one of the most important, yet complex questions imaginable. How can Kryon tell you of principles that are foreign to your reasoning? How can Kryon give you a picture of something that would not make sense to you? If you are with a sightless human, can you suddenly explain the entire color pallet of nature? There is no experience that can give you a perception of a human soul. Without interdimensional sensory abilities to understand it, it is like so much nonsense.

Your humanness is temporary. Your soul is the "real" you. It resides in several places at the same time. One piece is within each cell of your body. Another is an energy "stamp" on the magnetics of the planet itself that indicates that you are here. Another part, which you call the Higher Self, is on the other side of the veil, creating solutions for your incarnation here, and responding to your enlightened, changing path with new planning sessions for your contracts.

Did you know you were interdimensional? Can you understand that you are in several places at once? In a time frame where your mind is "stuck" in a linear framework, can you understand the loop of real, spiritual time? What if I told you that your soul has the ability to *share* a human body with another (see walk-ins)? Only in your dreams and visions do you ever come close to the actual reality of existence.

Know this: Your soul is the blooming flower in the garden of the Universe. It is eternal and knows everything I know. It is far larger than you can ever realize. It survives in several places at once and many time frames at once. It is family. It is LOVE!

Now, you know all about it.

Human Vibrational Shift

Question: I have been doing bodywork for about fifteen years for friends and family (without pay, just as a service). Just lately, I have noticed that I can barely feel the energy from the people I facilitate, yet they all say they can feel my energy as I work on them. What causes this, and how can I get the feeling back?

Answer: Dear one, your work is indeed celebrated! We have mentioned before that the frontrunners of the New Age will often be the facilitators of the planet, those whose passion is to help others in so many ways. You are one of these.

The new energy paradigm for Earth is that the "torch has been passed" from the astral entities to humans. This means that much of what you "felt" in your work is being shifted to a new plane entirely. A direct answer to your question of *"How can I get the feeling back?"* is "You won't." It's now time for you to understand the mechanics of what is taking place, and for you to get used to other feelings that will help you with the "feedback" you need in order to know you are indeed plugged in to the energy.

Humans are now carrying all the energy of the whole for Earth. This is astounding, and it is the reason we celebrate your time now. Because of this, your work, the work of other body workers, and most meditators will feel a shift in what they got used to as a signal of knowing they were "in touch" with Spirit. Now the feeling will come from you and nowhere else (and never another human). This requires that you spend more time honoring the God within you, and start communications with your Higher Self to a degree that it will help you to know when you are at your peak of energy while working on others. Already you are beginning to have better results with your body work than before—and the joke is that you feel very little! Does this give you a hint as to the new mechanics? The incredible power passed to humanity can now be used for healing and co-creation in a very matter-of-fact way, and does not need the kind of ceremony or old feelings around it that it used to.

Those you work on will be very aware of your new power and your intuitiveness in the changes you will make within your procedures. Expect those you work on to feel a great deal! Tell them that they will, and stand back and trust Spirit to work through you. The new feeling is one of SELF-EMPOWERMENT. The only thing you will get from Spirit is a "love wash" from your Higher Self when you are in the middle of your work. Ask for it. Humans have reported that it is a very warm feeling of being honored and loved beyond measure. It is our gift to you for being in the right place at the right time. This is the "sweet spot" that we have spoken of repeatedly.

Question: Dear Kryon, you stated that the sphere in the Hale-Bopp comet was to "drop spirituality" on us. I am confused. I thought that we, as free willed beings, have the right to choose spirituality. I also thought this choice (spirituality) is something within each of us. Can you elaborate on the concept of dropping spirituality on us, and elaborate on the comet?

Answer: The 24-year window of potential as started in 1987 demands that more energy be brought to the planet in many ways. It's the reservoir that humans will use in the process of higher vibration and graduation. Perhaps it surprises many to know that three-dimensional physics is related to spirituality, and that energy for the purpose of human elevation must be provided. The planet simply does not contain this new energy quotient by itself. It needs more to allow for the humans to elevate themselves, like fuel is needed to win a race.

Your scientists just discovered one of the delivery systems. They now know where the gamma rays are coming from, and they are still reeling with the news (see science chapter). They found the most powerful energy source ever seen in the Universe—and it's also the farthest away! They are looking at the creative center! A short while ago, a very large asteroid brushed by you just outside of the orbit of your moon, shortly afterwards we gave you the comet. Each of these is a real three-dimensional delivery system of spiritual energy.

This spiritual energy is stored in the planet and on the grids (where else?), where all the Earth changes are occurring. This energy is waiting for humans to give intent for it. It, therefore, is a depository of new spiritual energy for any part of humanity that gives intent for it. With personal intent from within comes the new gifts of vibrational increase as drawn from the planet's attributes. This is free human choice! Now do you begin to understand how the planet is related to your own personal growth? It's actually your storehouse! Those who don't give intent for the energy will not receive it (their choice), and they will be unaware that it exists.

Question: *Dear Kryon, are we here on Earth for "experience" or "lesson"?*

Answer: Tomorrow when you awaken, are you going to "get up" or "get out" of bed? *Up* and *out* are very different, yet to you they mean the same thing. Your language is extremely limited when it comes to sacred interdimensional concepts. In actuality, you are here to "experience lesson"!

There is no either/or. You are here to *experience* remembrance of why you are here. The remembrance is of the past *experience* you had in other incarnations, which give you overlays of *experience* that you must now deal with. All of this experiencing is called *lesson* by some. Others call it karma. Others call it work!

Which enlightened one of you would tell any other human that you are walking around this planet to experience things and learn nothing? Tourists? The answer is none of you! Light workers recognize that there is a purpose and a goal. Therefore, the *experience* is to move forward and make a difference for the planet and the entire Universe. While many of you sit and ponder the meaning of the words, others will have already grasped the fact that the words are inadequate, and the power is really in the DOING!

Implant/Release

Question: After we take the implant and void our karma, does the co-creating happen immediately, or what? Second, I want to contact my guides and have one or more appear regularly. Is there a way to make this happen?

Answer: [with great humor] Each time humans ask if they should make a choice, and one of the choices is "or what," the humorous part of Spirit wants to tell them to choose "or what." We are interested in what that is, exactly!

We know the way you communicate, however, so the true meaning of your question is honored within this answer. Each of you is extremely different in your karmic path. As we have already discussed in many publications, some of you are ready right now to assume the new gifts of Spirit and start using them. Others might have to wait a bit to have them all in place. In either case, the gifts are yours now, but the implementation of them might take some understanding and practice. Again we tell you that your actions after giving your intent for the "implant" will make the biggest difference, as discussed in Kryon Book Three.

You might be interested in knowing that my partner, Lee, has never seen his guides. You might expect that the Kryon channel would have this ability, but he does not at the moment. Later, when he is more integrated, we have promised this for him. The same is true of you. Your personal vibration and integration with your Higher Self will totally determine your ability to see your guides.

Be aware that even if you do get to see them, it is not a normal physical happening, so don't expect it on a regular basis. Always be careful to stay grounded in these things. Part of you wants to be with Spirit and to go home! Seeing your guides is one step closer to that. Seeing them all the time is like asking to be removed from your lesson. For all of you, remember that asking for these things may tend to remove you so far from your three-dimensional human existence that it would not serve you or those around you. Any of you can slowly create a move to this side of the veil. In the process, you will lose touch with the reality of your lesson, and eventually will be alone in consciousness, having one foot on each side of the veil. You should know that there is no sacredness in this situation. Spirit wants you to stay grounded in the reality of your lesson and your own dimension. That's where the lesson is—and the work. It's far easier to leave your body than to stay in it!

This is the true reason that the "ascension process" for humanity now is so special and time-consuming in its accomplishment. To have ascension status and remain human is to have a dichotomous physical being walking the planet. Both body and Spirit have to understand being in a high vibration while being grounded on the planet. The ascension status, therefore, is a multidimensional one. The Avatar is an example of this, and shows the training necessary for such a state.

Believe me, dear ones, when you come home there will be plenty of time for celebration, humor, and family reunion. For now, we encourage you to concentrate on the purpose of your humanness, and continue changing your planet!

Question: Dear Kryon, having stated my intent about three months ago, I am trusting that I have the neutral implant in place. My area of doubt occurs when I find myself judging others. I catch myself doing it and think, "Oh, darn, I thought this wouldn't happen after the implant." Does having the implant mean judgments don't happen anymore? Fear doesn't arise anymore? Self-doubts don't reside in my thoughts anymore? Or is it that a wisdom should occur when I have these thoughts?

Answer: Having the implant gives you a clearing. Like a clearing in a dense forest that now gives you permission to move quickly instead of being bogged down by the thicket, it provides a potential for action on your part. The implant gives you nothing but tools to move forward. It does not change you without your intent. You must arise and move by yourself!

Your judgment is a habit, and now you can void it through intent. With the powerful tool you have called for, watch what happens when you have a small ceremony around this problem. Intend out loud that you wish it to be tempered until it is no longer an issue. Then watch that exact thing happen. First, dear one, you must give intent for its demise. Nothing in your life is going to change without your action of INTENT. The implant/release, therefore, is the catalyst for advanced spiritual action.

Light Workers / Warriors of The Light

Question: How do I know if I am a "warrior of the light"?

Answer: If you have given intent to marry with your contract and be everything you agreed to be in this lifetime, then you are a "warrior of the light." Your contract is everything. The intent to engage it and skip some of the lessons around it is the "implant," or "release" (as some have named it). Making this decision and giving your intent is an admission of responsibility for the New Age.

Question: What is the single most important thing I should be doing as a warrior of the light?

Answer: Continuing from the last answer: The recurring theme of the New Age is that the single most important thing you can do as a human being is to discover and implement your contract. "Why does that matter so much?" you might ask. The mechanics of your incarnation here are to see if you can discover your contract. If you can, and implement it, not only do you dramatically change your peacefulness, but you also change the vibration, or "tally," of the whole planet Earth. One human finding his contract creates a "graduate status." This status is worth a great deal of energy when the whole of the planet's energy and vibration is measured—and the measurement is what changes your planetary future!

Therefore, what you do at a personal level is responsible completely for changing the whole. Some humans fail to understand this, and they feel that their contract must be something bold and worldwide to accomplish a planetary shift. Just the opposite is true. Finding the contract itself is what does the work, not the substance of it. The world peacemaker is no more apt to change the vibration of the planet than the one who finds his passion writing a children's book, or one who realizes that her entire purpose this time is to make a peaceful family out of a chaotic one. It's not what the contract is that is important, only the result of the search for it. The treasure is in the discovery!

Question: Dear Kryon, you use the term "Warrior of the Light" to describe us light workers. Can you explain more about why you chose this term. Is there indeed a "war" of sorts going on? Inquiring minds want to know!

Answer: Indeed, we have spoken of this before. In addition, we have given metaphoric references to the sword of truth, the shield of knowledge, and the breastplate (armor) of wisdom. In these cases, as well, you will find the analogy to war or battle.

The metaphor is strong and must be related to a battle since it is the old energy that you are at war with. Some have felt that this is not a very spiritual attribute, and that war is something that men made for themselves, so why should Spirit reference it so often, including the term "Warrior of the Light"?

If the struggle is with the old energy, then in many cases you must use old-energy concepts to solve the struggle. The old energy that you face is definitely going to do battle with you, and you, in turn, must face them in the same way for them to understand the power you possess. They understand the symbols of the old battle, and it is what will solve the situation and create a victory for all.

Think of it in this way. Let us say that you as modern people landed on an island of primitive natives. You wished to give them peace, medicine, wisdom, and knowledge. They, in turn, were afraid of you due to their ignorance and didn't wish to know about your strange ways. They turned to what they knew worked in the past—battle! They attacked you en masse. It was not your wish to harm any of them, but it looked like you might have to. You drew your modern laser weapons—small, efficient, and deadly—and showed them your arsenal as a deterrent. They kept coming! Your up-to-date science was invisible to their consciousness. They had no concept of your power! To them you held something you might be planning to throw at them—like small rocks—and nothing more. Without something special happening very soon, it looked like they were headed for a bloodbath. You would have no option but to use your incredible power on the ignorant natives, who were only reacting to their own human fear.

Instead, picture this scenario: Even though you have the power of mighty thunderbolts at your disposal, each member of the team draws a magnificent sword—one that glistens in the sun with its power, and is huge! All of you produce armor and shielding and put it on. It is obviously going to protect you from the natives' pitiful spears. This would have stopped them cold! There would have been no battle. Your apparent strength in *an arena they understood fully* would have solved the problem, and the natives would have realized that the prudent thing to do was to either retreat or accept the peace. Either way, everyone wins. The ones who retreat have the choice to do so. They are not forced into one decision. The ones who decide to accept you take a step into their fear—the first step to enlightenment. No human is harmed, and everyone wins. Do you now understand why an enlightened group carried old weapons? A metaphor, perhaps, but a very real one.

The battle with the old energy has many forms. It is not always fought against other humans. Sometimes, many times, it is fought within the single human as he struggles to find the light inside, and balance it against that part of him that has no love. That is where the "dark side" lives. It is not some evil force that is apart from humanity. It is the part of humanity without love.

Dear ones, again we state this: There is no greater power in the Universe than love. It is your solace and your shield. The sword of truth is a symbol of your new power over the old ways.

Question: Dear Kryon, there seems to be a large group of light workers who were born in the mid 1950s. Was there anything significant about those years?

Answer: Well, well. Finally, someone noticed! Thank you dear one, for the insightful question. Yes! These represent the years that would allow humans to be able to have children in the 1970s and be in their forties (age wise) right now. All of you who were born in the 1950s were very excited to get here. The potential for change on the planet was at hand, and you knew it. You also knew that the potential for your children and grandchildren was going to make the difference for a graduate planet or not.

Remember that when you are on the other side, you know what we know. We have told you so often how excited we are at what has taken place in the last fifty years! The potential was here, but you would not know of it until the harmonics were converged in the measurement of the planet's willingness to move forward. All of you born in the 1950s would, therefore, be adults when that happened. The potential for the 11:11 and the 12:12 were also there. Is it any wonder you wanted to be here to be part of it?

The spectacular news is that it all happened! You asked to be part of a potential for one of the greatest changes in consciousness the planet has ever seen. It can actually change your time frame within the next fourteen to fifteen years! It has voided the old prophecies and changed your future, and you are here to participate in it—some will even create it!

Therefore, those of you of that age, represent the beginning of those who had the earliest potential to recognize their Higher Selves. There are more light workers of your age on the planet than of any other, but more and more young ones are also taking up the quest. You have allowed for that, and I salute those of you in that age group. Now do you understand why your age is what it is? Some of you have bemoaned the fact that you are as old as you are. You often wish you could be younger. If that had happened, you would have missed the opportunity to be in on "the ground floor," so to speak. Everything is appropriate! You are loved for your willingness to be some of the first!

Question: This past year seems to have been particularly intense and challenging for most light workers I know. Now that we're coming to the end of the year, how would you grade our progress, as light workers and as a planet in general?

Answer: You are correct. The closer you get to a critical mass of light workers able to raise the planet to the next vibratory step, the more you are going to feel. The intensity is not going to let up for a while. The secret is to understand and deal with the intensity in a way that will enable you to become peaceful with it. The challenges will still be great. They must be in order to produce the results that you wish. Dear ones, please do not fear these changes or challenges. The work you are doing by going through these things is more valuable than you can know.

Your work in this last year, including the challenges, has brought you far closer to the vibrational goal than when my new work started in 1989. It has accelerated so greatly that much of what had been foretold in the early 1990s by channelers and psychics is now misinformation. Your work has actually allowed you to "leapfrog" certain attributes of learning and Earth progression that might have been even more challenging for you. More than three times, the schedule for meeting your cosmic neighbors has been changed due to your quickening vibrational changes, and now these plans are again going to change.

This is why we again say that no entity—not even this one— can tell you the exact details of your future. It is a moving target and has moved very quickly past even what we expected.

The only constant is that your linear time still guides the master calendar toward a dimensional shift potential starting in 2012. You very well might be at that time potential as personal humans, but the linear time frame will remain the same for that window.

To answer your question: You have done well, indeed, and you can measure it by how challenging it has been! Change is now your norm. Challenge is expected, and peace is yours during all of this. As you change your vibrational rate, you will become far more peaceful with the very things that disturbed you last year. We honor you greatly for your work!

Live Essence Medicines

Question: I have always been interested in alternative medicines. I found the chapter on "Healing in the New Energy," Book III, very interesting. What exactly are "live essence medicines"? Are they bovine glandular essences?

Question: Recently, my sister and I started a "circle garden" and are making flower essences for vibrational healing. We would greatly appreciate your comments regarding this venture and any suggestions for this energy work.

Answer: Both of you are indeed working with New Age live essence medicines and are on the leading edge of very powerful healing. Let me first help define what is meant by live essence medicines, and second to give some direction to those of you working with them.

Live essence medicines (LEM) are substances or processes that directly use something that has (or had) life energy. Instead of an inert chemical or chemical compound, we are speaking of something that is alive or once was alive, but with great life energy. Within this definition, there are some excellent examples and some forms yet to come. It does not matter what process you are using with these LEMs, they are potent in their use. Some simply have their energy passed to the human individual, and some are ingested into the body. These LEMs, however, go far beyond what you currently know about plants and herbs. You will find many to be LEMs of a form unexpected, and able to hold a life energy that will co-create healing in your body with you. There are some LEMs that are locked into rocks—having the life energy of many thousands of years ago when Earth's energy was greater than today. Some are growing as very small life forms, ready to harvest, but have been "hiding" their great value to your biology. And finally, some are from the animal kingdom (animals are here to serve you—see the first question in this chapter), and will be biological and very helpful.

Here is some guidance as to what to look for: (1) Watch for any medicines currently in your society that are already known as "live essence." There is no mistake that this name was brought through my partner. His message was not proprietary for him, and many healers have already received this same message and named their substances accordingly. (2) If you are using LEMs, look for new ways to use them, and expect some powerful results. Part of the new gifts from Spirit are increasing awareness by facilitators using good body-balancing methods (which is what live essence medicines do). (3) Look for LEM systems—that is more than one in conjunction with other known balancing methods with color and sound. The New Age healer will be one that is very diversified in the use of many systems together for balance. As we have told you before, it is time you understood how your many diverse approaches to alternate healing combine into systems that will become much more powerful and productive.

These new healing techniques will feature human balance and wellness, which will keep away sickness and disease. Rather than just curing sick individuals, these new LEMs can become the accepted method to keep the body in touch with its cellular memory of wellness, actually feed it, and create a balance that will enable great strength in fighting off the new stubborn viruses that are presenting themselves to you.

Magnetic Mattresses

Question: Dear Kryon, I have seen ads for "magnetic blankets" in some of the New Age magazines. Are these beneficial? Is there the potential for "overdose?"

Answer: We have spoken of this in depth before, and now is not the time to repeat the details. The basics are that magnetic healing of any kind is to be treated with caution and care. Magnetics to the body are as powerful as the strongest curative herb, or live essence substance you can use. Would you continue taking the strongest herbs on the planet for your entire life—even if the biological curative reason you started taking them was solved? Would you continue the medication for a disease that you had cured? Would you then obtain a magnetic blanket or chair or mattress and use it for life? Remember that the body is designed to create balance by itself. Once it is helped into that state you need only to feed it properly and keep it healthy. Stimulating it for any other reason is inappropriate.

Yes, you can overdose. And the overdose has the potential for unbalancing the cellular instruction sets of the body. Some have reported feeling "stimulated" as long as the magnetics are around you with a device such as this. You can achieve the same thing by ingesting certain chemicals, too and they won't be balancing while they are stimulating your biology. Many call that "addition."

Use magnetics sparingly and wisely. Don't take large magnetic arrays (lots of magnets together) and metaphorically throw them at your biology in the hopes that somehow they might help you. In some cases, they may actually harm you!  Use discernment, and call on your gifts in this New Age to tell you what is proper for your own body.

Realize that magnetic aids are wonderful healing tools. Now go find out how many, what power, when, and how long! Active or passive? Singular or array? The puzzle is before you, and many are finding the answers.

Meditation

Question: In Book III, there is a mention of not having to meditate anymore. Many of us light workers use this for centering. Can you expand on this further?

Answer: Let it be clear that Kryon has never told a light worker to stop meditating. Instead, we have explained in the writings that the mechanics of your meditations have changed. (Book III, pages 28–30). Your centering techniques may not work the way they used to in the old energy, so we have described why, and we have given you advice on how to change them.

Many have felt this and have asked what they can do to get the old feeling back. Our answer is that the old feelings represent the old energy, and that they must now move on to finding the centering connections with new feelings. Like other learning, this new paradigm will come in time and may seem inconvenient at first. It is all part of your existence within a higher frequency on this planet.

You are greatly loved and honored for your questions as to how to better communicate with your God-self! Please continue to meditate! Learn the new energy methods and feelings, for they will greatly increase your power!

Music

Question: Dear Kryon, music has been around as long as man. It has been, and is, included in worship and celebration of all kinds. I am a singer and writer and would like to understand the mechanics of how music affects everything. Also, are there negative aspects of musical vibrations, such as heavy-metal rock? Can music be used for healing, and how?

Answer: What if I told you that as a singer and a writer, you were also a channeler? Did you ever wonder where that wonderful melody came from after you put it on paper? Some of you who write the lyrics for the music can also relate. *"Where did these beautiful concepts and words come from?"* you might ask when finished. You channeled it! It is an anointed gift!

Tones are vibration. Multiple tones in complex arrangements and harmonies have the absolute power to heal, create peace, make feelings deep within a human heart, and cause decisions and action! The vibrations are mathematical and resonate against both you and the Earth. Music, therefore, has substance, and it creates its own reality. It is important, and it is sacred.

Two answers also follow, one from a question you asked, and one you did not. (1) Can music be damaging? Just as the same healing chemicals mixed in a different intensity and proportion can also be poison, the answer is yes. Vibration sends a message. That's only fair, seeing that you have the ultimate choice, as humans, with respect to what to do with every attribute of your planet. The vibrations can be mixed to create chaos, control, and even sorrow—such is the power of tonal vibration on the planet.

(2) The second answer may seem like a joke. The philosopher asks: If a tree falls in the woods with no one to hear it, would it make a noise? Let me update that: If music happens in the forest, would

it make a sound? The answer is YES! A resonance that everyone and everything would "hear." For the very dirt of the planet also reacts to tonal vibrations, as well as every living thing in creation.

Is it no wonder that music brings up the emotions in you? It has the power to enhance any message and create a love atmosphere without one word being spoken.

Last, think of this: Why is it that on your planet you have hundreds of languages and dialects, yet when a musician from any country sits in front of his score, he understands a common language? Written music is common to all civilized cultures! It is one language, universal and understood by all. This was not an accident. The entire Earth "speaks" music in the same manner, with full understanding—just as it is with love.

Negativity and Fear

Question: How can I learn to release negative things in my life? I want to let go of hangups, bad habits, and dramas, but they seem so ingrained that it's difficult to move forward.

Answer: The first thing is to give verbal intent (out loud so your biology can hear it) that you wish these things to pass from your life. The hardest part is the next one. You have to take action to allow for these things to leave. Giving your consciousness permission to have them go is necessary, so you have to help the process by co-creating your new reality. You must also take responsibility for each of the negative (or seemingly negative) attributes that are now irritating you. See them as something you carefully planned before you got here. With this in place, you can then dismiss them as easily as you gave them to yourself originally!

You should know that all the things you wish to clear are actually waiting to be cleared! Nothing is impossible to change regarding your personality, but pay particular attention to the work with your inner child, dear one, for in your case the little kid within hasn't come out to play for a very long time.

Question: How can I overcome the internal "battles" I have within myself?

Answer: Read the last answer. Your internal battles were placed there for you to overcome them! List them, and verbalize that you wish solution to their presence in your life, then take some time to play.

These internal battles are most often the imbalance of the intellect. They represent one of the most serious stumbling blocks to enlightenment, for the intellect without the balance of the inner kid, love, and the Higher Self will try to defeat you every time. We have spoken of this many times in channeling. An internal battle is where part of you is actually opposed to another part, so you find yourself unable to move forward in any direction without feeling that somehow you have done something wrong, or at least disappointed part of yourself. In your case, the seriousness of everything you see should be a hint that there is an imbalance present.

When the Higher Self is in communication with you, the inner kid is stimulated, for joy and humor go together within the mind of Spirit. Did you ever wonder why no animals on your planet laugh at concepts? Humans are the only ones with the contract of a Higher Self and a personal Merkabah. Humor is a sacred attribute. Treat it as such, and understand that it is necessary for your inner peace. Inner peace is the energy that will totally replace inner conflict, and you are on the brink of having it happen! Let go of the things that your intellect cherishes, such as self-pity and self-criticism. Honor who you are, and start laughing more.

Question: I have an overwhelming urge to leave this planet on a daily basis! This is causing me much anxiety and pain. Why do I feel this way, and what can I do to soothe this?

Answer: You are in the process of great enlightened change! When this takes place, quite often those imprints that temper your abilities to tolerate your humanness are lifted for a short while. This is simple energy accounting, and it allows for the new overlays of higher vibration to be given to you. When this takes place, you will again relax with your condition of duality. Somewhere along your life, you asked for this change, and now you are in the middle of it. This is exceptionally common to many who wish to go through a vibrational change while they move up.

Dear one, Spirit does not want any of you to suffer or be in pain. It is exactly the opposite! Even within the process of moving from a lower vibration to a higher one, there doesn't have to be pain. A clear overview and understanding of the temporary situation will help, along with verbalization to Spirit that you claim the peace you deserve during this transition.

Your co-creative power is absolute in this new energy! Even within a guide change, you can co-create peace and can verbalize: *"In the name of Spirit I create peace in my life, and ask to feel the love of Spirit with each breath!"* Let this be your communication to Spirit when you are in this transition. Take responsibility for the change, and give yourself permission for peace during it!

Then thank your Higher Self that you find yourself in this condition at this time in your life, for it is a clear indication that you are on your path and have broken through karma that would otherwise have kept you from the higher vibration that you deserve.

Question: Sometimes life seems so full of loneliness, suffering, and pain. It would help if I understood the "bigger" picture of things. Why are we here in the first place? What's the purpose of our existence on Earth?

Answer: You are correct. If you could only see the bigger picture, you would be astounded! We have casually mentioned many times that what you are doing here by choice will affect the whole. By this we mean the WHOLE! All of creation, and everything you can see as far as you can see is going to be changed by what you do on this planet. Hidden from you are two grand facts: (1) The Universe (you and I included) have created Earth as a balancing catalyst that is constantly measured for purposes that are difficult to describe due to your duality. But simply, the vibration of this planet of yours is the driver of many things you cannot fathom, and which have been neutral (not dark or light) for eons. What you are doing here is bringing a light balance to a great portion of the entire Universe! (2) Your loneliness, suffering, and pain are part of the plan you set up in order to give yourself the chance to move through these things and play a part in the new energy. What you do with your life will make a difference for the vibration of the planet. What happens to the planet will then affect the whole. Will you take responsibility for your condition as it stands right now? Do you claim victimization as your plight? Will you walk into your fears in order to quickly get past them and move into your contract (the reason you came)?

Let me tell you this: A life that is filled with loneliness and suffering and pain is a life that has not yet seen the higher purpose for being on Earth and has not yet understood the great gifts that lay waiting. Imagine if you will that your Higher Self and your guides, and all the other entities that support you on Earth (including Kryon) are dormant, playing no part in your existence, because you have not given any intent for us to go to work! It's no wonder that you are uncomfortable. It is when you stand up and start using the awareness gifts of Spirit in this New Age that you will never be lonely, and your suffering will turn to peace, and your pain will disappear. If it were not this way, I would not tell you this!

Start associating with others who understand these things and who are positive in their approach to life. Also remember that each time you tell someone that you are suffering, your biology "hears" it, too. Think about it. You are actually perpetuating your discomfort by feeding this thought to your cells. Do you commiserate often, telling people how troubled you are? Start realizing that your entire being, both biological and spiritual, will respond to each word each action. If it hears you are dying, you will! That is why you have so much power through pure intent to heal yourself! You are greatly honored for your life—and for your question. Truly, a major change for you is imminent if you are seeking answers with pure intent.

Question: I am very critical of myself. Intellectually, I know it is invalid, yet I seem to keep on with negative self-talk and criticism. I have a gentle, compassionate love of others, yet little for myself. Is there a way out of this trap?

Answer: Sit in the chair, dear one! The chair we speak of is the one of SELF WORTH—the throne that is waiting for you in the temple that you call your inner chamber (as in Chapter One). Look at it! Someone else is always in that chair, and that is your problem. As in the question to follow, this is one of the most basic of all problems with those in the New Age. The reason? You have spent so much time on your knees in past lives wearing sackcloth and sandals that you bring with you the feeling that you are not worthy to be called a PIECE OF GOD! Until you claim your absolute right to be here, and claim the deserving qualities you came in with, you will not be able to move out of this condition. You stood in line to be here! Now are you going to deny that? Never verbalize in private or public that you are "less than," or that you "don't deserve" or that you "can't do this or that." Your body will "hear" it—AND WILL ACT ACCORDINGLY. Think of it as programming. You are powerful! And you can create your own demise, as well as creating your own graduation. Each thing you verbalize is being acted upon spiritually and biologically. What is it that you wish to tell your life force? That you are no good? Start telling it the opposite. See the instructions in the next question for additional ideas. You have the right to be here, and it's about time you told your biology the truth! It will work.

Question: I have asked my guides repeatedly for help in having the right livelihood, the right place to live, and the right place to work. I do not feel I am getting any answers that I can feel or experience. I have done all I know how to do, and it gets increasingly difficult to have faith and keep on going. What is the blockage that prevents wonderful change "in the twinkling of the eye"? How do I find joy when nothing seems to be moving?

Answer: When you find yourself "stuck," it's time to evaluate several things: You have been told that Spirit loves and honors you, yet you feel nothing. (1) TRUST: Time to take stock if you really believe all this spiritual stuff or not. *"Whoa!"* you might say. *"Do you mean that co-creating your own reality means you have to believe in something? Like clicking your heels to-gether?"* Not exactly. You will never sit in any chair if you know it won't hold your weight. Only forcefully will you be pushed down to sit in what you know to be a faulty chair. It's against all the muscles in your body. The process of trust and co-creation carries some of the same attributes. You absolutely must believe that this is real. If you do not, there is a block occurring that will keep you from moving forward—and sitting in the spiritual chair. Although you give good verbalization to the co-creation process, you don't actually believe it can happen to you. This is where the New Age facilitators come in. They can help "unstick" you, and enable you to move forward into what you can trust.

(2) UNWORTHINESS: As in the previous question, some of you can't possibly conceive of being worthy enough to have these New Age gifts in your life. We are providing more and more teaching in each channel about finding your worth. It is imperative for you to feel worthy at the cellular level in order to move ahead with your enlightenment and co-creation. Nothing is going to happen as long as you stand silent, feeling that you do not deserve any good thing. Dear one, this feeling is not that hard to void. Start verbalizing daily, *"I am that I AM. I AM worthy as a child of the Universe, placed on this planet to achieve great things! I*

deserve all that I came to be. Only good things will attach themselves to me. I am that I AM!" Study some of the works of those who have had great success with affirmations. Learn and use them. This process has been documented in this magazine many times, and in the books of Kryon. Your body will absolutely respond to these verbalizations. The very cellular structure of your biology needs to HEAR YOU TELL IT THAT IT IS WORTHY! As we said above, too many past lives as a pauper or a priest will take its toll during these times of vibrational change.

(3) NO FUN: It's time to relax with your spirit. Conjure up the kid within, and run through the grass. Ignore the "have to's" and make noise. Be inappropriate in a fun way—and show that spiritual aspect of laughter! So many of you are mired in the seriousness of life that you cannot extract yourselves from the mud of worry. You intellectualize yourselves right into the frying pan of fear, and there you continue to sit, hoping Spirit will deliver you. Time to do a puzzle, fingerpaint, sing songs. There is no greater healing than to return to a state when you knew who you were! The child that entered this Earth that you called yourself absolutely knew it was born of God...eternal...and powerful. Go back there, and feel it. Then you will understand why you are stuck.

Ouiji Boards

Question: Many people play with the Ouiji board. Would you explain the energy of using the Ouiji board and the effects of having one in your home and using it? What is the higher truth on this please?

Answer: It is a great irony that due to a game, you are suddenly able to suspend your reality and let the automatic body deliver messages! If you only would do this when healing! The Ouiji board is not evil but can be confusing. Why?

When used in a group, this device collectively uses the mass consciousness from the energy of the group. This is why there is often so much discovery involved, or secrets revealed. It is the psychic energy of the individuals put together that is being displayed. Therefore, sometimes there will be multiple conflicting messages. Sometimes there will be a powerful negative aspect involved. If that happens, you are in touch with the fear part of the consciousness of either the group, or one strong individual who is touching the board piece.

This game isn't a valid option to find spiritual truth—even if used alone. You would do far better with a pendulum, and we have discussed this before. The pendulum has a limited number of options, therefore, it requires less energy to use and is easier to read. It is also far less susceptible to corruption by unusual energy or fear. It is also a very personal tool, which must be used only by one person at a time—the key to why the Ouiji is not as good. Answers based in truth must come from the Higher Self. With proper verbalization and setup (defining in advance what the pendulum motion means from the energy of the person holding it), the pendulum is a grand tool for those kinds of answers. The Ouiji is likely to be misleading due to its fixed characteristics, and the energy needed to move its pointer over a predetermined surface to a system of letters and numbers—none of which are intuitive to your spiritual nature.

Relationships

Question: My husband and I do not share the same spiritual path. In fact, I wonder if he has one at all. This has caused quite a bit of tension between us because he also tends to be critical of my New Age activities. I would appreciate any advice about coexisting in peace with nonspiritual partners.

Answer: You are greatly loved for asking such a question, for this situation presents itself often as humans on your planet discover themselves and have to cope with what to do with their partners who are not in the same posture.

First, you must understand that your partner is as blessed and loved by God as you are. If he never once prays, or never once meditates, or never once speaks to his inner spirituality and dies without a clue to his real spirituality, he has made the journey and is as honored as anyone on the planet. It is the parable of The Prodigal Son again. I tell you this so you understand that he is never to be evangelized. You may feel that he would be a better person if he only had enlightenment, but this is his process. Let him ask you—never preach to him.

When a mate understands that you do not judge him for not being "in the fold" of your process, then he will tend to relax with what you are doing, as strange and odd as it might appear to him. Let there be no threat to the partnership from your work. Let your activities be for yourself alone, and don't bring them into his space. Also, be cautious about violating your community space, as well with your New Age dealings.

Now, what should you ask of a mate who does not share your ideas? And what should he or she ask of you? Here is the answer, and it can absolutely be accomplished if your love for each other is as proclaimed. Face off with him and ask this: "*In love, I ask you to not judge me in my ways, or verbalize your criticism of them. They will not interfere with my life with you.*" Then make sure you keep this promise! Indeed, you might not go to as many spiritual places or participate in as many New Age activities, but you are respecting the partnership first. Know this: You can work on your enlightenment personally and never have to go anywhere. Make the sacrifice to show him that your beliefs will not tear you both apart. What does he want from you? Tell him, "*I will never try to involve you in anything that you do not believe in, and I will not bring my beliefs into your space.*" Finally, take time to be together! Don't let your quest take over the partnership. You never have to speak of your New Age work. Let the changes in your personality speak for themselves. Let the healing in your body speak for itself. Let the peace of your countenance speak loudly to him. Believe me, the mate will notice these things first! There is plenty of time for you to grow in the New Age system and still relax with your mate.

Dear ones, you must understand that when you approach your partners with this kind of integrity, they will gradually change. They won't necessarily embrace the New Age, but over time they will absolutely see that what you have is not going to disturb the partnership, and has helped you. Most of the anger and disagreement is about fear—fear of losing you! Once you show a mate that you are sincere in the balance between your activities and the integrity of the partnership, the mate will relax and let you be.

The love between humans is directly related to the love of God. When you begin to use it in your partnership—nonjudgment, integrity of purpose, and sincerity of conversation—it cannot be ignored. Usually your partner will respond to it, and your life with a *nonspiritual* partner can not only be peaceful, but very loving indeed.

By the way, the term *nonspiritual* human is very funny to me! Cover a plant with a cloth and call it a rock. It thinks it is a rock, and walks through life doing "rocklike" things. But the one who covered it will always know it is a plant, and when the cover comes off in the end, everyone will have a good laugh. There is no such thing as a *nonspiritual* human...just humans who don't know yet about the cover.

Soulmates / Twin Flames

Question: I've heard a lot about "soulmates" and "twin flames." Could Kryon explain more about these, and what we should do to draw this energy into our lives?

Answer: In your karmic group, you cannot live lifetime after lifetime without sometimes "recognizing" humans as being something more than they seem. Suppose you had a wonderful mate or partner in a powerful lifetime of great experience and purpose. Even though it might have been many expressions (incarnations) ago, the karmic residue remains at the cellular level. In addition, your Higher Self knows everything, and you are invited to be closer to it in this New Age.

Suddenly a person (gender makes no difference) seemingly stumbles into your life and knocks you over with their presence. Perhaps they have said nothing or are not especially outgoing, but from your standpoint they are shouting, "I know you!" This is the soulmate or twin flame attribute.

There is much to say regarding twin flames and soulmates (and many good things have been channeled as well by Saint Germain, a true human alchemy specialist), but here is some basic advice. Please be aware that if you find this person, there is no astral ruling that says you should automatically be with him or her! Most of the time this soulmate attribute is something you feel from the past that really does relate to what your contract is now. You have played out parts with this person before, and this time you are resting from him or her. Meeting this person can be a real experience, however!

There are differences between what causes a soulmate in comparison to a twin flame, and these have been explained by others. The fact remains, however, that they both carry a "charge" of energy that you feel at the cellular level.

In some cases, there are some of you who have been waiting for this person for either relationships or business partnering—and time has been waiting for things to be correct for a union. Knowing the difference in what to do with a person such as this is part of your new intuitive power of communication with your Higher Self. Usually, the situation will be obvious as to whether to take action with this person. Don't try to create a situation or delude yourself into thinking you _must_ take action if you "recognize" a soulmate.

It is more often true that a soulmate or twin flame from a past life is only "recognized karmic energy," and not a sign or indication from the Universe for you to do anything romantically. This seeming romantic message is often a false one due to the amazing past-life energy present. Those who have ignored this advice have found themselves on the learning end of a very powerful and unpleasant lesson. Many times this person is the **last one** you will want to become personally involved with in your current lifetime! *Spark* is an English word that will give an idea of what can happen between the two of you. You are often magnetically opposite this time around, appropriately to keep you apart. Forcing the issue can create a feeling of stone against stone. That is why you didn't meet this person earlier. **How can you tell?**

The secret in knowing which situation is correct is based around synchronicity and ease of action. If you find yourself in chaos trying to put this "perfect" partner together, where nothing is going smoothly, then the situation is shouting that it is not appropriate! Call on everything within you to help make such a choice, to know if the sparks are going to repel—or attract. If the situation melds together easily and smoothly, without problem or drama, then you have indeed met someone special, someone who is worth the effort to bring into your life.

Dear ones, The love of appropriate twin flames or soulmates who have presented themselves synchronistically in your life is one of the highest loves between human beings. It can be between children and parents, or romantically between partners. If it is romantic, it can hold the charge of "first love," and the feelings thereof for an entire lifetime. If you find this, under any circumstances, cherish it and don't let it go, for it's anointed, and carries with it the seeds of Spirit itself.

Walk-ins

Question: I've heard of walk-ins, and the definition fits me! I had an experience when I was a child that seems to qualify me as one. What is it? Am I weird?

Answer: It would astonish many of you to know how many walk-ins there are in the New Age! Let me give you a very brief overview of the walk-in. There are many channels on the planet right now who are able to give you wonderful details about the soul mechanics of this spiritual attribute. They are specialists in this, and are available if you look.

The walk-in is a soul overlay, or meld of entities for the lifetime of a human being. When the answer was given regarding what the human soul was, I mentioned this very thing.

Imagine if you will a human who has agreed to come to the planet in order to spend seven to twelve years growing up for another entity who has only recently been human and who has made the "death" transition only recently—well within the life of the seven-to twelve-year-old. By agreement, the older more experienced human soul can then enter and "meld" with the original soul for the rest of a lifetime.

When this happens, the original soul takes the "back seat," but is still a participant in the ongoing planning session. This is not comprehensible to you—how a meld like this could work, and how two souls could carry on as one. It is so nevertheless, and the result is a walk-in. The original soul is dormant in contract, and exists for the life of the human. The new soul is the dominant one, and it is this one that slowly changes the very DNA of the human. Both exist as one—something else you find very difficult to believe. There is no energy fight, and no slit personality. It is a perfect spiritual meld, done in love and with great purpose.

It is extremely common in the New Age. Let me tell you why. The purpose for such an arrangement is so the older soul can return right away to continue life within a contract arrangement that is potent. In addition, the one coming in has better karmic equipment to carry out important work.

How can you tell a walk-in? It is usually very obvious. When there is an accident as a child, or a near death experience, it allows for the new soul infusion at the prearranged time. The child that emerges has all the physical characteristics and remembrances of the original soul, but also the contract and experiential attributes of an old soul that is now reborn. Quite often that human will go on to do amazing things at a young age, or change greatly in talent areas right before the eyes of their astounded parents. It usually happens before the teen years, so that their growth into an adult with be with the new overlay.

Can you look back and see this pattern in your life? Believe me, many of you can. Since you are reading this, you are probably among those who represent the leading edge of the New Age. Are you weird? Dear ones, if you could really see who you are, you would absolutely feel that you were weird (cosmic humor)! Many of you made this walk-in arrangement so that you could quickly come back and participate in one of the grandest times on Earth! Know that you find yourselves reading about the experience, and are finally understanding what happened.

World Financial Collapse

Question: For years we have heard stories of worldwide financial chaos. Where is our economy headed? Is a crash impending?

Answer: What you do with your political and financial structure is your society's karma. Kryon will never advise you on political issues. This is human-based decision making and will reflect the energy of your enlightenment as a race. It truly is your test.

However, we have given you some hints and reflections regarding the years to come that have a bearing on these questions. What did we say about those you will *meet* in the next decade? When you meet *them*, who will speak to *them*? If there is trade, what will be used? Will there be a commonality among the nations to allow for this?

Some of you fear this commonality, for you feel it has to be a world government, something that will take your freedom away, so you campaign against it at all costs. This is because you think it will be organized and structured in some way as to void what you have worked so hard to accomplish regarding freedom in your country. We have already applauded your society for its emphasis on the individual and its stated tolerance for all. Now do you think we will advise you to throw that away? NO.

Here is what to strive for: Think globally. Work on a system where your planet's countries may all exist within their own cultural systems, but where there is a commonality of value and trade. Work on a system that will allow you to agree on what your assets are worth to each other. Next, decide which council will represent the planet. **You never have to have a central world government to be a planet of uniform consensus.** Instead you will need organization, tolerance for your neighbor's culture, and the absolute certainty that you must have a mixed representative group that can speak for all of you quickly—not a world government.

The wiser of you will understand that for this to happen you must have (1) a more equal value system worldwide, and (2) peace between nations. Shortly you will see that those tribes that continue to insist on war will be outcast and controlled by the others, never to have a voice in the council. Peace will become a symbol of enlightenment, and consensus will be a sign of wisdom.

Whether you have a "crash" as you describe it will totally depend on your country's reaction to the natural economic evolution in this New Age world value system—**not a world government.** Will you resist coming to grips with a uniform valuation system, or help create it?

The precepts upon which your government was founded (speaking of America) were channeled and anointed. It is within your wisdom to continue to hold it dear, and still accomplish a planetary value system and a world communication council. We honor you for this endeavor.

Special question
Question: *Okay, Kryon, who are you, really?*

Answer: I have told my partner many times that by asking the correct question, much can be learned. Not everything will be told to you if you are still. Therefore, you show some insight within your question that perhaps Kryon is not simply the magnetic master. You are correct. I will give you two of my *qualities*:

Dear one, as I mentioned earlier in this book, I am one of the nurturing angels of the New Age. My cosmic *family* energy includes the one you call Archangel Michael. We travel together often, and again find ourselves partnering for the work on your planet. Some of you have suspected this and have recognized the energy. Now I confirm it because you have asked about the *family*.

I am also of the *work* and *specialty* of all spiritual entities you know who have the last spelling in your language of "on." List them, and you will see that they are all about science, physics, and love.

Long after the magnetic work is done, and the Kryon contingent leaves, I will remain to continue to love and honor and speak to you as I am doing now.

I love you dearly…

Kryon

THE NAMES, ATOMIC NUMBERS, AND SYMBOLS OF THE ELEMENTS

1	H	Hydrogen
2	He	Helium
3	Li	Lithium
4	Be	Beryllium
5	B	Boron
6	C	Carbon
7	N	Nitrogen
8	O	Oxygen
9	F	Fluorine
10	Ne	Neon
11	Na	Sodium
12	Mg	Magnesium
13	Al	Aluminum
14	Si	Silicon
15	P	Phosphorous
16	S	Sulfur
17	Cl	Chlorine
18	Ar	Argon
19	K	Pota...
20	Ca	Cal...
21	Sc	Sca...
22	Ti	Titan...
23	V	Vanad...
24	Cr	Chromium
25	Mn	Manganese
26	Fe	Iron
27	Co	Cobalt
28	Ni	Nickel
29	Cu	Copper
30	Zn	Zinc
31	Ga	Gallium
32	Ge	Germanium
33	As	Arsenic
34	Se	Selenium
35	Br	Bromine
36	Kr	Krypton

37	Rb	Rubidium
38	Sr	Strontium
39	Y	Yttrium
40	Zr	Zirconium
41	Nb	Niobium
42	Mo	Molybdenum
43	Tc	Technetium
44	Ru	Ruthium
45	Rh	Rhodium
46	Pd	Palladium
47	Ag	...
48	Cd	...mium
49	In	...
64	Gd	Gad...
65	Tb	Tb
66	Dy	Dy ...ium
67	Ho	Ho
68	Er	Er
69	Tm	Tm
70	Yb	Yb ...m
71	Lu	Lu

72	Hf	Hafnium
73	Ta	Tantalum
74	Tu	Tungsten
75	Re	Rhenium
76	Os	Osmium
77	Ir	Iridium
78	Pt	Platinum
79	Au	Gold
80	Hg	Mercury
81	Tl	Thallium
82	Pb	Lead
83	Bi	Bismuth
84	Po	Polonium
85	At	Astatine
		Radon
		Francium
		Radium
		Actinium
		Thorium
		Protactinium
		Uranium
	Np	Neptunium
	Pu	Plutonium
	Am	Americium
96	Cm	Curium
97	Bk	Berkelium
98	Cf	Californium
99	Es	Einsteinium
100	Fm	Fermium
101	Mv	Mendelevium
102	No	Nobelium
103	Lw	Lawrencium
104	Unq	Unnilquadium
105	Unp	Unnilpentium
106	Unh	Unnilhexium
107	Uns	Unnilseptium

2	He	Helium
3	Li	Lithium
4	Be	Beryllium
5	B	Boron
6	C	Carbon
7	N	Nitrogen
8	O	Oxygen
9	F	Fluorine
10	Ne	Neon
11	Na	Sodium
12	Mg	Magnesium
13	Al	Aluminum
14	Si	Silicon
15	P	P...
16	S	Su...
17	Cl	Chl...
18	Ar	Arg...
19	K	Potassium
20	Ca	Calcium
21	Sc	Scandium
22	Ti	Titanium
23	V	Vanad...
24	Cr	C...
25	Mn	Mn
26	Fe	F...
27	Co	...alt
28	Ni	Nickel
29	Cu	C...
30	Zn	...c
31	Ga	
32	Ge	
33	As	A...
34	Se	S...
35	Br	Br
36	Kr	Kr

38	Sr	Sr
39	Y	Y
40	Zr	Zr
41	Nb	Nb
42	Mo	Molybdenum
43	Tc	Technetium
44	Ru	Ruthium
45	Rh	Rhodium
46	Pd	Palladium
47	Ag	Silver
48	Cd	Cadmium
49	In	Indium
50	Sn	Tin
51	Sb	Antimony
52	Te	Tellurium
53	I	Iodine
54	Xe	Xenon
55	Cs	Cesium
56	Ba	Barium
57	La	Lanthanum
58	Ce	Cerium
59	Pr	Praseodymium
60	Nd	Neodymium
61	Pm	Promethium
62	Sm	Samarium
63	Eu	Europium
64	Gd	Gadolinium
	Tb	Terbium
66	Dy	Dysprosium
67	Ho	Holnium
68	Er	Erbium
69	Tm	Thulium
70	Yb	Ytterbium
71	Lu	Lutetium

73	Ta	Tantalum
74	Tu	Tungsten
75	Re	Rhenium
	Os	Osmium
77	Ir	Iridium
78	Pt	Platinum
79	Au	Gold
80	Hg	Mercury
81	Tl	Thallium
82	Pb	Lead
83	Bi	Bismuth
84	Po	Polonium
85	At	Astatine
86	Rn	Radon
87	Fr	Francium
88	Ra	Radium
89	Ac	Actinium
90	Th	Thorium
91	Pa	Protactinium
92	U	Uranium
	Np	Neptunium
	Pu	Plutonium
	Am	Americium
	Cm	Curium
	Bk	Berkelium
	Cf	Californium
99	Es	Einsteinium
100	Fm	Fermium
101	Mv	Mendelevium
102	No	Nobelium
	Lw	Lawrencium
	Unq	Unnilquadium
	Unp	Unnilpentium
	Unh	Unnilhexium
	Uns	Unnilseptium

Science

Chapter Ten

"Science"
Discussion and
Validations from Kryon

Sagan's Missing Element

I want to start this important science chapter by thanking the late Carl Sagan for all his important work regarding discovery within our universe. He also gave us lively discussions and made us THINK about some very important issues. It was Carl, in his intelligent dissertation regarding the science–God connection, that severely criticized channelers, psychics, the New Age movement, and religion in general for being so darn woo-woo, tentative, and ungrounded regarding his practical approach to what is *real*, **and what is not.**

You might think that I, as a channeler, would not follow Dr. Sagan's work very closely, but instead I find it refreshing. Naturally, I don't agree with his philosophy regarding many things, but his undying quest to make us think about real-world proof for intangible concepts fits neatly within this chapter, and within my quest as well.

Somewhat of a dichotomy, Dr. Sagan's life 20 years ago was filled with a search for extraterrestrial life. He wanted to believe it was possible, and he pestered NASA with his views that there had to be life on other planets! When the Viking Mars probe showed nothing, however, he began to change his tone, discarded his willingness to BELIEVE, and instead tempered his ideas into a "show me" attitude. According to his wife, Ann Druyan, a frequent collaborator in his work, "Carl never wanted to believe. He wanted to know."[1]

---

[1] *Newsweek*, March 31 1997, p. 64, "Unbeliever's Quest."

I expect that Carl's original passion to discover life elsewhere led to the writing of *Contact*. I also think that he never really left that hope of extraterrestrial life behind, and was always searching. In the dusty closet of his youthful mind was a party hat, just waiting to be worn at the revelation of life on other worlds, but the scientific adult was subdued. His children may see the discovery, and perhaps in some way they will celebrate for him. Even surrounded by his clergy friends, of which he had many, he refused to acknowledge God even on his deathbed. There simply was no proof for Carl.

As many of you know, I also search for real-world (three-dimensional) proof of spiritual concepts. I intuitively *know*, and search for validation in a world where to most, seeing is believing. My quest, a bit different than Dr. Sagan, is to validate what I already *know*. Dr. Sagan asks us to examine the intangible in a scientific way in order to discard it. The scientific method is that way, and in many cases you start with a hypothesis, then apply what is known to it in order to prove it or disprove it.

Carl, although you are gone, I know you are with us in spirit. I also know that you are celebrating on the other side, due to one of the last things that you left us—even though as a living human you might not have designed what happened exactly as it unfolded. One of the most lasting impressions of your work was the 1997 film *Contact*, starring Jodie Foster. For many of us "woo-woo" folks, it made up for the last book. Whatever happened to the script after your transition didn't exactly reflect what your concepts were while you were alive, but instead somehow got modified to bring us a powerful metaphysical film! It spoke to many of us about the intangible, and how, even if things cannot be proven, they may still exist—even for the practical scientist. This film's message was awesome, and the presentation was first class. (It also just happens to represent the theme of Kryon—that there is more *energy* around, and of different types than we can currently measure.) Carl, I know you were pleased, as your energy touched the film from beyond the veil and made it come alive.

Woo-Woo Baloney

Dr. Sagan's books are being promoted and sold even after his passing, so I believe that I have the right to discuss my viewpoint, too. Even though he is not here to read my thoughts and form a rebuttal discussion, I still think his writings can be examined fairly. I don't intend to blast him. Hardly! I honor his life greatly, and I believe that his last book, *The Demon-Haunted World,* presents a scientific premise that I wish to address from the latest metaphysical standpoint. I feel I have the right and the freedom to disagree, but with valid scientific discussion (in the Sagan style). Without Dr. Sagan's argument, there would be less presentation of another valid viewpoint—one that today even many scientists hold. Therefore, he has provided a catalyst for the logical examination...of the woo-woo!

Dr. Sagan used to point out, "Science requires a strange mating of two contradictory tendencies: a willingness to consider even the most bizarre ideas, and at the same time, a most rigorous skepticism, requiring hard evidence to back up every claim. A scientist must hover in a strangely divided state of mind—open to all, yet closed to anything but the most rigorously proven. Both perspectives are critical to scientific inquiry, and neither works without the other." [2]

Dr. Sagan disapproved of Ramtha. He might have been open for a moment to the bizarre idea of channeling, but he was closed to it when he could not prove it with his Earth-based techniques. He used the channeler J. Z. Knight as an example of how the process was flawed, unreliable, unscientific, and probably fake. Again, I don't agree, but before I present any of my ideas regarding Dr. Sagan's main assertions, I would like to address this issue. I really don't think that Dr. Sagan ever interviewed Ms. Knight personally. Some of the answers to the questions he asked within the pages of *The Demon-Haunted World* have been available for some time. Dr. Sagan questioned how a 50,000-year-old entity could have an accent in English, when obviously Ramtha didn't speak English while he was on Earth. What accent is it? Where does it come from? Dr. Sagan asked other questions as well, guiding the reader to a conclusion that Knight's work was probably a show.

You know what? That's a darn good question! Here is an answer, not one that features empirical proof in the Sagan style, but my truth, nonetheless. First, a question of my own (for Carl and you): Why is it that most (if not all) out-of-body channelers who channel in the English language have the exact same accent? Even if they have never heard any of the others, they have the same funny-sounding Scottish type voice affectation. Why? Why is it that even though they might have come from northern America or Australia or England or South Africa, the vocal accent does not reflect those areas, but rather is the identical "channeling" accent? Without some mass agreement, channeling manual, teacher, or global primer, how is that possible? If they copied each other, then who copied who? Odd, isn't it?

J. Z. explained it years ago. The affectation is the "accent of Spirit" while using the vocal chords of the human body. Can I prove it? No. However, let me quote some dialogue from *Contact*, the film based on Dr. Sagan's book.

"Did you love your father?" [asks the minister]

"Of course." [replies the scientist]

"Prove it." [silence]

Intangibles such as love, faith, spiritual emotion, envy, anger, and even God cannot be put into the same *proof mold* that has been developed by humans for the known elements and the behavior of matter as we have seen it. Before this discussion is finished, I wish to show how the intangible is actually becoming more tangible than ever! Back to J. Z. for just a moment.

[2] *The Los Angeles Times*, Thursday August 7 1997, p. A23R, "SCIENCE: In Quest for Truth, Argument Is Part of the Equation."

Whether a result of Dr. Sagan's book, or just because it was time, J. Z. has begun a campaign to scientifically show the changes that occur within her body when she channels Ramtha in an out-of-body fashion. A recent news magazine featured these efforts, and the beginning findings actually bring up more questions than they answer! Is there a change? You bet! Why? What does a "meld with Spirit" create biologically? What is normal? What should we expect to see? Whatever the answers, Knight's INTENT was to show that there is a real, physical change in her physiology during channeling, and there was! I'm certain there will be more to come on this. By the way, she invited real M.D.'s, not New Age friends (just thought I would mention it).

I also did something similar, but very unscientific. I only bring it up here for comparison. My channeling is conscious *in-body*, but I know that there are also physiological changes, because I feel them. I asked an auric photographic team I trusted to do a test. Now, auric photography itself is suspect to many as being fake, but I figured that whatever the camera was measuring, this test would at least show if anything was changing with me, in or out of channel. Even if this photography method isn't auric, and is something else— if there was a change in what it "saw" and measured, there would be a significance to ponder. I had two photos taken five minutes apart. One out of channel, then one immediately after I *brought in* Kryon. I remained in the photo chair, unmoving, for the pictures. The photos were absolutely dramatic! I published them in Issue 6 of the *Kryon Quarterly* for all to see. Whatever was going on was picked up and we all got to see it. I had multiple colors around me out of channel, which changed dramatically to one solid color the instant I brought in Kryon.

In his book, Dr. Sagan has given us a "baloney-detection kit." Supposedly, if you apply the principles outlined in the "kit" to anything you are examining, it will help give you a "yes" or "no" answer as to the reality of the examined phenomenon or hypothesis. As you might expect, the kit is a list of do's and don'ts for good, logical problem solving that would help lead to solid, empirical proof of a theory or idea. To a scientist, anything less is suspect and falls into the category of unfounded speculation. I guess if you wanted to prove a principle such as gravity, or how something physically observable works, or a hypothesis on how something might work that you can't test, this kit would be quite helpful. I tried something. I applied the logic procedures in the kit to *love,* and it failed! Oops. Guess love isn't real. Next, I applied it to my **belief** in *God.* It failed again! Then I applied it to the **existence** of God. It failed again. Guess God is fake, too? This is really the crux of Sagan's quest. Again, I think he wanted desperately to prove God, but as a first-class scientist, he couldn't.

If God is fake, then 80 percent of the population of Earth has really been duped! What is going on? Is the kit that bad? Actually, it's a good kit for physical things and logical thinking, but when you apply it to concepts, even ones we accept and experience daily (like the passion of love, for instance), it fails! Therefore, I believe the kit is incomplete—not bad—just incomplete. I am not one to provide the protocol for the additions to the kit, since I am not a scientist, but I would like to give you the missing kit element, **as disclosed by scientists**. Before that, however, here is a summary of Sagan's kit.

Sagan's Baloney-Detection Kit [3]

Do's: (all of them presented)
1. Provide independent confirmation of facts.
2. Encourage substantive debate on evidence by knowledge-able proponents.
3. Spin more than one hypothesis. What else could it be?
4. Don't get attached to your original hypothesis. It creates bias.
5. Quantify. Don't get vague. Find things to measure.
6. Make certain that each chain in the hypothesis argument works.

7. *Occam's Razor*—Simpler is better. Most answers fall into a less complex scenario when finally proven.

8. Ask if the hypothesis can be falsified. "Propositions that are untestable, unfalsifiable are not worth much." If you have proof, then let others make the same experiments to verify it with control experiments.

Dont's: (Mostly arguing and logical thinking techniques—not all presented here)

1. Don't attack the arguer (the one with the weird idea).

2. Don't argue by trusting an authority base that is not provable (e.g., *get this president back in office because he has a secret way of balancing the budget—which can't be revealed at the moment*, or *trust God in this matter—He knows things better than you do*).

3. Don't argue from adverse consequences (e.g., *find this man guilty; if you don't, it will encourage others to murder*).

4. Don't appeal to ignorance (e.g., *there is no proof that UFOs are NOT visiting us, therefore they must exist*). Proving that something is NOT happening doesn't prove that it IS, either. Absence of evidence is not evidence.

5. Don't use "special pleading" (e.g., *you can't understand this because God works in mysterious ways*).

6. Don't beg the question, also called assuming the answer. This is a statement in an argument that seems to give proof within the verbiage (e.g., *institute the death penalty—it will discourage violent crime*).

7. Don't just expose favorable circumstances—counting the hits and ignoring the misses.

8. Don't use a small database to prove anything.

9. Don't misinterpret complex statistics.

10. Don't be inconsistent

11. Don't be illogical (*non sequitur*—Latin for "it doesn't follow").

[3] Sagan, Carl (1997). *The Demon-Haunted World, pp. 201-218/* Paraphrased.

As I stated earlier in this book, I believe that science has been missing a vital new element to the mixture of their *energy realities*. I contend that the missing element is **human consciousness**. There IS energy in human consciousness! (more on that in a moment). Energy and power don't simply exist without reason. Whether in the smallest atomic particle or a black hole, energy has a process connected with it. Where there is proven energy being created, science looks for some physical creative process going on. Patterned (nonrandom) energy denotes a process of sophisticated energy creation. This energy is being generated or is being trans-mitted or is being delivered by some process—even if we simply call it physics, or "the way things work."

Gravity is an example. Because we know where to look, and because it is all around us, the *baloney-detection kit* easily proves that gravity exists (no baloney). What IS gravity, however? No scientist yet really knows, and the exact mechanics that create it is still a hypothesis. Question: Do you BELIEVE IN gravity, or do you only KNOW gravity exists? To believe in something denotes a recognition greater than its simple existence. Even though the process is not specifically known that actually creates gravity, it is accepted as real (of course). It is acknowledged that gravity is not CAUSED by mass. Gravity is the result of some mechanism in physics that is related to mass (possibly by the elusive *graviton*, but that's for another book). Even though we don't understand it, it's accepted as "the way things work," since it's all around us and very common (like love, for instance). Proving the existence of gravity using the kit is easy. The hypothesis behind what causes it, however, doesn't pass the kit! No amount of logical thinking and correct examination brings us verification regarding the process. Is gravity baloney? No. Only the hypothesis regarding what causes it. But I still BELIEVE IN gravity, even though I don't know what causes it. I still TRUST in the way it works, even though I don't know how it operates.

I contend that God and love are the same as this. They exist for all to see but cannot pass the test of the examination of the mechanics of their operation. Nothing I present here is going to change that. I can, however, provide some *kit-like* proof of the existence of the **energy** of human consciousness. It's a good start. Perhaps this is love? Whatever it is, it has substance! If I can demonstrate that there is actual designed (sophisticated) energy associated with human consciousness, then doesn't it make sense that we should consider it a player on the stage of real-world energy science (as in "the way things work")? Let's find some real science (documented by the kind of experiments and sources that Dr. Sagan might invite as part of his testing) regarding human consciousness. Let's show that it displays measurable energy, that it affects known elements around it, and that it has consistency in this display—a display that can be duplicated over and over within a controlled scientific venue. Wouldn't that take it out of the woo-woo department a bit? Perhaps we could even go further, later on and examine love in the same way?

First of all, I have to laugh at the premise I am about to present. There are certain potent emotions whose energies are undeniable to every human alive. Like gravity, it is all around us, yet here we are forcing it into some confined experimental matrix (designed by humans) so that we can "prove" it exists, then examine its workings—such is the logic of our scientific thinking. It's like jumping through logic hoops to prove that it's raining outside. Some of us want to violate the protocol and just open the window and look.

Have any of you ever been grief stricken? Can you even for a moment deny the tremendous energy around this process? As you sat there drained of all human desire to live, with all your bodily functions being affected, and those around you in dramatic response, how would you like to have someone ask you to prove that your body is radiating some kind of energy (a punch in the nose might be the result)? Although extremely unscientific for the purpose of this discussion, I have to tell you that to a psychic, this person is like a beacon in a crowd—easily picked out due to the energy around them radiating dramatically. It's the same with rage, by the way.

Were you ever deeply in love? Believe it or not, these two energies of human consciousness are very related in their effect on you. Your body stops functioning as designed, and you seem to disengage from everything you know to be "real." In this state, also, there is a great amount of energy blasted out for anyone or anything with the right kind of antenna needed...to *see*. You actually glow to a psychic! (very unscientific, I know)!

Can any of us really sit there and deny the energy of such things? What about the love of God? Billions of humans all around the globe feel this at the cellular level, and react. They worship, celebrate, pray, sing, and dance about due to the energy they feel regarding the love of God. They feel reciprocation, and claim miracles, too—all due to this highly charged energetic attribute. Is it all fake?

We absolutely do not know the scientific mechanism behind the energy of human consciousness, but we all see it. Unlike gravity, however, it does not fit within the parameters of measurable physical earthly phenomena. This is not the time to totally revisit one of my basic principles (as mentioned in my other books), but I will quickly review for the new reader that simply because we can't measure something does not mean that it does not exist! Did radio waves exist in the cosmos before we could measure them? Yes, but we couldn't prove it. Dr. Sagan's *baloney-detection kit* would have concluded their possibility to be very tentative 100 years ago. Baloney—or real? Right now I believe there are other attributes arriving daily from the cosmos that we have no concept of. They would not pass the *baloney-detection kit* either, because the ability to measure or understand them has not yet been realized and is not part of our *reality*.

Like an IQ test (which is said only to measure what an IQ test measures—not real intelligence), therefore, Sagan's *baloney de-*

tection kit might only measure designer baloney—a preset concept biased in the human reality of what **current** *baloney* must be. It will be interesting to revisit this in 100 years to find out how much of today's baloney has been labeled as real science due to new discovery.

I set out to show that at least human consciousness can be measured—or perhaps transmitted. I thought, certainly by now our science has done this? Where do I look for such things? Then I found that my request had partially been granted, and by a New Age worker at that! In her book *The Lightworker's Way*, Doreen Virtue, Ph.D. (Hay House—1997) has included specific chapters on this exact subject. In fact, reading her book would "shake hands" very nicely with this entire subject matter, and I highly recommend it. I bought the book just to find what I was interested in, but I couldn't put it down. I was thrilled with the information, and it's not all science.

Dr. Virtue graciously gave me permission to include her name regarding this subject, and I am also going to paraphrase some of what she has reported, and also give the credits from sources she developed, as published in her book. Here are just three scientific discussions (of many) that fit into a venue that Dr. Sagan might be more comfortable with than the heretofore woo-woo.

The Power of Human Thought

Since we are talking about gravity so much (as being very real and provable), let's see if there is any positive empirical evidence that human consciousness (something that isn't thought to be provable energy by science), can actually change gravity (something that absolutely IS provable as energy).

Princeton researchers Robert Jahn and Brenda Dunne decided to try it. In a controlled experiment, they asked many volunteers to participate in two specific tests regarding matter response (or non-response) to human concentrated thought. In one test, the volunteers sat in front of a machine that randomly flipped coins. They were asked to concentrate on influencing the machine to make the coins all land "heads up." The results showed that the thoughts of the humans indeed made a difference, and that most of the volunteers provided a statistically influential bias—with their thoughts alone—and far more coins were coming up heads than a control without the human influence. This, of course, was a repeatable test.

Another experiment was with 9,000 marbles and a pinball machine. It dropped the marbles from a center point, and the volunteers were asked to concentrate on having the marbles go only to the outer bins only. Again, the results were absolute, repeatable, and significant. Human thought affected matter.[4]

Can one mind affect another? When you pray for someone (concentrated thought), can they feel it? If so, would that show a communicated energy? When you meditate in a room with like-minded people, can you concentrate energy with a combined effort, as if all the people had some kind of synchronized larger mind?

Scientific evidence, measuring brain waves, heart rates, and emotions of those being concentrated on, have shown that the answer was YES! Those meditating in a group, asked to concentrate on one thing, were also measured (brain waves). The results showed an exact brain-wave match with others in the group![5]

---

[4] Dunne, B. J., Jahn, R. G. (1992). "Experiments in remote human/machine interaction." *Journal of Scientific Exploration*, Vol. 6, No. 4, pp. 311-332.

[5] Hirasawam, Yamamoto M., Kawano, K. & Furukawa, A. (1996). "An experiment on extrasensory information transfer with electroencephalogram measurement." Journal of *International Society of Life Information Science*, Vol. 14, pp. 43-48.

Radin, Dean I. (1996). "Silent Shockwaves: Evidence for presentiment of emotional futures." *European Journal of Parapsychology*, Vol. 12.

Honorton, C., et al. (1990). "Psi-communication in the Ganzfeld: Experiments with an automated testing system and a comparison with a meta-analysis of earlier studies." *Journal of Parapsychology*, Vol. 54.

Varvoglis, Marlo (1986). "Goal-directed and observer dependent PK: An evaluation of the conformance-behavior model and the observation theories." *The Journal of the American Society for Psychical Research*, Vol. 80.

At Cornell University, Daryl Bem and Charles Honorton were skeptics regarding the energy of human consciousness. They developed a tightly controlled experiment that simply could not be faked to disprove the idea of psychic powers. They believed that those claiming to have them were simply using good human nature techniques and some clever tricks. To their astonishment, the experiments ended up supporting psychic power—not disproving it! It was real, and they had the scientific results to show it. They continued, and with 11 experiments between 1983 and 1989, they changed the minds of other scientists and fueled thoughtful discussion with respect to the concept that there is an energy within the human mind that is far more than what it seems! Needless to say, they themselves were among those converted. [6]

Why do I show all of this? It is to attempt to bring the formerly weird and woo-woo subject of psychic power into focus as a reality. The term *psychic power* may get in the way of your logic mind, since for so long it has been the language of many who are considered strange, if not fake. So call it the *energy of human consciousness*. That's more accurate.

In these studies, it has been shown that human consciousness can change physics. Not only does this fly in the face of the "baloney-detection kit," but it also supports the basic premise that Kryon brought to us starting in 1989. To ignore this energy and to claim to provide a testing kit that is absolute without it is not logical. I know that someone in the future with far higher credentials than I, will complete this kit. Then we can "prove" that love is real! With this, I wish to wrap up the Sagan discussion and move to something directly related to human thought and enlightenment, but far larger in the scope of our own planetary shift, and more directed to the metaphysical readers of this book.

---

[6] Bem, Daryl J. and Charles Honorton (1994). "Does psi exist? Replicable evidence for an anomalous process of information transfer." *Psychological Bulletin*, Vol. 115, pp. 4-18.

Science News, January 29 1994, Vol. 145, No. 5, p. 68, "Scientists Peer into the Mind's Psi."

The Grand Gift—We Gave Ourselves

Now that we have given the basic premise of consciousness changing physics and have presented some science behind it, I am going to shift into a purely metaphysical discussion. I will speak of something that I firmly believe has taken place that many of you are not aware of—and it continues to speak of the power of human consciousness.

Since 1989, Kryon has told us that we have changed the future of our planet. He has told us that we can throw away the doom-and-gloom predictions of what was heretofore a very frightening coming millennium change. He has told us that human consciousness has raised the vibration of the planet and that our future is now a moving target—known by no entity and controlled by the critical mass of enlightened humanity, right now as you read these words. What a message! Now, for the first time in any Kryon book, I wish to alert you to something I feel we have done, and give you a scenario to ponder that is astounding and profound in its implications.

Doom and Gloom—Our Future?

As metaphysicians, for many years we have had solid evidence that something alarming was going to take place on the planet.

1. Nostradamus, a 400-year-old prophet, gave us very accurate predictions. His profound quatrains from four centuries ago actually spoke of Hitler, and Nostradamus missed that famous name by only one letter (his quatrains spoke of Hister)! He also accurately foretold the assassination of President John F. Kennedy. It would make sense, therefore, to also look to his wisdom and accuracy to see what he has to say about our immediate future. It's scary. Nostradamus has indicated that our continents will have altered their shorelines by hundreds of miles! Water will be covering major cities that have been on the coasts of most of the world's land masses. Is some major catastrophe going to create this?

2. Gordon Michael Scallion, a New Age visionary (and doom and-gloom-specialist), has been telling us for many years of the same scenario as Nostradamus. He also had visions that support the Nostradamus assertions, and he has published maps that give us the detailed effects of the result of whatever is going to happen. The coastlines on his maps are frightening, and my town is underwater—and perhaps yours, too.

3. The indigenous American Hopi Indian tribe has ancient predictions also, and (you guessed it) their map looks just like the above two, with the water encroaching over much of what is now coastal habitation.

What is going to happen? Can we change it? Should we be hunkering down in fear? If you watched the doom-and-gloom TV special *Prophecies and Predictions*, you might think so. Remember that program? David McCallum—with a flashlight under his chin, spooky music, and swirling smoke—very scientific (I'm being facetious)! Those types of programs are absolutely designed to scare you silly, and use pseudo science and lots of sensational rumors (and Gordon Michael Scallion) to do it. The television program *Millennium* tells us (using loosely based facts added to hearsay) that the Earth is going to tilt on its axis in the year 2001 due to a unique alignment with the other planets. If you remember, Kryon told us in 1989 that this very old predicted tilt is actually the new grid shift (the reason Kryon is here), and not an actual shift. Still, to many, Kryon is simply a woo-woo channel, so why believe it? Instead, why not believe the validated soothsayers? Read on.

A Changed Future

Something is happening on the planet globally regarding predictions in general. They are not happening as *scheduled*. Take a look around you. Those of you who make a study of those who have solid prediction records (and those who don't)—take a look.

1. The prophet Edgar Cayce has had a validation track record in the 60 percent or higher ratio, but within the last few years it has dropped to less than 30 percent. Does this mean Cayce was wrong? What is happening to alter this?

2. Sheldon Nidle, who brought us dramatic and potentially fearful information regarding the photon belt in the book *Becoming a Galactic Human*, misfired completely, and the photon belt experience simply didn't happen. None of his other ET predictions have either, making him 0 for 0 in the prediction department. Does that mean Sheldon was wrong?

3. The quatrains of Nostradamus, by the report of experts in that field, are now off by over four years. His predictions are not happening on schedule. Was Nostradamus wrong? He wasn't before.

4. Gordon Michael Scallion issued his startling maps of altered coastlines many years ago. The dates on those maps indicated that our "doom and gloom" would be here in the late eighties and early nineties. When it didn't happen, for whatever reason, Mr. Scallion issued and published new maps with UPDATED doom-and-gloom information. What happened? Was Gordon wrong?

These visionaries and channels all had visions that to them were extremely real. In the case of several, a track record of validation accompanied them. Were they wrong? The answer is NO. If we have changed our future as Kryon said, then it is indeed possible that these men of vision accurately reported a future that didn't happen. They channeled a POTENTIAL future that Kryon has been telling us is now gone and passed, due to our work on the planet. Therefore, they accurately reported an old-energy future, one that has now been changed forever. It is interesting to see what the ones who are still alive will do with their personal predictions that fail to take place. So far they seem to be in denial and have stated that for whatever reason, the bad news has simply been *delayed*. So they continue with the fearful information, updating the dates and events (sometimes in a national venue), creating fear and unrest. I disagree with this. I think we can look at our three-dimensional world with God-given human discernment and common sense, and clearly make a correlation to something that took place recently that made the difference—a big difference.

Consciousness Changed Physics – May 1996

Time magazine, June 3, 1996, blazed a frightening message on page 61: *A SHOT ACROSS THE EARTH'S BOW*, it proclaimed. Evidently in May 1996, we were almost hit by a very big asteroid! Listen to what *Time* had to say:

A Shot Across The Earth's Bow

"Early last week…this celestial interloper whizzed by Earth, missing the planet by 280,000 miles—a hairbreadth in astronomical terms. [*The moon is only 240,000 miles from us.*] Perhaps a third of a mile across, it was the largest object ever observed to pass that close to Earth. Duncan Steel, an Australian astronomer, has calculated that if the asteroid had struck Earth, it would have hit at some 58,000 m.p.h. The resulting explosion, scientists estimate, would have been in the 3,000-to 12,000-megaton range. 'That,' says astronomer Eugene Shoemaker, a pioneer asteroid and comet hunter, 'is like taking all of the U.S and Soviet nuclear weapons, putting them in one pile and blowing them all up.' "

If this asteroid had hit us, it would have probably been in one of Earth's oceans (greater than an 80 percent chance of that). Do you know what that would have done to us? Can you imagine the result of an explosion equal to all the nuclear weapons on Earth being concentrated in one spot in the ocean together? It would not have been subtle, and it would have affected us ALL greatly!

This was a scientific report, but what did this mean metaphysically? Could this huge rock have hit us? Was it *scheduled* to hit us? I asked Kryon, "*Could this asteroid have hit us?*" Kryon told me YES. I pondered it. "*But it didn't! Why?*" This is when I received the Kryon "wink," a giant "love wash," and he again said to me, as though I had never heard it, CONSCIOUSNESS CHANGES PHYSICS!

"*Kryon,*" I said, "*do you mean we changed the math of orbital mechanics, and changed the path of an asteroid?*" Again came the answer: YES!

This was difficult to believe. Did this near miss stated in a national magazine "conveniently" fit into the Kryon work, or was there more to it? Within this question, you may continue to see the workings of my "show me" mind. I was skeptical, even though I am the channel. I wanted more. I got it.

The Complete Ascension Manual, by Joshua David Stone, is published by Light Technology Publishing (the same publisher as the *Sedona Journal*). On page 246 is a startling channeling by an entity named Vywamus. When the book was published, Vywamus was being channeled by the now late Janet McClure.

In these pages, Vywamus said that an asteroid a mile in diameter (slightly off from the real one) was heading toward the Earth. He said it should arrive around 1995 (again, slightly off). "From a consciousness point of view," he said, "it could actually be a very positive thing, a new kind of energy being integrated into the Earth's system." He said, "The asteroid would be carrying a great amount of spiritual energy. **If humankind has gotten to the point where it can use this energy, the asteroid won't be destructive.**"

I couldn't believe it. There, in black and white, was a channel who had predicted our asteroid's near miss! The small differences in size and time didn't bother me any more than Nostradamus's missing Hitler's name by one letter, for the prediction was made years ago. It was right on—extremely close to the reality of what had happened! Look at what it was saying. It predicted the asteroid (within a year of its actual arrival), but more importantly, the ability of our human consciousness to change the asteroid's path, just as Kryon said WE INDEED HAD!

There's more to this than meets the eye. My assertion is that had this astronomical body hit us at 58,000 m.p.h., it would have been responsible for the outlines on the frightening map of Nostradamus, and the map of Gordon Michael Scallion, and the Hopi Indian map. This asteroid's visit was just one of the events that voided out an old-energy future, and we all got to see it—not from a New Age magazine that might have been suspect by many, but from a national source reporting scientific discovery. Start getting used to this method. Spirit, and the predicted workings of our New Age, will be reported for ALL to see in this manner (see "The Kryon Validations" starting on the next page). The asteroid DID NOT hit us, since we had an elevated human consciousness. The doom-and-gloom team can keep going, but just like the asteroid, we will never see it. This is indeed a time for celebration!

Dear reader, as you read these words, Kryon has something to say about this:

"Dear ones, now do you understand the love we have for you? Now do you understand what you have done? It is the humans who have the power in this New Age! Even with the evidence in front of them, there will be those who will continue to shout that all is coming to an end. As their fearful predictions dwindle into a tentative reality, and nothing takes place as they say it should, celebrate the love of Spirit that partners with you in this grand new future for the planet Earth! Celebrate the new millennium and the graduation of the human race! Celebrate our love for you!"

I can add very little to this. So I won't.

The Kryon Validations

Kryon doesn't give predictions. To do so would be to violate the already stated Kryon premise that no one knows our future, and that a brand new one is being developed as we go. What Kryon DOES do, however, is to give us hints as to WHAT to look for, and suggestions as to WHERE to look to facilitate our own self-discovery. He also delights in giving us phrases within channelings that are often printed later within the pages of national magazines, reporting scientific discoveries. This is one of the many cosmic humor aspects of his work, where often the verbiage of the channeling is repeated verbatim.

The following subjects are brought to you (as in every Kryon channeling book since Book Two) in order to validate what Kryon has said in certain live and transcribed channelings of the past. I believe that this element in a Kryon book is important and neces-sary. It is my opinion that any New Age channel should be able to do this, and let it stand for the record to see. Spirit is not proprietary. Information is given through a channel that is universally accurate and true, and does not belong to Kryon or the Kryon work. If channelings are the inspired and anointed messages from God for humans, then the information imparted should be able to be validated over time, and also appear in other channeled works as well. I am happy to say that the Kryon work meets those criteria.

Radioactive Waste

In Kryon Book II, page 223, the question was raised about what to do about radioactive waste. One of the solutions that Kryon put forward was "Look to your biology." In Kryon Book III (page 249), we spoke of this again and told you that bioremediation was beginning to develop all over the globe. A biological solution to radioactive waste didn't seem to be common knowledge until recently, how-ever. Now I wish to quote portions of an article in *Science News* that absolutely validates the fact that this is being worked on at the highest level, and will give credibility to a heretofore fanciful Kryon channeling originally given in 1989. The following appeared along with a photo of a platform of plants in a pond.

Botanical Cleanup Crews

"Rafts with sunflowers growing on them float on a small pond at the Chernobyl nuclear accident site in the Ukraine. No, it's not some touching monument to the 1986 disaster. The plants are helping to clean the pond; their roots dangle in the water to suck up the radionuclides **cesium 137** and **strontium 90**.

... Exxon Corp. and DuPont are testing a variety of plants to see if they can do some of the dirty work of cleaning up such pollutants as **radioactive material**, lead, selenium, and oil. Many plants, it turns out, have a taste for these stubborn contaminants." [7]

Crop Circle Validates DNA Base-12

On June 17, 1996, a 648-foot-long crop circle appeared overnight in the famous East Field at Alton Barnes near Oxford in the U.K. It is pictured for you on the facing page.

Is there any doubt that this is a double-helix? If you don't believe that crop circles are real communications from another source, then you can simply skip this section, but you will also have to pass over the next crop circle section where Euclidean geometry and mathematics experts got a surprise or two—your choice.

---

[7] *Science News*, July 20 1996, Vol. 150, p. 42, "Botanical Cleanup Crews." Entire article not shown.

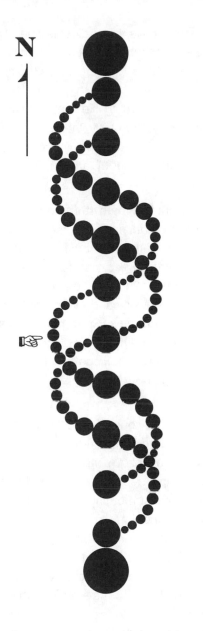

Double-Helix
With Twelve Chakras

by Peter Sorensen

This spectacular formation arrived June 17th, 1996, in the famous East Field at Alton Barnes (SU115-625), near Oxford, pointing at Adam's Grave to the North and Woodborough Hill to the South. The official length is 648 ft. long, and consists of 89 circles forming twin strands of "thought bubbles" (77 total) spiraling around a central backbone of **12** large circles in a line. Everyone who sees it agrees that the design represents DNA.

Note, where the double-helix strands cross over each other, it is implied that in 3D, the near strand hides one of the circles on the far strand. Hence, there could be ten circles accounted for in each of the eight loops (except one of the loops indicated by the hand, which has eleven). Thus, if we count overlapping circles and the extra one, there is a defacto total of **93**.*

*Interested in a great **web page** with crop circles and other cosmic stuff?*

http://www.cosmic-connections.com

This "energy stamp," as Kryon calls the circles, is one of the best validations I have ever seen of the ideas presented in Kryon Book III regarding DNA, and Base-12 math (page 292). You might recall that in a live Sedona, Arizona, channeling, Kryon began speaking about the elegance of base-12 math. He related it to many things around us, including geometry, Astrology, the Jewish calendar, the sacred number of tribes in the Jewish lineage, music, spiritual hints (like the 12:12 and the 144,000), and finally, human DNA.

Let's get something clear about this math stuff: Kryon doesn't want us to suddenly stop counting on our fingers (base-10), but he keeps speaking of base-12 math as being the math for physics. He wants us to know that much of what we see around us is already base-12. He gives us hints that base-12 calculation and examination is going to reveal much about physics and even simple math that has been difficult or hidden up to now. From prime-number computations to the better understanding of Tesla technology, Kryon encourages us to experiment with it. Hopefully, by the next book, I will have some news to print about this very subject. It can't hide forever.

The crop circle on page 363 is obviously DNA. If you want an interpretation that is a summary, here it is: *"We understand your DNA, and it's base-12!"* How's that for a simple interpretation? Kryon tells us that the energy stamps are sent to us from *"those we are going to meet."* I want to clear up something about crop circles and ETs. These crop circles are not being made by the little gray guys with slanted eyes who abduct us, or who are lately trying to gain our confidence (since abduction is getting bad press—see page 92). These guys desperately would like to know all about our DNA (especially the hidden, non biological parts—more on this later in this chapter). If you have followed the stories about communications regarding these ETs, it's all about their quest to examine us.

The message in the grass at Alton Barnes is from those who absolutely know about our biology. It is from those who represent the actual seeds of our DNA. Everything about the circle "yells" base-12. Kryon told us that as a starter, our DNA was a pattern of four, repeated three times—an obvious base-12. In the same communication, he spoke of the 12 strands of DNA—all 12s! Now, here is validation of that fact.

The double-helix is 648 feet long (by the way, that's over two football fields for those who want a better grasp of the size). This wasn't made overnight by two guys with sticks and ropes and a case of beer! Think about it. The math, and the numerology, is important. The analysis is that 648 is divisible by 12. That equals 54; 54 reduces to 9 in numerology, which is the energy around *completion*. If you read the commentary by Peter Sorensen (with the circle on page 363) you know that the de facto number of circles is 93. This also adds to 12. Remember also that 12 in numerology reduces to a 3, which has the energy of *catalyst*. Remember in Kryon Book I about the *power of the 3*?

Finally, there are also 12 main *chakras* (large circles) along the spine of the diagram, indicating again to look at the significance of the 12. This was a fine communication, indeed. Keep reading this chapter. There's more about base-12 DNA coming.

Crop Circle Gives Mathematicians New Theorems

It finally happened! Crop circles—kind of a no-no in science circles—get it? *Science circles? Well, they* made it into a scientific publication. Not *just* a scientific publication, but the MATH section of a scientific publication! It seems that the circles are now giving theorems that even Euclid did not give us. What follows on the next page is a story as quoted from *Science News*.

Take a look at the disclaimer in the last paragraph of this math article. Wow! Suddenly, not only can two guys with sticks and ropes, under the cover of darkness, make dozens of crop circles (some of them two football fields long), but now they are first-class mathematicians, too—giving new theorems that have never been reported on Earth yet—even by Euclid!

Mathematics
Crop Circles: Theorems in Wheat Fields

Several years ago, astronomer Gerald S. Hawkins, now retired from Boston University, noticed that some of the most visually striking of the crop-circle patterns embodied geometric theorems that express specific numerical relationships among the areas of various circles, triangles, and other shapes making up the patterns.

Hawkins found that he could use the principles of Euclidean geometry to prove four theorems derived from the relationships among the areas depicted in these patterns. He also discovered a fifth, more general theorem [on his own] from which he could derive the other four.

Curiously, Hawkins could find no reference to such a theorem in the works of Euclid or in any other book that he consulted. When he challenged readers of *Science News* and the *Mathematics Teacher* to come up with his unpublished theorem, given only the four variations, no one reported success.

This past summer, however, "the crop circle makers showed knowledge of this fifth theorem," Hawkins reports. Among the dozens of circles surreptitiously laid down in the wheat fields of England, at least one pattern fit Hawkins's theorem.

The persons responsible for this old-fashioned type of mathematical ingenuity remain at large and unknown. Their handiwork flaunts an uncommon facility with Euclidean geometry, and signals an astonishing ability to enter fields undetected, to bend living plants without cracking stalks, and to trace out complex, precise patterns, presumably using little more than pegs and ropes, all under cover of darkness.[8]

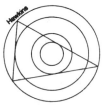

Hawkins's fifth crop-circle theorem involves a triangle and various concentric circles touching the triangle's sides and corners...an equilateral triangle produces one of the observed crop-circle patterns; three isosceles triangles generate the other crop-circle geometries.

[8] *Science News*, October 12 1996, Vol. 150, p. 239, "Crop Circles: Theorems in Wheat Fields." Entire article not shown.

The Gamma Ray Puzzle Revealed

In both Kryon Book II and Kryon Book III, I reported unexplained gamma-ray activity and quoted science sources. Why? On page 67 of Kryon Book II (1994), Kryon told us to look for this exact activity as an indication of the **arrival of spiritual energy for the planet**. "*Look for short, highly intense, unexplainable gamma ray activity.*"[11]

Years went by with the scientific community asking where the rays were coming from. Naturally, science did not suddenly find that they were coming from God (hardly). Instead, they found an even greater paradox—one that actually goes further in supporting Kryon's assertion that these great energies are from the *great central source*.

It is accepted science that the Big Bang theory (which Kryon says is false), places the source of the "wave" of the expanding universe at about 11 to 12 billion light years away from the planet. That, simply put, is where the beginning *stuff* of the origin of the universe is thought to be, still expanding outward.

Suddenly on February 28,1997, an Italian-Dutch Beppo-SAX satellite *accidentally* was able to record the exact position of an 80-second gamma ray burst. The position of the burst has been labeled as GRB 970228.[9] NASA turned its orbiting Compton Gamma Ray Observatory (GRO), which carries the *Burst and Transient Source Experiment* (BATSE), toward the source and began recording something that is simply unexplainable to scientists.

Cal Tech scientists have said that it represents "the most powerful bursts of energy in the universe."[10] Astronomer Shri Kulkarni said, "It Boggles my imagination to think what it means to be a billion billion times brighter than the sun."[10] *Scientific American*, who reports the energy at an astounding 10^{51} ergs, says that "it must be very far away, near the outer reaches of the observable universe. In that case, gamma-ray bursts must represent the most powerful explosions in the universe."[9]

What is puzzling to scientists is the following: (1) It is further away than anything they have ever observed, but with more energy than anything they have observed. This was unexpected. Normally energy arriving from 7 to 11 billion light years away is extremely faint (as you might imagine). This energy is just the opposite, and (2) It doesn't seem to fit the protocol of an object moving away from us.

The first thing the astronomers wanted to establish (besides where it was and how much energy it was pushing at us), was if the source for this energy was indeed moving away from us like almost everything else in the heavens (supposed proof of the Big Bang). This is normally done with spectrometry, measuring the "red shift." Before I tell you what they found, I want you to know what Kryon said (again, and at the end of this section). This energy is cosmic and is part of a spiritual delivery system. It didn't take 11 billion years to get here. It is instant (see the next section of this chapter), and is not moving away from us. Here is what *Scientific American* says about the telltale red shift: "At such a distance, the bursts should show the effects of the expansion of the universe. Galaxies that are very distant are moving away from the earth at great speeds; we know this because the light they emit shifts to lower, or redder, frequencies. Likewise, gamma-ray bursts should also show a "redshift," as well as an increase in duration. Unfortunately, BATSE does not see, in the spectrum of gamma rays, bright or dark lines characterizing specific elements whose displacements would betray a shift to the red."[9]

[9] *Scientific American*, July 1997, pp. 46-51, "Gamma-Ray Bursts: New observations illuminate the most powerful explosions in the universe."

[10] *The Los Angeles Times*, May 15 1997, front page A1, "Cal Tech Captures Key to a Mystery of the Heavens."

[11] *Don't Think Like a Human,* Kryon Book II (1994), p. 67.

Oops! It doesn't seem to fit the expected pattern. There's more consternation: Astronomers have leaped to their cosmic physics, trying to create hypothetical patterns of what this could be. *Scientific American* tells us that these theories vary, but the best one is a "cosmic catastrophe," where a fireball is involved. Binary neutron-star system collapse was mention, as well as white dwarfs colliding with black holes (I wonder if Snow White is aware of this?).

"There are some problems, however: the binary collapse does not explain some long-lasting bursts. Last year, for instance, BATSE found a burst that endured for 1,100 seconds and possibly repeated two days later."[9]

Well, folks, the puzzle continues. Will science ever admit the spiritual aspects of this physical attribute? Probably not, but the more they find out about it, the more it seems to verify the Kryon information about what to look for, given in 1994—that this great energy is from the creative source, and that it is more powerful than anything we have seen, and that it's being delivered in real "now" time, and that Its essence is LOVE!

Faster Than the Speed of Light?

How can energy, or anything else for that matter, travel faster than the speed of light? The speed of light has been thought to be the absolute universal speed limit. Nothing that is observable with our scope of scientific understanding goes any faster than light waves (or light particles).

In Kryon Book II (again in 1994), Kryon gave us some hints about physics, in that there are indeed things to measure that go faster than the speed of light. In fact, Kryon called it instant communication and referred to it as the basis for Spiritual communication. I hope you are "plugging" this in to the last few pages as well, since it all relates. Here is what Kryon said.

Kryon's "Twins" Message in 1994

"There will be new parts to discover as well. One of the most interesting things, however, will be when you discover the *twins*.

Hiding within common atomic structure is a marvelous peek at something that will totally and completely mystify you, for it will seem to break all the laws of time and space. The *twins* are a pair of atomic parts that always relate to each other and are always found in pairs—stimulated correctly, they will always move together as a pair. When you start separating them by distance to experiment, they will continue to move exactly together. No matter how far you remove them from one another, they will exactly move together... If one's energy is converted, then the other will do the same...

This instant communication between the parts of the *twins* is the basis of communication of all universal Spirit entities in the Universe."[12]

In July of 1997, an ongoing experiment at the University of Geneva in Switzerland researching (of all things) cryptology, has remarkably discovered the exact attribute that Kryon said to look for! On the facing page is the article describing it. Compare it to the Kryon information. You have to understand, as you read it, that it was given first in Swedish, then translated to French, and then taken from the Internet and translated into English! My thanks to Yves Vidal for finding this information and translating it into English!

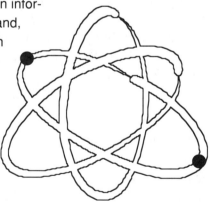

---

[12] *Don't Think Like a Human,* Kryon Book II (1994), pp. 220-221.

Photons Jemeaux: Enigme Quantique, Solution Technologique - 1997

The *New York Times* scientific issue relates a very strange experiment that deepens the mysteries of quantum physics, although very promising in the domain of cryptography and coding.

Some researchers from the University of Geneva have measured the behavior of *twin* photons (created by decomposition of a unique photon) after making them diverge on perfectly identical trajectories along many kilometers.

The orientations taken by each of these two photons (measured with interferometers located at the end of each trajectory) should normally follow the laws of independent random distributions. In fact, the *twin* photons are showing an identical behavior, as if each photon was informed of the orientation taken by the other one. The size of the Swiss experiment warrants that no information could have transited between the *twin* photons during their orientation decision (or choice). Scientists are totally bewildered by such a mystery and cannot explain it. They are already searching, however, for some technological applications.

Continued Cool, with Occasional Tsunamis

Honest! That's the title of an article that appeared in *Outside* magazine. Okay, okay...I guess you don't really have to read in these pages that we have been undergoing tremendous planetary weather changes! For some, all you have to do is open the window and look outside to know that. Some of you are still cleaning up from flood damage.

Still, I just wanted to mention that in 1988, when the first Kryon book was being channeled, this was the exact theme of what was going to take place. Channel after channel referred to the upcoming earth changes—and here they are!

Kryon said, *"Certainly there will be floods and quakes and eruptions in your future...some will be a reaction to my new work..."*[13]

What you are seeing now is exactly what Kryon told us would happen. Even as I write this, my town (San Diego) is expecting the *storm of the century* for the **second time** in 15 years! In review: Kryon is here to change the grids. The grids posture our enlightenment, and a critical mass of humanity vibrating at a higher level causes earth changes. See any lately?

It's important, though, to realize that Earth is responding to US! None of the changes are being dumped on us. We have asked for the planet to increase in vibration, and it is! The article below was about the year 1996. The writer had no idea that 1997 would bring even more!

Continued Cool, with Occasional Tsunamis

"Golly, it was a super year, wasn't it? We're speaking of last year, which wasn't that long ago if you run tardy on stuff, like government meteorologists do. They're the folks who tally up the world's weather-related disasters, and as we mentioned, 1996 was a really super year. Hurricane Fran, drought in Mongolia, an Old Testament barrage of rainstorms, tsunamis, and typhoons throughout southern Asia—not to mention volcanoes and earthquakes, the planet's own internal weather. According to the world's largest reinsurer, 1996 managed some 600 major natural disasters, wreaking $60 billion in damage—a net disaster increase of 400 percent since the 1960s! That's good weather?" [14]

[13] *The End Times,* Kryon Book I (1989), p. 22.

[14] *Outside* magazine, April 1997, p. 106, "Continued Cool, with Occasional Tsunamis."

...speaking of Earth Changes

The entire work of Kryon is centered around the fact that we changed our future, and he is here to adjust the grid because of it. Within the scope of all this we find that our future continues to shift as we increase the vibration of the planet. Unknown to us in 1989 (when Kryon Book I was originally written), some attributes of the physical planet Earth itself were changing. The Schumann resonance, a measurement of the standing wave within the current between the bottom of the ionosphere and the surface of the Earth, has been consistent at approximately 7.25Hz to 7.8Hz for eons. It has been so consistent that even some scientific instruments were calibrated to it. Gregg Braden, noted author of *Awakening to Zero Point*, indicates that this resonance is currently (as of 5/97) being measured at 10Hz to 11Hz! The Earth is not only changing its spiritual attribute as a result of our work, but also physically changing its vibration, and science is showing it in these areas. All this activity is a strong reaction to the fact that consciousness changes physics...do you remember that theme at the beginning of this chapter?

The Shumann Resonance

The Schumann resonances are quasi standing electromagnetic waves that exist in the cavity between the surface of the Earth and the inner edge of the ionosphere 55 kilometers up. The standing waves represent several frequencies between 6Hz and 50Hz, with the fundamental being 7.8 and a daily variation of about +/- 0.5 Hz. For more information on the Schumann resonance, see Handbook of Atmospheric Electrodynamics, Vol. I *chapter 11 by Hans Volland - 1995 - published by the CRC Press.*

The Big Bang Comes into Question

In a 1995 channeling in Sedona, Arizona, Kryon told the audience that the Big Bang theory wasn't accurate, as many of today's scientists would have you believe.

Kryon's Big Bang Message in 1995

It seems as you sit here in this modern age, your scientists are convinced that all the matter they see in the universe—the Earth, the solar system, the galaxy, and all other galaxies as far as they can be seen—were all caused from one expanding event. They have called this event their *Big Bang.* This is indeed a very illogical scientific premise, although metaphorically it makes the same kind of sense that it did to those three hundred years ago.." (speaking of the notion that everything we saw in the heavens rotated around us—with math to prove it).[15]

Kryon goes on to give examples of the illogic of the idea, with some simple examples to look at—including the ages of the stars themselves at long distance—and the uneven distribution of matter. Now it seems that Kryon isn't alone. In the last two years, more and more scientists are beginning to question the theory and are finding some of the same things, just as Kryon said they might.

New Thinking about the Ages of Old Stars

Whether it's truly a crisis in cosmology or just a matter of incomplete knowledge, astronomers are up against a conundrum: The universe, according to several observations, appears to be younger than its oldest stars.

To resolve this paradox, researchers must prove that the universe is older than recent estimates of 9 to 11 billion years or that the oldest stars in our galaxy are younger than 12 to 8 billion years.[16]

---

[15]*Alchemy of The Human Spirit,* Kryon Book III (1995), pp. 284.

But wait...there's more!

Turmoil in the Heavens

Suppose you learned on good authority that your mother is younger than you are. Obviously that would be impossible to accept. You'd be thrown into a quandary and forced to contemplate the possibility that you're a lot younger than you thought you were. Astronomers have been thrown into similar upheaval—the universe turns out to be 8 to 12 billion years old. So far, so good. But that makes the universe much younger than the oldest known stars! [17]

Does the Cosmos Have a Direction?

East side, west side, all around the cosmos: No matter which way an observer looks, the vast reaches of space appear the same. Indeed, direction is meaningless in the simplest version of the Big Bang model, which holds that the primordial universe expanded uniformly, like a perfectly spherical balloon.

A controversial report now challenges that long-held tenet. An analysis of the polarization of radio waves emitted by distant galaxies suggests that the universe may have a preferred direction after all... .

The results of the study, if verified, could have startling consequences. One possibility is that the Big Bang gave rise to a nonuniform distribution of matter and a somewhat lopsided expansion... .[18]

---

[16] *Science News,* December 14 1996, Vol 150. "New thinking about the ages of old stars," p. 374. Entire article not shown.

[17] *Discover* magazine, March 1995, "Crisis in the Cosmos," p. 66. Entire article not shown.

[18] *Science News,* April 26 1997, Vol 151. "Does the Cosmos Have a Direction?" p. 252. Entire article not shown.

Human Biology

The Key in the Lock

I told you that sometimes Kryon tells us what to look for, only to have the news media print the very words or analogies Kryon used! This is verification of the highest order, and difficult to accept as *coincidence*. In Kryon Book I—*The End Times*, written in 1988, Kryon spoke of human disease: "*Within the symmetry of repeating parts that make up the whole disease organism there are specific parts that are special. These specific parts have extensions and depressions which 'look' for the opposite extensions and depressions within similar systems in the human body. Like a deadly **key in a lock**, if the extensions and depressions fit each other from disease organism to human organism, then the disease attaches itself and begins to grow... Know this: Even after the **key** in is the **lock**, it is not too late to change things. This is because: (1) the key is constantly growing new keys that continue to mate to other locks within the body, and (2) **the key is never in the lock for good.**" [19]

Now take a look at the following article:

Keys to an Antibody's Near-Perfect Fit

A lock that can be opened with many different keys wouldn't do a very good job of protecting a house. Yet a new study suggests that antibodies—the immune system proteins that tag foreign invaders—begin life as adaptable locks, changing shape to accommodate many different molecular keys. When the antibodies mature, they become like traditional locks, accepting just one key.[20]

---

[19] *The End Times*, Kryon Book I (1989), pp. 117-118.

[20] *Science News*, June 14 1997, Vol 151, "Keys to an antibody's near-perfect fit," p. 366. Entire article not shown.

The True Nature of DNA - Magnetics plays a part?

Those in metaphysics have been told that DNA has 12 strands. Kryon agrees, and has gone on to describe much about our DNA. In summary of his information, Kryon tells us that besides the two biological strands, we have some that are MAGNETIC! Surprised? These magnetic ones are part of the **programming** of the biological ones, and are part of an electromechanical-chemical system of the human body.

This is extremely difficult to prove, and in the brief discussion that follows, I will only offer some compelling evidence that indeed it might be so. Kryon tells us that we will never be able to see the magnetic DNA strands, but we may be able to see their "shadow." (Perhaps a later Kryon book will validate this as well?)

As you read this, it is going to start making sense why magnetics affects the body at all. Also, as you read this, you are going to realize that what I am offering from this point is pure science, with no other sources. I feel that we are on the verge of understanding the electro-magnetic mechanisms of our human DNA. If this is so, then I return to the basic premise of the **power of human consciousness**. If human consciousness is indeed measurable energy (as demonstrated in the first portion of this chapter), and DNA has an electromagnetic complement, then we are just beginning to realize why INTENT works for our own healing! Suddenly, the "woo-woo" attributes of energy healing are being transformed to understandable science. It's about time! Not that we needed it for energy healing to work, but it's nice to have the validity from the rest of the world.

In 1996 I received a letter from a researcher. This M.D. (I found out later) was *number one* in his class of 1,800 at Northwestern University in Evanston, Illinois. at the time of his acceptance into an accelerated medical training program at Johns Hopkins University. After receiving his M.D. degree from Johns Hopkins he did his residency at Georgetown University Hospital in Washington, D.C. While at Georgetown he was voted "the best of all the residents across the board." I give you this information to let you know that this researcher is firmly grounded in the methods of science. He also MEDITATES, however. His letter to me said the following:

"Dear Lee, I have just read the first two Kryon books and am amazed for a number of reasons. I have been conducting a line of electromagnetic research which follows very closely and gives earth level physical support to the principles outlined in Kryon's writings...Just as Kryon suggested it would, this strategy works."

I met Dr. Todd Ovokaitys and have been his friend ever since. He firmly represents good, logical science at the highest level, yet is willing also to listen to his "higher self," which is starting to give him wild, incredible information regarding the workings of DNA. Before I go on, can I again quote Carl Sagan? *"Science requires a strange mating of two contradictory tendencies: a willingness to consider even the most bizarre ideas, and at the same time, a most rigorous skepticism, requiring hard evidence to back up every claim. A scientist must hover in a strangely divided state of mind—open to all, yet closed to anything but the most rigorously proven. Both perspectives are critical to scientific inquiry, and neither works without the other."*[2]

As this chapter is in its closing pages, it comes full circle. I present a scientist who is willing to consider bizarre ideas—and this one is proving they are viable!

Dr. Ovokaitys has a concept that is truly bizarre for the times: He postulates that DNA has a magnetic complement, and that through a proprietary invention he has developed, he is getting extremely promising laboratory results with respect to disease elimination. His work has been examined by others in his field, and has been found to be sound. The experiments are repeatable, and even as I write this, new frontiers are being broached that seem to be pointing to a positive conclusion that indeed DNA is responding to designer-like manipulation using complex magnetics in a form that has never been seen before. His work is absolutely unique.

Dr. Ovokaitys has eradicated both cancer and HIV using live diseased cells in the lab, and has had it verified by others. Remember, this isn't drugs or chemistry—it's physics! When I speak to him about what is happening in the lab, he is cautious (as any researcher is), reminding me that this process is in its infancy, and only happening in test tubes. When I asked him, *"what is it exactly, doctor, that is happening in the test tube with your process?"* there was a pause. Then he ventured a guess. *"I think it's DNA rejuvenation—a magnetic reprogramming of the cells,"* he said.

Rejuvenation? Magnetic? That was Kryon's message back in 1988 as something we indeed would find, similar to the Temple of Rejuvenation in Atlantis (as indicated in Kryon Book II), which he also told us was magnetic. Kryon told us we could balance our cells using magnetics, and actually eliminate disease and live longer. Now we are seeing it being developed in a scientific venue—right on schedule.

I would be remiss if I didn't also mention the fact that Dr. Ovokaitys is experimenting and producing products that use this balancing technology in other ways, with reports from those using the products of better memory, weight loss, and a greater sense of well-being. Brain scans are also being used to demonstrate physiological enhancements in this group.

We are beginning to see the meld of the former strange and unprovable, into a venue of Sagan-like scientific protocol, and in the process, the New Age is being validated. I can't tell you how excited this makes me. If you are interested in knowing more about the work of Dr. Ovokaitys, or know of those who might be interested in helping to fund his work, I am not ashamed to stand up and tell you where you can find him. The Kryon work does not gain by these funding efforts—in fact it's just the opposite. I was one of the first to contribute when I saw the potential of Dr. Ovokaitys's work. It fit what Kryon told us to look for, like a "key in a lock." I am very proud to present this information in this publication.*

Again, I quote something said about Carl Sagan. *"Carl never wanted to believe. He wanted to know."*[1] I believe Dr. Ovokaitys is the same way, and now he *knows* that DNA is magnetic.

> * Dr. Todd Ovokaitys
> Gematria Products, Inc.
> 2075 A Corte Del Nogal
> Carlsbad, CA 92009
> Phone: 760-931-8563
> Toll free: 888-838-8877
> [www.gematria.com]

Cloning Shows DNA's Magnetic Complement

No matter what you think of cloning and the moral implications of it, the recent success was a miracle breakthrough of science. I bring this to the book at this time to verify that, indeed, there are discoveries going on that validate what Dr. Ovokaitys found to be true about the electromagnetic property of DNA—a second validation.

Scientists have been trying to clone for a long time, but it always failed. They could never implant the nucleus of an unfertilized egg with an adult cell and have it live. They were trying to create an adult cell and grow to full-term. It didn't work. They have been trying since 1938, gradually getting better at nuclear transplantation.

Science had grown to believe that the embryonic or "growing" instructions of DNA somehow died or were voided after development into an adult, and that the instructions were no longer in the nucleic make-up of an adult cell. All the *growing-up* information was seemingly gone, and no amount of experiments seemed to be able to "wake it up" or bring it back. Cloning simply didn't work. There were even those who assigned religious reasons for this, calling it the "Jesus factor," where God would not let mankind do this kind of thing.

Suddenly, however, it worked, and in Scotland in 1997 the world got to see "Dolly," the first cloned sheep! What did they do differently? It wasn't simple, but let me quote some of what the Scottish scientist said:

> *"The key to nuclear transplantation with adult cells seems to be a phenomenon that scientist call **nuclear reprogramming**...*
>
> *Such a **rejuvenation formula** seems to exist inside the egg cell.."* [21]

Then I was astonished when I read of something different they did to help facilitate the rejuvenation:

> "The feat is typically performed by removing the egg's nucleus with a fine hollow needle. A donor cell is fused to the egg by **pulses of electricity**." [21]

---

[21] *Science News*, April 5 1997, Vol 151, p. 214, "A Fantastical Experiment, the science behind the controversial cloning of Dolly." Entire article not shown.

Electricity? Magnetics? Wow, no wonder! It did my heart good to read about the concepts of *reprogramming* and *rejuvenation* in the article, and then I became amused when I read how they did it all with help from electromagnetics.

Is there any doubt that DNA has a magnetic complement? There undoubtedly is more coming, but even at this point in time, the evidence is clearly mounting.

The Grid Un-Lock
Earth Magnetics and Our Changing Consciousness

The magnetic grid is the focus of the Kryon work. Indeed, Kryon has reminded us that he is the "Magnetic Master," here to change the magnetic grids in response to our changing consciousness. Early in Kryon Book I, Kryon stated that, *"magnetic fields are very important to your biology! In addition, magnetic fields can (and do) affect your biology. The magnetic field of your planet is necessary to your biological health, and is fine tuned to fit within your spiritual scheme"* (p. 18). Several pages later, Kryon adds, *"As the grids adjust over the next few years, you will be given more enlightenment. As I told you earlier, your restrictive implants are aligned to my grids. The grid alteration will free you of certain restrictions, and you will be able to control what you do from here to a degree that you never had before."*

Powerful words! Yet it is difficult to relate to something as conceptual as the magnetic grids when we are faced with the daily challenges of life, such as dealing with family and co-workers, paying bills, getting over the flu, etc. Imagine telling a not-so-enlightened friend that you're having a bad day because the magnetic grids are changing! Your friend may just choose to stay away for a while!

Yet those who are reading these words understand that there ARE changes going on—we ARE moving into new times—and there ARE many unseen forces behind these changes. So if Kryon's words are correct, where is the evidence of the changing of the grids (other than the immediate changes we witness in our own lives)?

The first "clue" that something was going on occurred in late 1996 when I was flying into Casper, Wyoming, for a seminar. Our hosts, Karen and Frank McVay, greeted us inside the small airport terminal. Before we had a chance to settle our stomachs from the turbulent flight on the 30-seat airplane, Frank excitedly pointed out that the airport runway numbers had been recently repainted. At the moment, his observation was over my head. But with Frank's help, the implications soon hit me: The runway heading—a magnetic reading used as a navigation aid—had been repainted to reflect the compass heading change!

It is a well-known scientific fact that the magnetic North Pole is prone to movement, but this runway incident was like a wake-up call from Kryon to look deeper into the "evidence" of the grid changes.

First, we checked with several airports to see if the Casper incident was an anomaly. It turned out that the airport in Billings, Montana, had also changed their numbers. Next, we checked with the Federal Aviation Administration, who confirmed that numerous runway numbers had changed recently, but added that it was just a "coincidence" that so many numbers were changing at this time.

Further investigation brought us to the Jeppesen Sanderson, Inc., forerunners in the aviation map and chart business. Jeppesen uses government information to create the maps and charts used by pilots for navigation. Jeppesen also confirmed that there were numerous airport runway heading changes in the past few years, too numerous for them to track. They suggested that we talk with the National Atmospheric and Oceanic Administration (NOAA).

We spoke to Allen Hittleman at the NOAA office in Boulder, Colorado. When asked how many airport runway numbers had changed in the past decade or so, his response was simple: "100 percent!" He noted, "The rate of decreasing (of the Earth's magnetic field) is increasing." In other words, the magnetic field is getting weaker, faster. And the grids are changing at a faster-than-normal historic pace.

It seemed that the more answers we got, the more questions we had. Through these expert sources, we learned that 1) the grids were indeed changing, 2) the magnetic field strength was weakening, and 3) the strength and movement of the magnetic field were changing in an unusual manner. None of the sources we checked with, including geologists, scientists, and government officials, seemed to know WHY these changes were occurring. There was speculation that the changes are caused by weather patterns, solar storms, or even the "wobbling" of Earth on its axis. But nobody knew for sure.

As our next step, we charted the movement of magnetic north over the past 160 years. It appears that the magnetic North Pole has shifted 150 kilometers (or about 90 miles) in that time. The unusual part is that the pole has moved 60 kilometers in the past 15 years alone! It took 145 years for it to move the other 90 kilometers!

Then we compiled a list of 20 U.S. cities and charted the change in magnetic characteristics since 1960. The characteristics included magnetic declination, inclination, north component, east component, vertical component, horizontal component, and magnetic field vector. As the computer crunched away the numbers, we began to notice unusual patterns in certain time periods. In other words, the magnetic changes were not constant—not even predictable!

Our curiosity was heightened as we delved into the subject. I can report to you now that we still don't know the answer, but we have formulated a theory. If the theory proves correct, it could go a long way in helping us to understand the relationship between the grids, our consciousness, Kryon's service, and our move into the new energy. Unfortunately, the amount of research and tabulation required for this project is so massive that it could not be finished in time for this book. We plan to publish the results in an upcoming issue of the *Kryon Quarterly*.

Here's the theory: When we analyzed the magnetic changes in 20 U.S. cities since 1960, we discovered some unusual spikes within certain time periods. These spikes indicated a rapid change in the magnetic composition, or even a complete reverse in direction. At first glance, we were left scratching our heads as to what this information meant. But after a more careful review of the years in which the events took place, it dawned on us that these were years of significant social, cultural, and consciousness changes in our society.

We plan to do a more in-depth analysis of cities all over the planet, going back some 200 years, then overlay this information with a historic timeline. For instance, will we observe a "spike" in the World War II era? Or something around the time of President Kennedy's assassination? Or perhaps when the Berlin Wall came down?

If our theory proves true, this could indicate several things. First, that human consciousness affects the strength and movement of Earth's magnetic characteristics. Second, that the magnetic grids help define our focus on this third-dimensional planet. And finally, Kryon states that much of our consciousness and greater Self are held in the grids, until such point as we can handle more of who we are (that is, our ascension within our current biology). Therefore, if we change our consciousness and change the grids, we will change our focus in this time-and-space dimension. We can literally unlock the hold of the magnetic grid. Perhaps this is what enables the transition into the new times? Perhaps this is why the Mayan calendar ends in the year 2012, marking the end of our grip on the current magnetic focus?

There is much research to be done on this subject, involving specialists in geology, Earth sciences, mathematics, history, and magnetics. As soon as we have new information to report, I'll get the word out to you!

Lee Carroll

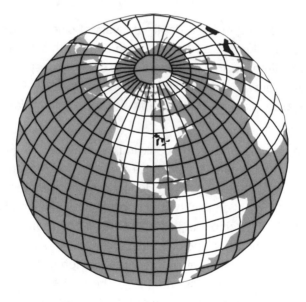

Chapter Eleven

Kryon News

The World Finally Notices HAARP!

Playing the Wrong HAARP

"Last January (99), The European Parliament took a stand on electro-magnetic weaponry, nuclear hazards, land mines, and environmental refugees. In its decision, the EP considers HAARP (High Frequency Active Auroral Research Project) by virtue of its far-reaching impact on the environment to be a global concern.

"It calls for HAARP's legal, ecological, and ethical implications to be examined by an international independent body before any further research and testing."

Canadian Journal of Health and Nutrition
As reported by Jean Manning in Alive magazine
#203; September 1999; page 42.

See HAARP information, page 243

Passing the Marker

Kryon Book Eight

Understanding the New Millennium Energy

The Eight Kryon book, published in 2000. This book is filled with channellings before and after the millennium shift (year 2000). It prepares us for what is ahead, and reveals what is now obvious after the fact. Kryon speaks of the potential of "Spiritual Rage," and defines the new times with a phrase: "No more Fence-sitting!"

"Read about new gifts and tools, new energies and potentials for the Earth - even new dimensionality! What are the latest scientific advances that fit right into what Kryon told us could happen 11 years ago? ... also a full alphabetized master index of all eight of the former Kryon books. Profound messages are given, some of which are very startling."

■ **The Leading Edge Review**

Published by Kryon Writings, Inc • ISBN 1-888053-11-9 • $14.00

Books and tapes can be purchased in retail stores, by phone, and on the Internet at [www.kryon.com] ~ Credit cards welcome ~

1-800-352-6657 - <kryonbooks@kryon.com>

At Home
with

Get together for a personal afternoon or evening with Kryon and Lee Carroll. It's called *At Home with Kryon*, an intimate venue for joining in the Kryon energy. What started in the homes of Kryon readers is now held in small hotel conference rooms and community centers. The special meeting starts with an introduction and discussion by Lee Carroll regarding timely New Age topics, then it continues with the latest information from Kryon, usually involving an AV presentation. Next comes a live Kryon channelling! Group size is typically 50 to 80 people. Often lasting up to five hours, it's an event you won't forget!

To sponsor an *"At Home with Kryon"* event in your home, please contact the Kryon office at 760/489-6400 - fax 858/759-2499, or E-mail <kryonmeet@kryon.com>. For a list of upcoming *At Home with Kryon* locations, please see our Website at [http://www.kryon.com].

Robert Coxon

Prelude to Infinity
Robert Haig Coxon

Robert Coxon, best-selling musical artist, Kryon international team member, and composer extraordinaire, has at last released a new, much awaited album. Best known for *The Silent Path*, Robert has gone to the next step in his musical evolutionary process with *Prelude to Infinity*.

With sacred composition and strong inspiring melodies, *Prelude to Infinity* paints on a canvas that is interdimensional, out of the normal expectations of New Age music. Think *healing....*

Drop By and visit our
HOME-*page*

The *new re-designed* Kryon website allows you to find the latest information on seminars schedules, and Kryon related products. Browse through portions of Kryon books, read some of the most profound Kryon channellings, reference, inspirational and educational material. Mingle with the Kryon family and meet facinating people from around the world, of like mind. Also, enjoy the new on-line magazine *In The Spirit*.

Kryon's re-designed website offers the latest in technology and is easy to navigate. Each page allows you to view in an animated or non-animated format allowing for maximum internet speed.

Find the latest Kryon information at:
www.kryon.com

www.kryon.com

Would you like to be on the Kryon mailing list?

This list is used to inform interested people of Kryon workshops coming to their areas, new Kryon releases, and Kryon news in general. We don't sell or distribute our lists to outside parties.

There are three ways to be give us your name: (1) Phone (858) 792-2990 and leave your information. (2) Use the Internet and go to [www.kryon.com] Find the "Kryon on-line" button, and select it. Then select "Synchronicity." You may then enter your information under "cosmic connections." (3) Simply drop a post card to us that says "LIST," and include your clearly printed name and address.

The Kryon Writings, Inc.

1155 Camino Del Mar, #422
Del Mar, California 92014
[www.kryon.com]

Index

Index

Index

The Rest of the Kryon Book Series

■ **THE END TIMES**
ISBN 0-9636304-2-3 • $12.00

■ **DON'T THINK LIKE A HUMAN**
ISBN 0-9636304-0-7 • $12.00

■ **ALCHEMY OF THE HUMAN SPIRIT**
ISBN 0-9636304-8-2 • $14.00

■ **THE PARABLES OF KRYON**
ISBN 1-56170-663-9 • $10.95

■ **THE JOURNEY HOME**
ISBN 1-56170-552-7 • $13.95

■ **LETTERS FROM HOME**
ISBN 0-9636304-2-3 • $14.00

■ **PASSING THE MARKER**
ISBN 1-888053-09-7 • $14.00

■ **THE NEW BEGINNING**
ISBN 0-9636304-2-3 • $14.98

■ **A NEW DISPENSATION**
ISBN 1-888053-14-3 • $14.98

■ **THE INDIGO CHILDREN**
by Lee Carroll/Jan Tober
ISBN 1561706086 • $13.95

■ **AN INDIGO CELEBRATION**
by Lee Carroll/Jan Tober
ISBN 1561708593 • $13.95

Books and tapes can be purchased in retail stores and by phone: **1-800-352-6657**
Also through our Website store at: **www.kryon.com/store**
Credit Cards Welcome